Praise for

GEORGE ANDERS'S
YOU CAN DO ANYTHING

"The career stories of liberal arts graduates provide the best argument for the value of their education. George Anders, in his thoughtful book *You Can Do Anything*, tells these stories in a compelling manner, weaving the threads of their education into the tapestry of their lives, demonstrating over and over why employers should seek out these unique thinkers. An interesting read and valuable for any liberal arts graduate or recruiter!"

—Dr. Katharine Brooks, author of *You Majored in What?* and executive director of the Vanderbilt University career center

"For a parent about to send her second child off to college—this one has a theater major—George Anders's book was not just a good show topic but a balm to my soul."

—Krys Boyd, host of *Think* (NPR)

"George Anders has provided a compelling and decisive answer to the recurring question 'What is the value proposition of a liberal arts education?' Students should have this book in their backpacks or on their iPads. So should their parents and teachers and our policy makers."

—Frederick M. Lawrence, CEO of the Phi Beta Kappa society

"Give this to anyone who is questioning the value of a classical education in today's fast-paced world."   —*Booklist*

"*You Can Do Anything* is part how-to for humanities types...It also tells stories about liberal arts students made good...These are important words of wisdom from a skilled storyteller and a sharp observer of the human condition."

—Adam Lashinsky, *Fortune*

ALSO BY GEORGE ANDERS

The Rare Find

Perfect Enough

Health Against Wealth

Merchants of Debt

YOU CAN DO ANYTHING

The Surprising Power of a "Useless" Liberal Arts Education

GEORGE ANDERS

BACK BAY BOOKS
Little, Brown and Company
New York • Boston • London

For Betsy, Matthew, and Peter
and all the adventures still ahead

———————————

Back Bay Books / Little, Brown and Company
Hachette Book Group
1290 Avenue of the Americas, New York, NY 10104
littlebrown.com

Originally published in hardcover by Little, Brown and Company, August 2017
First Back Bay Books paperback edition, January 2019

Back Bay Books is an imprint of Little, Brown and Company, a division of Hachette Book Group, Inc. The Back Bay Books name and logo are trademarks of Hachette Book Group, Inc.

The publisher is not responsible for websites (or their content) that are not owned by the publisher.

The Hachette Speakers Bureau provides a wide range of authors for speaking events. To find out more, go to hachettespeakersbureau.com or call (866) 376-6591.

ISBN 978-0-316-54880-9 (hc) / 978-0-316-54888-5 (pb)
LCCN 2017932050

10 9 8 7 6 5 4 3 2 1

LSC-C

Printed in the United States of America

Contents

Part One

Your Strengths

1

The Explorers

When Josh Sucher graduated from Bard College in 2007, he had no idea how to find a job. He had spent four years—and large amounts of his parents' money—studying anthropology. He knew how to conduct ethnographic studies as an insider or outsider; he could tell you the most amazing things about witchcraft in different societies. His senior thesis had analyzed the "constructivist underpinnings" of a one-hundred-dollar laptop computer, which he described as "a machine with political implications hard-wired into it." Within the context of Bard's liberal arts campus, Sucher had done everything right. Judged by the harsher standards of America's leading employers, he was as useless as an orchid in a snowstorm.

Similar frustrations gripped many of his classmates. Bard's free-spirited culture didn't seem to connect with the lucrative careers college graduates were supposed to find. Sucher's father treated this predicament as a comic disaster, remarking at one point: "Why don't you go down to the anthropology factory? I hear they're hiring." Even Bard's graduation speakers couldn't make the gloom go away. They offered the usual salutes to the life of the mind—and then winced at the perilous future each graduate faced. Bard president Leon Botstein bemoaned the extent to which higher education nationwide was souring on the liberal arts. Commencement speaker Michael Bloomberg warned that finding a job "can be scary," adding: "Some of you may take a little longer to find a job."

All the same, Josh Sucher has prevailed—and he has done so without ever needing to stifle his personality, his interests, or his take on life.

Sucher's story opens this book because it showcases a fundamental truth that's in danger of being lost amid our national anxiety about the value of a college education. Curiosity, creativity, and empathy aren't unruly traits that must be reined in to ensure success. Just the opposite. The human touch has never been more essential in the workplace than it is today. You don't have to mask your true identity to get paid for your strengths. You don't need to apologize for the supposedly impractical classes you took in college or the so-called soft skills you have acquired. The job market is quietly creating thousands of openings a week for people who can bring a humanist's grace to our rapidly evolving high-tech future.

Imagine a spreadsheet with human strengths capping all the columns across the top of the sheet...and technical disciplines supporting all the rows at the side. Each intersection defines a new type of job. Curiosity + data science = market research. Empathy + gene sequencing = genetic counseling. Creativity + information networks = social-media manager. It's a rich, wonderful grid. In the course of this book, we will explore all sorts of ways your liberal arts education and society's needs can fit together.

The central insight is this: The more we automate the routine stuff, the more we create a constant low-level hum of digital connectivity, the more we get tangled up in the vastness and blind spots of big data, the more essential it is to bring human judgment into the junctions of our digital lives. It's easy to get mesmerized by the digital tools that surround us: Snapchat and Facebook for socializing; TripAdvisor and Airbnb for travel planning; camera-toting drones for who knows what. It's natural to lionize the software engineers who build these tools. But each technological breakthrough is just an empty framework without people to coax, confide, persuade, debate, teach, agree, rebel, and interact. Fundamentally, we're social animals. We compete; we make friends; we crave respect and we punish our enemies. We behave in ways that baffle engineers and make perfect sense to humanists. That's been true ever since someone in the Cave of Altamira twenty thousand years ago looked at a crude sketch of a bison and told her neighbor: "That's clever! You should draw some more."

The more our labs and engineers innovate, the more jobs we create for people who can make the human dimension work. Technology may be a job killer in warehouses or on the factory floor. There's no denying robots excel at predictable chores, carrying them out faster, cheaper, and more reliably than we can. Yet in so many other aspects of life, the machines (and even software-based artificial intelligence) are clumsy intruders. They don't know how to handle subtler situations, where feelings matter and the rules haven't been written. We do.

If childhood habits foreshadow adulthood destinies, the starting point for Josh Sucher can be found in a family photo of him as a toddler standing on a chair, screwdriver in hand. He is trying to take apart a wall socket. The little boy looks so earnest—and so confident—that you want him to succeed, even if your prudent self is about to scream: *Get off that chair now!* Keep that image in mind. I've spent a lot of time trying to figure out why adventurers

2

It's 480 B.C. — You Have an Ax

Snow is falling hard in Hanover, New Hampshire. It's a January morning at Dartmouth College, and mobs of students are forming outside Loew Auditorium. The snowball fights and bonfires of Winter Carnival haven't started yet; no campus outrage needs protesting at the moment. Yet for some reason, more than a hundred students are jostling one another. Backpacks are bumping into backpacks. Something is about to happen, and no one wants to miss out.

The reason for all this excitement: Classics professor Paul Christesen is about to start teaching his renowned introductory course Antiquity Today. He's a broad-faced man in his late forties with a deep-seated interest in both the loftiest and earthiest elements of ancient Mediterranean culture. Over the next ten weeks, Christesen will march students through the significance of *nomos* and *physis*. He will explain how the Olympics began. He will discuss what it means for a nation to go to war, then and now. And he will spend an entire lecture exploring the sexual quirks of Roman citizens. In his hands, the ancient cultures of Greece and

like Sucher keep gliding into career opportunities that other people don't see. Part of his good fortune (and yours too!) can be
traced to the merits of keeping a dash of youthful wonder in your
life.

As Josh Sucher grew up, curiosity kept tugging him in unpredictable ways, including an ill-advised attempt to bicycle to school—
as a seventh-grader—by zipping onto the expressway. When it
came time to choose a college, he ignored the vocational pathways
his more prudent classmates preferred. Instead, he picked Bard, a
famously iconoclastic school a hundred and ten miles north of
New York City. Its alumni include the founders of the rock band
Steely Dan and dozens of well-known painters, artists, actors,
and composers. Its writing faculty over the years has featured the
likes of Toni Morrison, Saul Bellow, Chinua Achebe, and Ralph
Ellison. At Bard, there is no business school.

For Sucher, Bard became a nonstop source of enchantment.
The first week of freshman year, he found himself in a cultural
anthropology class where the instructor pulled out a nail clipper,
snipped off a few scraps of her own keratin—and passed them
around for student examination. Her point: What looks clean and
nice on the tips of our fingers suddenly becomes disgusting when
it's removed. Terms such as *dirt* and *filth* aren't absolutes at all;
they are hugely dependent on context and culture. For an excited
freshman at a seminar table, this was a thunderbolt of truth. The
professor's message "completely reframed the way I view the universe," Sucher later told me.

After four years at Bard, Sucher knew how to create a short
play from scratch in a week. He knew how to stage theater in the
most improbable locations, ranging from campus mailrooms to
abandoned barns. He had amassed a splendidly impractical col-

lection of skills without any obvious way of turning them into a respectable job. Stalling for time, he decided to try law school. That turned out to be a dead end; law was his father's calling, not his.

To help pay bills during law school, Sucher set up Block Factory, a side business providing tech support for small companies using Mac computers. He became a man with a tool kit, advertising on Craigslist and getting paid for installing video projectors, Internet cables, and other gear. His "office" consisted of a $450-a-month rented desk in a co-working facility near Brooklyn's Gowanus Canal. His home: a bed in the attic of his grandmother's house. So be it. "I knew my way around a computer, and I liked taking things apart," Sucher later explained.

If you had met Sucher then, you might have dismissed him as an aimless soul. In reality, he was sharpening a vital skill that Bard had taught him: how to listen. His new clients — particularly a cluster of Manhattan art galleries — needed more than a better A/V connection. They wanted a friendly listener who could soothe their spirits and deliver tech with empathy. "Most of my customers were anxious," Sucher told me. "Something wasn't working and they'd start berating themselves. They'd say: 'You're going to think I'm an idiot. I feel like a failure.' There were a lot of talking-them-off-the-ledge moments. I'd say: 'It's not you; it's the technology. This thing is terribly designed.' I'd get things fixed and then we'd talk shop."

After a couple years, however, Sucher yearned for a different kind of job, one that let him address tech's failings in a broader way. "I started burning out," Sucher told me. "I was becoming dissatisfied by devising clever workarounds for minor IT problems over and over again." His new goal: teaming up with like-minded people to create user-friendly tech built properly from the outset.

In his free time, Sucher started hanging out with digital designers and usability experts. Without ever sending out a résumé, Sucher was networking his way toward his next job. He popped into a Manhattan party to celebrate the launch of a book about market research and user interviews—and found himself rubbing shoulders with noisy, spirited people who appreciated great design. Inspired by the encounter, he signed up for a program in Interaction Design at Manhattan's School of Visual Arts. At SVA, Sucher paired his long-standing empathy and curiosity with new skills relating to design, market research, and a smidgen of computer coding. "It was a magical moment for me," Sucher said. "I had found my tribe. At one point, there were tears in my eyes." It didn't take him long to realize that technology's latest zigs and zags actually made his college training more valuable. Fast-growing new companies needed generalists who knew a little bit about tech—and a lot about human nature.

Three different paths led Sucher to Etsy, a Brooklyn-based company running a billion-dollar online marketplace for artisans selling everything from greeting cards to jewelry. Several of his SVA friends and instructors worked there. At a conference, he had heard Etsy's chief executive, Chad Dickerson, share the company's story. And he took a liking to the way Etsy's marketplace supported small businesses trying to make it in the arts. When he learned the company had an opening, he applied.

Not only was Etsy hiring, it also radiated a fondness for people with eclectic backgrounds. Dickerson himself had been an English major at Duke. Many of Etsy's software engineers and data analysts had spent their college years in fields such as literary history, Japanese studies, and psychology. This was a company where liberal arts majors needn't hide their pasts. They could banter about

Jenny Holzer's conceptual artwork and turn theory into praxis. To Sucher, Etsy sounded like home.

Today, Sucher conducts a digital-age version of ethnography and field research for Etsy. By using GoToMeeting and Google Hangouts, he connects with artistic creators and buyers around the world, finding out how they use Etsy and what would make it work better for them. He's the patient listener, drawing out details of the ways artists set up their studios or the reasons why they feel compelled to create. His curiosity and warmhearted manner help him gain insights into Etsy customers that administering standard questionnaires wouldn't reveal. "Each person is his or her own story," Sucher explained to me. "There are a million of them, and they never grow old."

Think of him as an anthropologist in action, mindful of buyers' preferences that can be as stark and hard to explain as the way we think about fingernails. Colleagues value his discoveries, which help guide new services and features. "I put myself in the shoes of our buyers and sellers," Sucher told me. "I'm constantly opening my mind to the way they experience technology." We can argue forever about the reasons why Sucher's unplanned journey worked out so well. What's clear is that the curiosity, creativity, and empathy you develop in college help you make your own luck. Rapid, disruptive change doesn't ruin your prospects; it can actually play to your advantage.

In 2006, economists David Autor, Lawrence Katz, and Melissa Kearney published a landmark study looking at the way technology was changing people's incomes, destinies, and ability to hold jobs. The scholars (based at MIT, Harvard, and the National Bureau of Economic Research, respectively) combed through a quarter century of data from the U.S. Census Bureau, the Labor Department, and other government agencies, decoding the secrets held in every American pay stub since 1980. What Autor, Katz, and Kearney uncovered has influenced public discussion of technology's allure and perils ever since.

While new technology is barely touching low-paid manual labor such as busing dishes, it is hammering millions of predictable, task-based jobs that traditionally provide tickets into the middle class. Factory workers have known this for decades, as machines keep displacing assembly lines full of human welders and fitters, but Autor, Katz, and Kearney demonstrated the degree to which tech's Grim Reaper has been targeting stores, offices, banks, and other bastions of white-collar work too. Payroll clerks keep being replaced by software. The same holds true for proofreaders, bank tellers, executive secretaries, and switchboard operators. McKinsey researchers estimate that 45 percent of workplace tasks in modern society are at risk of being automated. Or, as venture capitalist Marc Andreessen observed, "Software is eating the world."

When the U.S. economy careened into the troubles of 2008 to 2010, 8.8 million Americans were thrown out of work. Eventually the economy got better, but many of those jobs didn't come back. Autor, Katz, and Kearney had nailed it: technological progress was squeezing routine-centered jobs out of existence. Even *MIT Technology Review*—a magazine whose very name spoke to a fondness for cutting-edge engineering—raised a ruckus in 2013 with a cover story entitled "How Technology Is Destroying Jobs." In the piece, MIT management professor Andrew McAfee nervously ruminated on a future full of self-driving cars and warehouse robots. "When all these science-fiction technologies are deployed," he asked, "what will we need all the people for?"

As public anxiety grew, an idea took hold that the tech sector itself might provide the answer. If we could just train enough software engineers, the argument went, a new generation could find gainful work. Hundreds of coding academies sprang up in cities ranging from San Francisco to Detroit. During his presidency, Barack Obama repeatedly urged teenagers in all walks of life to load up with science, technology, engineering, and math (STEM) courses so they could become programming wizards too. Movies like *The Social Network* glamorized late-night coding binges. Even our language reshaped itself, like a plant twisting toward sunlight, with computing-related terms such as *open source, backward-compatible, hackathon,* and *hackerspace* writing themselves into the dictionary.

Here's the painful twist: The software sector makes no attempt to shield its own workers from automation; instead, it constantly squeezes out its own older jobs almost as fast as it creates new ones. Much of what programmers did by hand a few years ago has been turned into automated tool kits, libraries, or subroutines. Of the 10.1 million net new jobs the United States added from May 2012 to May 2016, only 5 percent, or 541,000, are in the computing sector. Being able to write business software, run a computer network, or create a smartphone app has turned out to be the answer for less than one-tenth of job hunters. For everyone else, success has been happening elsewhere.

What tech enthusiasts overlooked were the broader consequences of digital advances that kept rippling through the rest of the economy. Once or twice a century, a wave of innovation changes not just an industry, but an entire way of life. We saw this in the first half of the twentieth century, when the rise of the automobile industry inspired far more than a hiring spree at Henry Ford's factories. From the 1920s to the 1950s, millions of newly defined jobs sprang up across the country, brought into existence by what a motorized America now needed or desired. Towns everywhere reshaped themselves to make room for auto mechanics, road-construction crews, driving academies, car dealerships, car washes, motor-insurance agents, traffic-safety officers, parking-lot attendants, mapmakers, and personal-injury lawyers.

It's happening again.

Take a close look at job creation since May 2012, and you will see that the fastest-growing fields often turn out to be ones *indirectly* catching the warmth of the tech revolution. Thanks to the rapid rise of cheap online surveys and big-data analytics, for example, America is now graced with more than 550,000 market researchers and marketing specialists. That's a 30 percent leap from the level in 2012. It didn't take many software engineers to provide us with instant, low-cost polling services such as Qualtrics, Survey-Monkey, Clicktools, and FluidSurveys. The big impact lies in the ways these ubiquitous tools have been put to use. We poll ourselves constantly now. You probably clicked your way through at least a dozen such surveys in the past year, whether you wanted to or not. Companies need data on everything from airline service to your puppy's latest visit to the vet. In the process, market research has been transformed from an obscure specialty into a field more densely populated than the city of Cleveland.

Remember the figure of 541,000 jobs added in the computing sector from May 2012 through May 2016? Look at what happens if we tally job growth during the same period in the following thirteen areas, all of which are tech-influenced but hardly tech-centered: compliance officers, entertainment producers and directors, event planners, fund-raisers, genetic counselors, graphic designers, human-resources specialists, management analysts, market research analysts, marketing specialists, school administrators, technical writers, and training specialists. We're at 626,000 net new jobs, with many of these fields creating work at double or even quadruple the pace of the overall U.S. economy.

What's more, we're just getting started. Add in big categories such as general management, finance, legal work, sales, and teaching, and we're looking at a further 1.7 million net new jobs, or a grand total of more than 2.3 million over the past five years. To put this giant sum in context: it's more than *triple* the new-job contribution from the computing sector during that period. Or, if you prefer, it's equivalent to the entire population of Pittsburgh, Miami, New Orleans, Atlanta, and Seattle combined.

Surprised? That's totally understandable. Most of these new jobs have tiptoed into the U.S. economy with no fanfare whatsoever. They don't fit into the conventional story lines of media coverage or the major political parties' slogan wars. We aren't talking about *The Wolf of Wall Street* or single parents working the night shift at minimum wage for soulless multinational corporations. This resurgence of meaningful work is happening in the forgotten middle. It involves an eclectic mix of high-skill but low-profile areas that just happen to be hungry for talent.

If you're looking for entry-level jobs straight out of college, chapter 4 highlights a multitude of opportunities where your bachelor's degree can be put to work right away. If you're taking the longer view, with a focus on turning your liberal arts background into a fast-track career, chapter 7 shows you how people with degrees in the humanities and social sciences have risen to the top in fields as diverse as finance, government, nonprofits, and the entrepreneurial economy.

In all these sectors, tech makes us nimbler and quicker-witted. By spending less time on routine chores, we become more productive, which makes us more desirable. Our opportunities expand. Society keeps creating more room for people who do what we do. Put Google's search engine at your fingertips, and your productivity soars in any field calling for instant access to fresh information (examples range from medical research to sports announcing). Embark on a fund-raising campaign, and software tools like the Raiser's Edge become booster packs for your brain. The list is endless. LinkedIn has become the professional equivalent of steroids for recruiters; LexisNexis does the same for lawyers; AutoCAD for industrial designers; Final Cut for filmmakers; Houzz for architects; and so on.

Think of Josh Sucher's situation. He couldn't have found work at Etsy by proffering the old-fashioned ethnographer's approach of traveling around the United States with a notepad and a microphone, collecting one or two user stories a day. Such a method would have been unbearably slow and expensive for Etsy to endure. With GoToMeeting and Google Hangouts, everything changes. Suddenly it becomes easy to carry out virtual visits to artists' studios anywhere in the world, without the burdens of traditional travel. Sucher can arrive at Etsy's Brooklyn headquarters at 9:30 a.m. and begin a digitized chat with an artists' collective in Toronto a few minutes later. Customers in Arizona become just as accessible. For that matter, the whole world is within reach. Colleagues at Etsy headquarters can watch his conversations and suggest additional questions to ask. Technology might be eradicating other jobs, but it is simultaneously creating new openings that couldn't have existed twenty years earlier.

Most of these opportunities call for a modicum of technical literacy, but nothing that can't be picked up in a few months of concentrated effort. (You don't need a computer science degree.) Average salaries range from $43,000 to $90,000 a year—the sort of pay that commands college graduates' attention. Most important, these jobs are in the heart of the U.S. economy. They arise in big sectors such as management, teaching, sales, and education, which together employ nearly half of the 140 million Americans at work. By contrast, computer-related fields employ less than 3 percent of the workforce. Starting pay for the best software engineers can be stunningly high, but that's true for athletes and pop stars too. For the vast majority of Americans who will win new jobs in the years to come, programming won't be the answer.

What do we call this exciting new category of jobs? Many center on an ability to read the room—and get different people on the same page. Let's dub this "the rapport sector." Other opportunities call for wise decisions amid the ambiguity and murky information that machines can't stand. Such settings make the most of our ability to pick up signals machines never see or balance priorities in ways equations can't describe. Now we're talking about "the ingenuity economy." We might even want additional labels acknowledging the value of old-fashioned communication retooled for a digital age. People have been storytellers since long before the days of Aesop or the *Ramayana*. Even if modern cultures have traded in parchment for Pinterest and Prezi, the demand for people who can inform, entertain, or inspire is endless.

What unifies all these jobs is something more fundamental: an explorer's spirit. America's most interesting jobs are going to be ones that haven't been done before. The opportunities are bigger; the bureaucracy smaller. Find (or invent!) one of those jobs, and you control your own destiny. Your best ideas will take hold faster; your mistakes will disappear from sight more quickly. Such opportunities exist not just at start-ups, but in thousands of big companies too. Old work practices are fading away. New opportunities are arising, and fresh perspectives are needed. Look at the way advertising, public relations, and marketing have been upended by social media to see how vast and rapid this transformation can be. Everyone from Walmart to Wally's Bait and Tackle now needs an influx of social-media talent in order to connect with a new generation of customers.

Be like Josh. Come at your career with a pioneering spirit, and you gain the confidence of steadily building up your strengths. Just as important, when unexpected change happens, you have the experience and the temperament to make the most of whatever comes next. As the philosophical writer Eric Hoffer once observed, "In times of drastic change, it is the learners who inherit the future. The learned usually find themselves beautifully equipped to deal with a world that no longer exists."

Job hunting has changed a lot since the 1970s and even since the 1990s. Predictable career paths are rarer; the opportunities to improvise are greater. Irving Trust and Sperry Rand don't come to campus anymore looking for raw talent that can be slotted into multiyear executive-training programs. In fact, those particular companies don't even exist today. They have disappeared in a wave of corporate mergers and restructurings. Everything changes faster now—and so be it. In the creative chaos of everyday life, resourceful people still reign supreme. To borrow a phrase from MIT's David Autor, when success centers upon "problem-solving, intuition and persuasion," it's the explorers' turn to win.

Of all the classes I took in college, the most valuable one had nothing to do with the career I eventually found: writing business books and crafting cover stories for publications such as the *Wall Street Journal* and *Forbes*. Instead, this course transported me to nineteenth-century Russia and the life's work of a brilliant, tormented soul. The subject: someone who spent seven years in

Siberia's czarist prisons, who repeatedly skated on the edge of bankruptcy because of his gambling problems, and who, even so, managed to write two of the world's most renowned novels along with at least a dozen other books.

You've probably deduced that this was a Russian literature class focused entirely on Fyodor Dostoevsky. I signed up as a naive freshman at Stanford, having been blown away by *Crime and Punishment* in high school. Awed by my first taste of Dostoevsky, I wanted to see what else the man had written. Our professor did not disappoint. On the first day of class, the professor, William Mills Todd III, explained that we would spend the next ten weeks reading nearly everything of scale that Dostoevsky ever wrote. Not just *The Brothers Karamazov* (944 pages) and *Crime and Punishment* (another 560), but also *Poor Folk, Notes from the Underground, House of the Dead,* and *The Possessed,* as well as excerpts of other Russian works from the same period. All told, we would be assigned nearly three thousand pages of Dostoevsky's passionate (and sometimes chaotic) text. A six- to eight-page midterm paper would be a small part of our grade. The main event would be much tougher: an extended final paper that seized on some aspect of Dostoevsky's work and analyzed it across all of his fiction. I was stunned. How could I get everything read? How could I make sense of it all? I felt like a traveler in the opening scene of a survival movie, stuck in some remote forest after a bus crash, not sure what to do next. Was this what college was supposed to be?

At first, I relied on ordinary study habits, mixing dorm-room chatter with intermittent efforts to turn pages in the late afternoon. I fell behind. Too many pages; too many Ilyushas and Alyoshas that I couldn't keep straight. I did settle on a racy topic for my final paper: "Intemperance and Debauchery in Dostoevsky's Fiction." That was fine; it allowed me to savor many, many scenes involving drinking and reckless sexual choices. The more I perused, though, the blurrier it all became. I was going to fail.

In desperation, near the end of the term I cobbled together a radically new approach. Now I read late at night, hunched over a desk, with no distractions. I skimmed through long passages in which everyone was sober and fully dressed, making time to note each new moral transgression as it happened. Instead of gently dabbing key passages with a yellow Hi-Liter, I began attacking the text with a ballpoint pen. Soon Dostoevsky's work was splattered with an impudent teenager's commentary. Half my comments were inane, but it didn't matter. Later on I could refine the best insights and shed the rest. At least I would make it to the finish line.

Decades later, those unruly habits are still with me. In fact, they define my biggest projects and my most productive moments.

Learning how to wrestle with big, half-formed ideas—and how to keep fighting in the face of fatigue—was the best lesson of all. I don't mean to malign the standard preprofessional courses that college offers. Basic journalism classes taught me how to turn someone's speech into a news story; economics and accounting courses schooled me in how to read a balance sheet and think through questions of supply and demand. Those career-minded classes not only made me employable; they ensured that I would sail through those awkward probation periods when employers wonder: *Can this newbie actually do anything?* Yet a decade out, when I began to dream of writing big, ambitious feature stories or full-length nonfiction books, Journalism 101 wasn't going to get me there. The habits learned in the Dostoevsky course did.

Essentially, our professor had turned us loose on a big project with inadequate preparation—and then left us alone. We had ten weeks to stare failure in the face and come up with our own survival strategies. How would we stay afloat when we were being overwhelmed with too much information? How would we stay organized? How would we take all this material and shape it into something that was coherent, believable, and surprising? He wasn't going to spoon-feed us the answers. We had to find the solutions, which meant inching ahead on our own, week after week, without any outside assurance that we were on the right track.

Knowing how to prevail in such murky moments is the hallmark of a liberal arts education, and you can benefit from it even if you don't attend an ultra-selective school such as Harvard, Stanford, or Amherst. Your grades don't matter as much as your willingness to stretch your ideas and aspirations. In the chapters that follow, you will meet graduates of Mississippi College, the University of Nevada, and San Francisco State who parlayed their liberal arts beginnings into winning careers. Regardless of whether you're studying philosophy, English, sociology, or any of a dozen other disciplines, you're being introduced to a wider way of engaging with the world. Payoffs arise later in all sorts of jobs. As the nineteenth-century British educator William Cory put it, the benefits of such an education consist of "the habit of attention... the art of expression... the art of assuming, at a moment's notice, a new intellectual position... the art of entering quickly into another person's thoughts"—and even the willingness to accept that you might be wrong.

Aren't life's biggest challenges always that way?

In the movie (and novel) *The Martian,* there's a scene where astronaut Mark Watney discovers that he has been left alone on Mars by his crewmates with at least a four-year wait until any space probe might return. He's not dead yet. He has three hundred days of food, as well as an erratic but diverse assortment of supplies and tools. At that point in the film, Watney starts to envision a way out, declaring: "I'm gonna have to science the shit out of this." The movie is a beautiful tribute to the power of science and engineering if you're ever stuck on another planet needing food, shelter, and oxygen.

Inspired by his example, I'm going to do everything possible in this book to help you "humanities the hell" out of similar situations on Earth—when it's your mind and soul that need sustenance.

It's hard to say exactly how or why the pioneering spirit forms in people. Psychologists' research suggests that personality is very fluid in childhood, begins to take shape much more clearly in the high-school years, and is largely settled by early adulthood. How much is determined by genetics, parenting, educational exposures, socioeconomic standing, and peer interactions isn't fully understood. Perhaps it never will be. Even so, the relationship between personality and success is one of the most keenly studied subjects in the social sciences.

In recent years, society has embraced grit as the greatest virtue of them all. Traits such as tenacity and conscientiousness have been admired for decades, and a wealth of academic research now demonstrates how broadly these strengths pay off. The full linkages are elegantly explained in *Grit: The Power of Passion and Perseverance*, a bestselling book by University of Pennsylvania psychology professor Angela Duckworth. But even the best ideas can be taken too far, especially when careful scientific research is turned into click-bait headlines. There's a difference between saying grit is important (it is) and deeming it the only trait that matters (it's not).

A second path can also lead to success, and its power is grievously underrepresented in the current public debate. Hundreds of psychological studies have found that people with a high level of what's called "openness to new experiences" fare somewhat better in school and, by extension, later life than those who have lower levels of it. Our world needs people who color outside the lines. When colleges (or even high schools) encourage such exploratory thinking, students benefit in two ways. If you already radiate curiosity, you can make the most of your talents. And if you are still sorting out attitudes toward the new and unfamiliar, you might discover a strategy for success.

One word of caution: Well-prepared explorers fare better than hasty travelers, people who count on raw enthusiasm to solve every problem. That's literally true in the wilderness, where your odds of success improve if you bring sufficient food and water as well as some form of navigation. And it's metaphorically true as you travel from college to career. In the chapters that follow, I'll talk about the extra elements of a college experience that can help you become fully career-ready while still making the most of your liberal arts strengths. Touch points will cover everything from why you should get to know your professors and the school's recent alumni to the importance of picking the right summer jobs and the right electives. (Yes, curiosity, creativity, and empathy will pay off once you start working, but a few practical skills will help you land that first job.) A generation ago, when tuition costs were lower and almost any undergraduate diploma was good enough to impress employers, college officials could joke that a liberal arts education "trains you for nothing but prepares you for everything." Today, you want to be brilliantly prepared and properly trained too.

You're probably wondering whether the explorer's track favors students from affluent, well-connected families, people who can afford to take risks that others dare not try. We haven't achieved perfect equality of opportunity yet, but a lot of people are working hard to knock down barriers. In the chapters that follow, you will see how students in many traditionally underrepresented groups—first-generation, Latino, African American, Pell Grant recipients, and so on—have created compelling careers from a liberal arts beginning. Technology is helping in a big way, as it's becoming easier than ever to strike up online conversations with potential allies, no matter what your own background might be. (See chapter 9 for an extreme example of what a single Skype contact can accomplish.) Life's imbalances related to money won't ever go away, but a handful of colleges with a conscience are helping lower-income students try promising career options without going broke. Such pilot programs are overdue; they should be expanded as rapidly as possible.

In part 1 of the book ("Your Strengths"), you will see why supposedly impractical classes can turn into superb launching pads for ambitious students' careers. Part 2 ("Your Opportunities") will explore four powerful new career strategies that have helped explorers with "tainted" degrees end up in terrific jobs. You will see why IBM counts on a sociology major to explain some of its most complex technology to customers, why a philosophy major has created one of Silicon Valley's most successful start-ups, and why a leading ad agency hires English majors, not data scientists, when it wants to tell stories with numbers.

In part 3 ("Your Allies"), we will look at broader changes that could help our country and our companies make fuller use of this pioneering spirit. You will learn how campus career offices and recent alumni can make the job hunt less frustrating. You will be introduced to several dozen major companies that "get it" in a big way when it comes to the merits of hiring liberal arts graduates.

Some are in tech-influenced fields; others are in traditional strong-holds of humanities and social science majors, such as govern-ment, education, and media. Part 4 ("Your Tool Kit") will provide tactical advice on how to tell your story and how to get paid properly.

In the summer of 2015, I wrote a *Forbes* cover story headlined "That 'Useless' Liberal Arts Degree Has Become Tech's Hottest Ticket." I didn't realize until near the very end of my reporting and writing that this project was really an ideological manifesto cloaked in the safer garb of a carefully reported magazine feature. We as a country were in danger of isolating and marginalizing some of our most valuable talent. We needed freethinking pio-neers more than ever, yet in many sectors, we were mocking the very people that we should have been celebrating.

Taunting liberal arts majors had become an ugly sport. "If you're planning to major in English, see if you can't get a job at Starbucks instead," nationally prominent columnist Megan McAr-dle wrote in 2012. It was philosophy majors' turn to be rebuked a few years later, when Florida senator Marco Rubio declared in a presidential debate: "We need more welders and less philoso-phers." Former Florida governor Jeb Bush suggested in a 2015 speech that universities warn new students: "Hey, that psych major deal, that philosophy major thing, that's great, it's impor-tant to have liberal arts…but realize, you're going to be working at Chick-fil-A." Individually, such jibes can be shrugged off. In aggregate, they sting.

Ironically, these critics' own careers disprove their pessimistic views; all three hold liberal arts degrees themselves. McArdle studied English literature at Dartmouth; Rubio majored in politi-cal science at the University of Florida; Bush specialized in Latin American studies at the University of Texas. Their own lives reveal the power of this academic path in widening your horizons and preparing you for leadership. The virtues of independent thinking, curiosity, and bold, clear communication may be incubated in college campuses—but they run deep throughout America's heritage. When Gutzon Borglum was hired to carve presidents' faces into Mount Rushmore, three of his four heroes (Thomas Jefferson, Abraham Lincoln, and Theodore Roosevelt) were the epitome of free spirits. They remade themselves multiple times; they chased after the new; they did everything possible to help meandering earn its good name.

And then the nation lost it.

Somewhere in the late 1980s or early 1990s, we became a more cautious country. The culture of Jack Kerouac's *On the Road* and Bobby Troup's "(Get Your Kicks on) Route 66" gave way to a nation of homebodies. People's willingness to relocate to a new state fell by half from 1980 to 2015. Open lawns gave way to gated communities. Parents turned nervous and protective. College tuition rose to the point that few administrators dared talk anymore about developing students "trained for nothing," regardless of how well these jaunty originals might succeed over the long term. Instead, campus leaders vied to make the undergraduate business and engineering programs as robust as possible. At many campuses, marketing, accounting, management, and finance became more popular majors than English and history. Families lost patience with the long-term benefits of college education, regardless of academic focus. Instead, everyone fixated on vocational majors associated with the highest starting salaries. Finally, liberal arts departments sometimes became their own worst enemies, retreating into a narrow form of scholasticism that made getting a job seem like selling out.

Yet our country's original curiosity and desire to explore is inextinguishable. Within my own family, I think about my father-in-law, Jack Corcoran. Shortly after World War II, he came home from Japan with a military discharge and a chance to go to college on the G.I. Bill. Instead of working in the Connecticut factory towns that had employed his relatives for decades, he decided to try his luck at Wesleyan University. He studied biology and English, slicing his way through the tormented novels of Romain Gary. If his girlfriends didn't care for such books, he shrugged and looked for new companions.

By the time I met Jack, he had been working in military engineering for more than twenty years, but his job alone never fully defined him. Throughout his life, he has continued to seek out challenges that stretch his curiosity. One year he read up on neural networks, fascinated with computers' ability to mimic the human brain. A few years later, he tried his hand at short stories with a science-fiction twist under the pseudonym Virtual Jack. Video editing…documentaries…the projects just kept coming. College infused him with the explorer's mind-set, and that indomitable spirit never left him.

We all need to find it again.

Rome aren't ancient at all. They are reborn as pulsating, provocative counterpoints to the way we live today.

Students can't get enough of it. In the winter of 2016, more than two hundred undergraduates signed up for Antiquity Today. Several dozen were turned away; there wasn't room for them. When official enrollment settled at 159, Christesen found himself teaching one of Dartmouth's most heavily attended classes. He had corralled the equivalent of 14 percent of the freshman student body.

Don't let anyone tell you liberal arts education is dying. Standout professors are revitalizing the humanities and social sciences at colleges across America. At Harvard, philosophy professor Michael Sandel pulls as many as eleven hundred students into his wide-ranging course on justice. At the University of Texas, crowds form when English professor Elizabeth Richmond-Garza teaches Victorian literature. At schools such as the College of Charleston, San Francisco State, and Appalachian State, the most admired professors (according to student assessments) reside in the Spanish, music, and psychology departments.

Great teaching alone isn't enough, though. Fewer students are majoring in the traditional liberal arts disciplines (humanities and social sciences) amid concern such specializations will hurt their prospects after graduation. The liberal arts path doesn't guarantee a big starting salary, and the tactics that can help you make rapid headway after graduation aren't as well known as they should be. The horrifying stereotype of liberal arts majors ending up in green smocks pouring coffee at Starbucks has become a trope that won't go away.

Consider what happened when Steve Pearlstein, a professor of public affairs at George Mason University, invited honors students to read an eight-hundred-page biography of Andrew Carnegie. Everyone liked the book, with its deep insights into human character and economic struggle. Buoyed by this warm response, Pearlstein asked how many of his twenty-four students had chosen to major in a field such as history, English, or philosophy. The answer: only one. The explanation from half a dozen others: "My parents wouldn't let me."

The sheer cost of college is causing many families' time horizons to shrink. After adjusting for scholarships and tuition discounts, the average family needs to muster $27,000 a year for a student to attend a private four-year college; $14,000 annually for the in-state public equivalent. We've had hardly any inflation in most other sectors of the U.S. economy since the early 1990s — but colleges never got the memo. Costs keep rising as much as 3 percent more than the overall inflation rate year after year.

If you're a long-term thinker, the case for college as one of life's best investments remains strong, no matter what major you choose. Over time, in fact, some liberal arts majors can take you further than even the seemingly hot ticket of a computer science degree. Many parents, however, can't wait. They have become understandably fixated on starting salaries and the supposedly safe majors that will make college pay off (at least in economic terms) the fastest.

Such shackles exist even at Ivy League schools. Jill Lepore, chair of Harvard's history and literature program, periodically hosts information sessions at her house so undergraduates can learn about her interdisciplinary initiative. At one session, as Lepore ruefully recounted to the *New York Times*, an optimistic attendee was bombarded with dire text messages from her parents: *Leave right now. Get out of there. That is a house of pain.* It's easy to imagine the alarmist thoughts running through such a parent's mind: *Build your own meth lab, hitchhike across America, just don't ever set foot inside a historian's house again.*

The warier our society gets, the more we treat learning for its own sake as a fragile form of magic suited only to the confines of high schools, colleges, and universities themselves. Think of Robin Williams's recklessly enthusiastic English instructor in *Dead Poets Society* or the mathematician Alan Turing's struggles in *The Imitation Game.* These geniuses try so hard, only to discover they can't fix everything wrong with the world. We view their work with admiration and pity. Even in real life, there's a tinge of wistfulness on graduation day whenever a professor in a famously impractical field receives an award for distinguished teaching. Thousands of engineering and business graduates pocket their diplomas and race off to become rich, or so it seems, while the admired instructor must keep looping through the same academic routines, endlessly surrendering his or her gifts to an unappreciative world.

Perhaps the academic establishment has built its own cage. In the 1970s and 1980s, as college enrollment surged and newcomers gravitated toward vocational programs, faculty who taught "impractical" subjects took a stubborn pride in learning for its own sake. People who studied civil engineering might be getting trained to build bridges, people who studied nursing might be readied for careers helping patients heal in hospitals — but people who studied the likes of English, philosophy, or sociology were supposed to be operating on a higher plane, learning the purity of independent thought. Jobs would take care of themselves. Besides, for the brightest undergraduates, further education and faculty careers beckoned.

By the late 1990s, though, the old certainties were failing. Too many newly minted PhDs were chasing too few tenure-track openings at universities—creating a fresh crisis of underemployment among the most educated. Meanwhile, undergraduates who didn't want to become professors weren't sure where to turn. As liberal arts leaders took stock of society's not-so-scholarly priorities, they felt betrayed—but didn't know how to respond. Professors, deans, and provosts wanted all their undergraduates to succeed; these leaders believed what was being taught on campus was intensely valuable. They just didn't know how to connect campus-honed values to workplace needs. The more vexed these academic leaders became, the more they risked sounding both brittle and smug.

What's so poignant about this mismatch is that a winning campus-to-career alliance is within reach—if only the combatants could talk about their values, needs, and achievements in a shared language that makes sense to one another. Instead, scholars, students, and employers are at odds because of an agonizing translation problem.

Where's the common ground? Employers want to hire college graduates who write well, speak clearly, work effectively in teams, and know how to analyze complex problems. All those virtues are central to a good college education, particularly in the liberal arts. All of them are embedded—eight levels down—in the concept of *critical thinking*, which is a term much loved in academic circles. But if you ask university leaders to explain critical thinking in detail, what ensues is a cacophony of overlapping, conflicting— and self-interested—responses.

It's painful but true: when academics try hardest to define critical thinking, they inadvertently play into their detractors' stereotypes.

I've read university presidents' testimonials going back to 1935. Academic leaders keep portraying critical thinking as the ability to examine assumptions underlying an argument and the capacity to consider competing perspectives without rushing to judgment. Invoke such abstract, languid phrases in a job interview, however, and you poison your chances. When the academic community talks about what it does best, it spends too much time celebrating the processes by which scholars develop knowledge, too little time championing the real-world payoffs.

To redeem the liberal arts' good name, we need a fresh way of talking about critical thinking, this time with your postcollege career in mind. We need to showcase, as crisply as possible, the aspects of your liberal arts education that will help you make a significant difference in the world. This means translating the airy descriptors of a commencement speech into another language — the job-market phrases that will help you get hired, gain greater authority, and advance in your career. Critical thinking's renamed strengths should help you return to campus for your twentieth reunion with the knowledge that you've become everything you wanted to be long ago.

I've done my best to crack the code. The starting point: Every job ad in the United States that offers a salary of at least a hundred thousand dollars a year while also requiring strong critical-thinking skills. Most of these want ads are well-crafted manifestos of five hundred words or more. They start with detailed job descriptions and crisp lists of formal qualifications yet include some much more human touches toward the end. One of the grim beauties of the American capitalist system is that when businesses are on the brink of spending a lot of money, they tell you, quite candidly, what they want. Before long, a comprehensive picture emerges of what *critical thinking* really means to a wide cross-section of companies that need graduates like you.

Tapping into the job-ad repositories at Indeed.com in the summer of 2016, I found more than fifty-six hundred listings that offered six-figure pay while calling for critical thinking. The employers ranged from Apple to Allstate; from start-ups and consulting boutiques to the U.S. Department of Labor and Deloitte. It's a rich medley with something appealing for everyone and a powerful reminder that liberal arts values remain keenly in demand. Each time I opened up a job listing, I made a note of the specific strengths that appeared within ten lines of the key phrase *critical thinking*. It didn't take long for clusters of similar attributes to emerge.

When employers ask for critical-thinking skills, the term serves as shorthand for five crucial factors. These start with a confident willingness—perhaps even eagerness—to tackle uncharted areas where nobody knows the rules yet. You bring imagination to your job; you adapt well to new situations. Let's call this Working on the Frontier.

Next on the list, well-honed analytic methods that make you good at Finding Insights. You thrive on spotting the less obvious answer. As you gain experience and rise in power, you will start synthesizing insights in ways that make you a trusted expert when complex decisions need to be made. Let's call this higher-level power Choosing the Right Approach.

Finally, you understand group dynamics and other people's motivations in an unusually deep way. You're good at Reading the Room, and also at Inspiring Others. Your campus leaders weren't hopelessly wrong when they tried to describe these capabilities in more academic terms. But you're now better positioned to make your case in language that aligns harmoniously with what employers want. Master this framework, and you will be surprised how many of your seemingly esoteric liberal arts achievements can be retold in work-friendly contexts. Even something as offbeat as a visit to the ancient Greek battle site of Thermopylae can be relevant. You've thought hard about a momentous decision — and all the factors that play into it. If your interviewer has even the haziest familiarity with the movie *300*, you're ready to talk about what it's like to stand at a narrow pass, imagining that it's 480 B.C., the enemy is massing — and you've got an ax.

Whatever your stage in life, the analysis that follows will show how your liberal arts identity can become a strength, not an embarrassment, as you approach new jobs. You may even develop a smuggler's pride in the secret, campus-honed skills that serve you well in the outside world. You know how to ace a job interview, how to run a meeting, and how to find a nugget of truth (or a dangerous lie) in a mountain of data.

Let's take a closer look.

Working on the Frontier

Are you highly self-directed? Can you think outside the box? Can you adapt to a changing environment? Do you thrive on challenges? If you're nodding your head in response, you've got the explorer's mind-set that enterprises such as Deloitte, Humana, and the Federal Reserve are seeking. These organizations are constantly growing in unexpected directions, making them eager to hire people who embrace the new.

Since the early 1990s, psychologists have been talking up the virtues of boundary-less, "protean" careers, in which individuals write their own job descriptions and chart their own paths. When field researchers ask about actual workplace attitudes, however, it turns out most people aren't so brave. In one notable survey, the majority of subjects' self-described profiles fit researchers' categories of "solid citizens," "hired guns," and "trapped/lost." Less than a third of respondents chose the self-reliant, protean path. We're still a society that cherishes predictability, as you can see in jobs ranging from making hamburgers at McDonald's to reading X-rays at the Mayo Clinic. That's why automation and globalization frighten so many people. Both those forces keep assaulting the world of repetitive work.

Choose the liberal arts path in college, and you're throwing your lot in with the adventurers. Within the first few terms, you will be building your own interpretations on controversial topics, looking for something *new* to say, rather than parroting back your professors' views. You'll find joy in the times when you make a winning argument. When your first attempts are a bit of a mess, you will learn how to survive and regroup. By senior year, you will take charge of your own learning, picking projects, gathering data, and defining your own reading list. No matter how narrow your immediate topic of interest may be, the deeper you go, the more you acquire the universally useful skill of *knowing what to do when you're on your own.*

The most energetic professors will stretch your comfort zones in playful ways that make it easier for you to experiment. Think of them as Pan with a presentation clicker instead of a flute. Dartmouth's Paul Christesen plays that role at freshman orientation, delivering a rebel's talk in which he tells students "the best moments in life are when you are just starting something fantastic." He lets slip that he proposed to his wife, history professor Cecilia Gaposchkin, a week after they met. "Everything has worked out!" he says with a grin. Like many liberal arts colleges,

Dartmouth doesn't offer preprofessional degrees in fields such as accounting and physical therapy—and he makes no apologies for this omission.

If anything, the digital revolution makes humanistic learning more valuable, Christesen asserts. "The rise of the Internet and smartphones means that if you need extra facts, you can find them quickly," he points out. "That reduces the value of fact-packed heads that can't analyze well." He prefers to prepare people for an unpredictable future by developing universally useful ways of analyzing situations and by instilling an open-minded confidence about exploring the new. Get that right, he contends, and you've gained expertise that will pay off no matter how many times you change careers.

When Ally Begly arrived at Dartmouth in 2007, she thought she would focus on premed classes and become a doctor. In her first few months on campus, she was unsettled by how many premeds treated learning as an unpleasant chore. Her peers fixated on finding shortcuts to earning the As medical schools demanded. Begly wanted something different out of college. Having enjoyed Latin in high school, she decided the classics department might provide a better academic home for her. "It was really hard to do well in classics," she recalled. "You couldn't open a research book, learn the content, and pass it off as your knowledge. You couldn't regurgitate."

This new tempo, Begly decided, was her path to a better future. Her first major term paper in the field was a twenty-page examination of a small subset of Greek funeral urns; it explored the question of whether ancient amphorae were customized for each person's remains or were largely standardized. No textbook offered her the answer. She spent long evenings in the Dartmouth library, analyzing details and building a theory. "It was my introduction to the misery and the magic of trying to do something original," she recalled. "When I got an A, it felt really great. I was in a field where it was safe to be enthusiastic."

Since college, Begly has transformed this enthusiasm into a successful, and meaningful, career as a teacher. She is becoming an expert on the ways fourth- and fifth-grade girls learn science — and why they often experience a sudden loss of confidence academically as they approach the middle-school years. She thinks a lot about the impostor syndrome. An anxious question from one of her students stays on her mind too: Why hasn't any woman walked on the moon? "There's room for change," Begly said, "and I'd like to be part of the process."

A few years ago, Christesen asked his undergraduates to ponder why Athenian art never paid homage to naval victories in the fifth century B.C. The academic community hadn't solved that one, and Christesen wanted to see if fresh, inexperienced minds could make any headway. "Most scholars aren't any smarter than students," he later explained to me. "We simply know more, which can be a handicap if we've grown used to certain ways of thinking about things."

Undergraduate Sarah Murray seized the opportunity, developing such arresting answers that she was invited to present her findings at a major conference of classics scholars. Momentarily flustered just before going onstage, she looked to Christesen for reassurance. "I told her she would be in a room with the world's leading expert," Christesen recalled. "She looked even more aghast. And then I explained: 'It's you. You know more than anyone else.'"

A dozen years later, Murray is an academic in her own right

with faculty experience at Notre Dame and the University of Nebraska. She continues to work on the frontier, pushing ahead the new discipline of digital humanities. By introducing modern-day data analytics to antiquity's murkiest problems, she's once again finding insights no one else anticipated.

Finding Insights

Are you naturally curious? Are you good at connecting the dots? Can you filter and distill information? Are you calm and productive in the face of ambiguity? Those questions come from employers as diverse as the movie creators at Sony, the digital-storage enthusiasts at Dropbox, and the thermostat makers at Johnson Controls. Practically every organization is wrestling with the information age's awkward disparity: too much data, not enough clarity.

It takes training to feel at home with mountains of incomplete, haphazardly organized information, to become confident you can distill everything into a few powerful insights. When Hui Min Chang arrived at the University of Chicago as a freshman in 2009, she knew she could gain some of this mind-set by studying economics. To her surprise, though, further breakthroughs came in an entirely different field: nineteenth-century French art.

"I did a paper for my senior seminar on Édouard Manet's *Olympia*," Chang told me. It's a provocative painting that has scandalized generations of viewers, partly because the central figure is a naked French woman with no trace of shame on her face, but also because the secondary figure is a black servant in a jarringly deferential pose. The painting, the historical context, public reactions — Chang reveled in each aspect. "I ended up explaining the context of that nude vis-à-vis French attitudes toward salons, liberty, prostitution, and more," Chang recalled. While she didn't discuss *Olympia* specifically in her interviews for finance-industry jobs, she frequently talked up her art-history interests as a sign of an inquiring mind.

Employers bought her argument. Today Chang is an associate investment analyst at Morningstar, a Chicago financial-research firm. She specializes in writing about quant investments, approaches that use intricate computer models to predict trends across capital markets. The job, as she explains it, challenges her to sort through many complex factors at once, just as she did in her undergraduate days. "In the markets, it's not obvious what the driver is for the next six months," she told me. "It's similar to art history. You can't cover everything. You have to pick and choose."

A liberal arts education is hardly the only way to master such challenges. Keep the number of unknowns under control, and a specialist's background in business or engineering may prove better. Graduates from either of those programs are well-trained problem solvers too. The foundations of critical thinking aren't monastic secrets unknown outside the humanities and social sciences. Yet in the most turbulent fields, everything is in flux and nobody's model works perfectly. When the extent of what's unknown hasn't been established, the fluidity and highly developed lateral thinking of liberal arts training can carry the day. A background in the humanities and social sciences helps you get comfortable working with scanty data when nothing better is available. You become good at building provisional inferences when others are stuck. Often your early guesses prove right, making you unusually good at spotting emerging patterns before others do.

Consider how much can be extracted from a few snippets of military history in any culture. The texts don't just recount a battle; they share clues about what people ate, what they wore, and how each side's social hierarchies worked. What's omitted can be revelatory too. (Where are the women?) You could spend hours picking at one short passage before you are sure you've extracted as much as possible. Step into a business setting a few years later, and you will discover the same game is alive again. Everything from negotiators' terse e-mails to a competitor's ad copy can tell you a lot more than the surface reveals if you just pay close enough attention.

Evan Golden has settled into Los Angeles as an independent screenwriter. His scripts focus on modern-day dramas involving everything from women's professional wrestling to failed marriages. He studied classics in college a decade ago and says it helps him in his current work. "When you're trying to establish a character's motivation, it's surprisingly similar to inferring why people moved an ancient city from low ground to high ground," Golden told me. "I've spent a lot of time analyzing famous films, but it isn't the same. All the decisions have been made. All you see is the finished product. You can't really reconstruct all the choices the screenwriter or director had, and why he or she went down a particular path." Confronting open-ended uncertainty—and then deciding what to do about it—is "a rare gift that classics provides to everyone."

Arthur Motch started college as an economics major, thinking it would prepare him for a career as a professional investor. To his chagrin, he didn't like econ's large lecture classes or its rigid curriculum. He went hunting for a different field that invited students to develop fresh ideas in small seminars. Classics fit the bill.

He could sharpen his mind by doing fine-grained text analysis for hours and then match wits with a handful of classmates in provocative class discussions. "I liked the sense of figuring it out, reaching the point where I realized something no one else knew," Motch recalled.

These days, Motch runs Sustainable Income Capital Management, a twenty-million-dollar hedge fund in New York, specializing in unusual types of debt instruments other investors ignore. (Think municipal-lighting-system bonds.) He's famous for finding tidbits in the back pages of financial statements that help him spot unusual value or avoid pitfalls. "I'm one of the very few people who reads all the footnotes," Motch quipped. "That's how you can spot the classics majors on Wall Street."

Choosing the Right Approach

Are you a problem solver? Can you act on opportunities? Can you find creative solutions? Can we trust you to make the go/no-go decisions? Organizations such as FedEx, McKinsey, and PayPal ask questions like these when their attention turns to critical thinking. The reason: Business is complicated. The higher you move in management, the more you deal with tough situations where the best solution isn't always obvious. Such circumstances require discernment, decisiveness, and the magic blend that goes by the name of good judgment.

One school of thought argues that good judgment can't be rushed. All we can do is stumble through life for a while, gradually learning from our mistakes. Yet a well-structured college education can provide a spectacular blend of case studies, teaching precepts, and iterative revisions of major assignments. Taken together, these experiences can accelerate the journey toward better judgment. Liberal arts classes, in particular, train students to keep taking the wide view, allowing them to pick up important factors on the periphery that they might otherwise overlook. That's how people read novels; it's how they build sociological models; it's the essence of careful history or political science. I can't find my college diploma anymore; it got lost somewhere in the course of ten postgraduation moves. But if I close my eyes, I can still hear a chorus of long-ago history and literature professors asking our classes: "What else? What else?"

Less than two years after graduating from the University of Michigan (BA, psychology, 2015), Isabelle Abrams found her judgment being tested in a big way. She had settled into a consulting job that involved face-to-face dealings with big consumer-products companies. One client wanted to understand why pet owners split their shopping across different stores. Everything sounded simple at first. Then the project got complicated. Was this mostly about dog and cat food or did food for other pets matter too? What about people who bought fish food from friendly experts in specialty stores but hunted for rock-bottom prices on dog food in grocery stores? Each client meeting revealed new subtleties that hadn't been on the table before. It took considerable diplomacy to keep redesigning the survey without leaving everyone feeling frustrated.

"We probably needed twenty hours of meetings to figure everything out—but we did it," Abrams told me. "I realized it was essential to ask *Why?* questions. We had to resist the temptation to race ahead to a quick answer. Everything was usually a bigger issue than what surfaced at first."

Michigan had prepared her well. As a college junior, Abrams had helped marketing researchers analyze people's perceptions of healthy and unhealthy foods with an eye to eaters' subsequent eagerness (or lack thereof) to work off the calories they had just ingested. That study required her and her research colleagues to think deeply about why study subjects held the food attitudes that they did, even if those views seemed illogical. Other psychology projects introduced her to the abrupt judgments that people make when deciding whether to be generous or stingy. She came out of college knowing a lot about the obvious and hidden factors that influence decisions; she was unusually well prepared for a high-stakes consulting job.

Such aspects of critical thinking become increasingly important as your career plays out. Entry-level jobs typically adhere to well-established rules. Someone older and more experienced will tell you what to do and how to do it. This quasi-parental oversight soon fades, especially if you are ambitious. Before long, it's time to make decisions on your own, even if the facts are hazy and the rules unknown. Your nominal bosses won't know any more than you do. It will be up to you whether to build a product or scrap it; whether to approve an edgy ad campaign or start over. Equivocating won't be an option. You get paid for your acumen; success will require you to be perceptive in a wide range of ways.

How can you train yourself for such challenges? Amy Pressman studied history—and a lot more—at Harvard in the 1980s, without any expectation of going on to a career in business. Today, she is president of Medallia, a Silicon Valley software company that partners with everyone from Google to Gallup. When I asked her how she developed the mind-set that makes her effective today, she started describing a chaotic term in college when she was taking classes in art, sociology, psychology, and physics. "All of them were stressing the concept of space from four completely different perspectives," she recalled. "It made me realize that no idea exists in isolation. I got in the habit of looking for connective tissue, even when it wasn't obvious."

Reading the Room

Can you build a team? Can you balance different perspectives and agendas? Can you understand the big picture? Can you manage through influence? Employers have been looking for these sorts of socially minded strengths since at least the 1930s. At first, this was an unambitious search, focused mostly on finding sales clerks with pleasant personalities. Not anymore. Financial giants such as BlackRock routinely cite team-building as a priority when hiring people for jobs paying a hundred thousand dollars a year or more. Leading Internet retailers such as eBay want candidates who know how to satisfy multiple agendas and still keep everything moving forward.

These are teachable strengths — and college is a great place to learn them. People are starting to jettison the well-traveled but condescending label *soft skills* in public discussion of these traits. I'm encountering a flurry of interest in *power skills*, which sounds far more apt. In the same spirit, *emotional intelligence* is a much-talked-about screening criterion in hunts for chief executives. All of these variants, of course, are very much in step with the liberal arts' emphasis on understanding different people's perspectives.

At Southwestern University, just north of Austin, Texas, English professor Helene Meyers asked some of her undergraduates in the autumn of 2015 to list the academic skills they had mastered. As she later recounted in the *Chronicle of Higher Education*, the students' lists began with writing and research but went on to include listening, speaking, managing a project, and "the ability to connect the small with the big picture." When Meyers asked what surprised students the most, "one of them excitedly blurted out, 'These are all marketable skills.'"

Indeed. Analyze literature, and you're digging deep into the main characters' competing motivations. During a course entitled Novel English Majors, Meyers introduced her students to a wide variety of careers in which well-read students of the human condition could thrive. Examples ranged from grant writing to managing restaurants and running nonprofits. Even the tech sector was in reach. As Meyers wrote: "If students have learned to connect diverse texts and traditions, they very likely have developed the skills needed to be liaisons between software creators and end users."

Study sociology, history, or political science, and the same dynamic is in play. You explore the tension between labor and management, immigrants and nativists, or any of the countless groups in opposition. You develop a keen sense of how coalitions form and conflicts get resolved. In any of these disciplines, you balance competing ideas in your own mind; you create carefully calibrated models that take the whole picture into account.

Know what makes other people tick, and you can steer through complex situations skillfully. "Most liberal arts majors have a conscience — or at least they have been taught the basis for forming one," a Chicago hiring manager told me in the midst of a long conversation about his firm's recruiting practices. He wasn't trying to malign people with preprofessional degrees. But he was trying to help me gain a deeper understanding of the reasons why an aptitude for reading the room makes business sense. Find people whose college educations emphasized taking a panoramic view of everyone else's concerns, and those fairness-first attitudes can prevent big trouble down the road.

Sometimes, humility is the hidden virtue employers want. During college, Joe Indvik struggled to pin down the accuracy or follies of Herodotus's ancient histories. Indvik came up with some intriguing ideas but also conceded that in certain areas, "We just don't know." Now he works in Washington, DC, as an environmental consultant, advising the Department of Energy and an assortment of start-ups. Many engagements involve bridging different viewpoints on the same problem, in the same way that a historian unravels conflicting narratives. "Sometimes, the right answer is the midpoint of all the viewpoints. Sometimes, a viewpoint is just plain wrong. I find that the best leaders are humble enough to understand when their behavior is part of the very problem they are trying to solve."

Immerse yourself deeply in another culture, and a more compassionate self emerges. Kari Dallas visited Greece as a liberal arts undergraduate more than a decade ago, but she still remembers a shocking incident that occurred in a Greek town while she was walking through the city streets beside a classmate with intensely blue eyes. "A young girl stared in horror at those blue eyes and crossed herself," Dallas recalled. "It was as if she had seen a devil." It's about digging into the way things are in a place, not just the way they seem.

Serving more recently as a lawyer in eastern Oregon, Dallas has dealt mostly with trusts and business transactions. "I work with clients who have limited English or who bring their children or friends along as interpreters," she told me. "My time in Greece has certainly influenced those dealings. It helped me understand what it's like to be the stranger... to be out of place."

Inspiring Others

Can you inspire confidence? Can you energize others to embrace change? Are you concise and organized? Can you convey information effectively? There's a new urgency in employers' wish lists when it comes to hiring the type of person who can connect with other people. Morale is more fragile, cynicism runs deeper, and hard-nosed assertions of authority end up being the opposite of leadership. Businesses don't run well when customers are confused, when employees become lethargic, or when everyone is dispirited. Strong leadership can't exist in a vacuum; it needs to take root in face-to-face, heart-to-heart communications, every day.

If your critical-thinking skills include the ability to speak or write persuasively, employers such as American Express, Cox Communications, and Genentech want you, now. One huge zone of opportunity involves traditional clusters in advertising, marketing, speechwriting, and public relations. There's equally strong demand in core business areas where leadership and communication have become so intertwined that it's impossible to separate those two traits. If you're interested in sales, strategic planning, recruiting, consulting, project management, or a host of other job categories, take note. Your ability to tell a story—or win an argument—will win employers' admiration.

As an English major at Mississippi College, Susan Farris focused on the emotional struggles we choose to hide. She won a campus writing prize for a short story about the bedside evasions associated with a dying woman's final days. When she graduated in 2013, she wasn't sure where to turn. Friends steered her toward EdgeTheory, a Mississippi social-media company scrambling to find high-empathy writers and editors.

In May 2016, I spent a morning watching Farris construct

messages of hope and hardship on behalf of a nurse-training program trying to reach new candidates via Twitter. "This is a long game," Farris explained to me. Getting the mood right was everything. With Farris at the keyboard, everything being transmitted spoke about saving lives...overcoming panic...fighting cancer... or staying alert on the night shift. The hard sell for the $425 training classes could wait. For now, the short-story writer was stirring people's feelings, and getting paid properly for it.

A few months later, I chatted with a cluster of recent liberal arts graduates creating digital-marketing material in Provo, Utah. They reinforced Farris's message of pride and relief; they weren't just comma-moving technicians trying to make corporate prose sound better—they were enjoying the freedom and authority to define a big organization's story. Power had shifted. In the noisy, jaded society of today, the ability to inspire other people is becoming more valuable than ever.

"I humanize things," explained Bryce Nobles, a 2015 graduate of Brigham Young University. To him, there was a natural path between his BYU days as an American studies major, reading Thoreau, Whitman, and Emerson, and his current job. He created the charts, e-books, and reports that Qualtrics, a market-research company, used in connecting with its customers. "What's the customer experience?" he asked me. "What's the American dream? They aren't so far apart."

Traditionally, the peak moments of a liberal arts education are defined by writing. College is where you struggle to master the demands of a twenty-page term paper or perhaps a much longer senior thesis. Within the world of the university, writing is still regarded as the highest form of communication. Away from academia, however, priorities are different. We've become a nation of talkers. The past twenty years have seen the rise of podcasts, webinars, talk radio, TED Talks, conference calls, Skype, and YouTube videos. Traditional barriers of distance and cost have vanished. New technology (especially dirt-cheap Internet band-width) has realigned the way we communicate. Speech is in the ascendant, while formal writing is struggling to hold its stature.

This transition shouldn't distress you. Even if your professors' grading metrics haven't caught up, the everyday nature of study-ing the humanities and social sciences will serve you well. Those freewheeling gab sessions late at night in the dorm weren't a waste of time after all. When the Association of American Colleges and Universities asked employers recently to list the most important skills college graduates should possess, *strong speaking skills* showed up at the very top. *Strong writing skills* was second.

I see the payoff in the workplace constantly. On the speaking circuit, at industry conferences, and in small meetings, certain presenters stand out. Their advantage transcends nice clothes, winning smiles, or well-modulated voices. They are "comfortable and charismatic," to borrow a phrase from a BlackBerry job ad. These speakers move smoothly back and forth between key points and supportive detail. They know how to make numbers and nar-rative work in harmony. They use wit quite skillfully. Analogies too. As for their majors—you know the answer.

Visit TED.com, and you will encounter hundreds of exciting onstage presentations by scientists, politicians, social activists, and other people of note. Several hundred talks at TED confer-ences have earned at least one million page views since being released online. As of early 2017, only three have crossed the thirty-million-view threshold—a level that makes them arguably more popular than any music single released in the past twenty years. Atop this list is a talk on creativity by English and drama major Ken Robinson, followed by a presentation on body language by social psychologist Amy Cuddy, and then a talk on the ways great leaders inspire action by anthropology major Simon Sinek.

Rhetoric, as it happens, was one of antiquity's original seven liberal arts. Mindful of that heritage, Dartmouth's Paul Christesen asks undergraduates in the Greece study-abroad program to deliver a half-hour talk at some point summing up their backgrounds, interests, achievements, anxieties, and ambitions. There are no other rules. Preparing for these talks becomes a soulsearching exercise that students vividly remember a decade later. Some admit to imagining themselves being back in Greece again and again, revising their youthful remarks each year as they redefine who they've become and who they want to be.

At another juncture, Christesen's students visit the ruined sanctuary of Delphi; each student has been assigned an altar or a statue to research ahead of time. On the afternoon of the visit, students walk the grounds together and take turns sharing their knowledge with as much zest as they can muster. The hallmark of a winning presentation: attracting a following of casual tourists who think official docents are providing a guided tour.

In 2009, Alexandra Maceda was a Dartmouth sophomore standing in front of the three surviving columns of what was once a twenty-column temple. "This is the Tholos," she began. In her black shorts and long-sleeved fleece jersey, she looked like just another college student. But as she gestured toward the temple's walls and benches, a crowd began to form. She knew so much! She was so confident! Australian backpackers wiggled forward so they could hear better.

Two years later, Maceda won a well-paying consulting job at Bain and Company right after graduation. With a bachelor's degree in classics, she didn't know as much about financial modeling as some of the business majors Bain had hired from other schools. She had a lot of catching up to do, but she was comfortable working on the edge. She could build bridges between different kinds of information. What's more, whenever she got up to speak, she radiated her own version of comfortable charisma. She was exactly what Bain needed.

3

You Can Start Anywhere

Growing up in Southern California, Mai-Ling Garcia acted like a teenager without any direction. Her grades were ragged; her long-term plans nonexistent. After marrying early, she moved to her in-laws' residence in San Jacinto, California, a working-class community halfway between Los Angeles and the Mojave Desert, where one-fifth of the population lives below the poverty line. In San Jacinto, the biggest private-sector employer is the Soboba tribal casino. Crime rates are high, and even legal forms of entertainment are not for the squeamish. Some years ago, the Soboba casino gave birth to King of the Cage martial-arts battles, in which combatants step into a pen surrounded by chain-link fencing. Something close to a prison brawl breaks out, with punches and kicks raging until one of the fighters gives up.

If you want a better life in this town, progress starts with community college. The two-year program at Mount San Jacinto College accepts anyone with a high-school diploma (and some people without). Popular classes include auto repair and English as a second language; a few strivers try Shakespeare and Veblen. Tuition is free and annual fees are minimal. Going back to school didn't interest Garcia until the Marines sent her husband to the Middle East for an extended tour of duty. Out of cash and tired of subsistence jobs, she was ready to try something new.

On a whim, Garcia enrolled at MSJC, signing up for psychology and sociology classes. At first, nobody pegged her for greatness. "She didn't sit in the front row," psychology professor Maria Lopez-Moreno recalled. "She would be in the middle of the lecture hall. I remember she had this cream-colored scarf with purple trim. She would play with the edges of it during lectures, or she would throw it back over her shoulder. She wasn't really focused."

Then something started to catch. The scarf-twirling student began asking insightful questions about the basis for hopelessness and criminal behavior. Intrigued, Professor Lopez-Moreno took this new student aside after class and asked: "Why are you here?" Garcia blurted out everything: marrying a Marine right after high school, moving to this desert town to be near his military base, seeing him head off to Iraq—and not knowing what to do next. Lopez-Moreno couldn't walk away. "I said to myself: 'Uh-oh. I've got to suggest something to her.'"

Apply for a place in Mount San Jacinto's honors program, the professor advised. Garcia did so, won admission—and began to thrive in a new environment of smaller classes and more motivated peers. During faculty office hours, Garcia and Lopez-Moreno had regular chats about classes, ideas, and life. The psychology professor pointed Garcia toward essays about ethics, morality, and crime. For the first time in her life, Garcia became a straight-A student, eager to master her course work. Drawing on her own multicultural heritage (Filipino and Irish), Garcia became a leader in campus diversity initiatives. She emerged as a confident, polite communicator with a knack for building coalitions.

Before long, the head of Mount San Jacinto's honors program, sociology professor Denise Dalaimo, emerged as a second mentor. "You should think about transferring to Berkeley or UCLA after you're finished here," Dalaimo said. "Me?" Garcia asked. "Yes," Dalaimo replied. It wasn't easy to leap from a community college to one of California's top universities, but it could be done. During Garcia's sophomore year, Professors Dalaimo and Lopez-Moreno coached their protégée on how to put together a winning application. Berkeley offered her admission and substantial aid. A brighter future awaited.

Today, Garcia is a leading digital strategist for the City of Oakland, California. She has made it to the big time. From her spacious ninth-floor office in Oakland's city hall, she enjoys a stunning view of a lush green plaza below. Her annual salary, benefits, and bonus top $130,000 a year. Best of all, she makes her living doing something she loves: cutting through procedural red tape to make city government more relevant and helpful for Oakland's four hundred thousand residents. "I like to think of myself as a bureaucratic ninja," Garcia told me over coffee at an upscale Oakland café.

Garcia's drawn-out, stormy journey to success isn't a disadvantage that she tries to hide; it's a valuable asset, even today. In city meetings, she's the voice of disadvantaged residents who don't own iPhones but still want to get on the Internet. "I know what it's like to be too poor to own a computer," Garcia told me. "I'm the one in meetings who asks, 'Never mind how well this new app works on an iPhone; will it run on an old, public-library computer? Because that's the only way some of our residents will get to use it.'" She knows firsthand what it's like to struggle with household bills while waiting for government agencies to send benefit checks. She has testified before the state legislature on inequities in veterans' benefits programs, sharing the results of her sociological research on military families from the San Jacinto area.

Take a close look at how liberal arts graduates make their way toward winning careers, and you will see that such gritty paths are common. Success isn't a straight line. Getting a bachelor's degree in English, psychology, history, anthropology, or other liberal arts disciplines doesn't guarantee you a predictable job at Amalgamated History Industries for the next forty years. You will need to keep improvising your future — and that's all right. You may switch cities two or three times in your twenties. You may switch employers five or six times. Each cycle of change expands your skills, your horizons, and your intuition for what should come next. You become both student and teacher, able to define opportunities that others can't see.

Even the Dartmouth classics majors cited in the previous chapter keep improvising their careers to an extent that would flabbergast their counterparts in engineering, business, or premed programs. Alex Maceda, the Greek-temple guide who won a postcollege job at Bain, stayed at that company for three years and then headed off to a San Francisco start-up, where she specialized in retail innovation and product management. She eventually left that job in favor of graduate school. Joe Indvik, the environmental consultant in Washington, briefly tried his luck as a venture capitalist. Ally Begly, the education innovator, spent eight months as a data analyst for the National Park Service before walking away from what had become a "soul-crushing" job.

Traditionally, our society admires people who go exploring with or without a coherent plan. We celebrate their journeys in movies, novels, and memoirs (such as Yann Martel's *Life of Pi*, Cheryl Strayed's *Wild*, and J. R. R. Tolkien's *The Hobbit*). Everything usually works out in these well-known stories, even if the tiger eats the goat — or the first pair of hiking boots ends up at the bottom of a ravine. Yet when it comes to the college-to-career pathway, well-meaning advisers refuse to see the advantages of improvisation or the rewards of being prepared for the challenges of a turbulent world. Instead, all they talk about are starting salaries, starting salaries, and starting salaries.

What's so baffling about this new pessimism is that it's out of step with what broad economic data tells us. Taking the explorer's path still works out well. In fact, the benefits may be increasing.

In 2015, the Bureau of Labor Statistics published data on the number of jobs people have held between ages eighteen and forty-eight, sorted by four different levels of education. Mobility ran lowest among people who didn't finish high school or who had nothing more than a high-school education. (They averaged 11.7 and 11.5 jobs, respectively.) For people with some college education or a four-year college degree, job mobility increased. (They averaged 12.3 and 11.8 jobs, respectively.) It's old-fashioned to regard a college education as a path to greater job stability. College provides something more precious: the ability to switch jobs successfully when new opportunities arise or old ones wither.

Fixating on starting salaries blinds us to the value of mobility. It's true that people with business, engineering, and other preprofessional degrees generally win higher pay straight out of college. Engineers frequently keep that lead for most of their careers, and good for them! For graduates in many other preprofessional fields, however, the earnings curve flattens out. It's liberal arts majors, particularly those in history, political science, international relations, and philosophy, who see their earnings rocket ahead. Full details on these trends and how to use them to your advantage can be found in chapter 13, "Getting Paid Properly." For now, it's sufficient to say that a decade or two after graduation, your liberal arts degree is likely to propel you ahead of many classmates with practical majors who thought they had seized an unbeatable lead at age twenty-two.

It's time to help meandering regain its good name.

This chapter will show how resilient the liberal arts' strengths can be, even in settings that hardly resemble the Ivy League comforts of the previous chapter. Take away the resources of Dartmouth's Baker-Berry Library with its two million volumes, and you can still tap into endless knowledge at any smaller college with an Internet connection. Take away the many benefits of a well-established study-abroad program in Greece, and you can create your own life-changing immersion program by doing field research in schools, hospitals, or police precincts within thirty miles of your campus. Take away the bracing experience of being surrounded by hundreds of valedictorians and National Merit Scholars who have won admission to the world's most elite schools, and you can still find classmates at less-famous schools who will stretch your horizons and inspire you to try harder.

Only one element can't be discarded without ruining everything: your own desire to grow. If you want to work on the frontier, sharpen your analytic skills, and embrace the best elements of a liberal arts education, you can make remarkable progress anywhere—and that includes schools that some cynic might refer to as Rustic College or Proletariat State. The mayor of America's tenth-largest city (San Jose, California) and a recent chief data scientist of the United States both got started at the same two-year institution: De Anza College. By contrast, if you sleep through classes, skip the reading, and pay someone else to write your papers, it's all a charade, regardless of how prestigious your school might be.

In September 2015, Richard Ekman, president of the Council of Independent Colleges, invited me to Washington to hear a daylong presentation on the virtues of small liberal arts schools such as Ohio Wesleyan and Emerson College. All the professional educators at the conference made appropriately worthy points. The showstopping moments, however, came when individual graduates opened up about their personal journeys. The recurring theme: how an open-minded spirit of inquiry brought them to a better life.

Bill Newsome concentrated on physics at Stetson University in Florida but also tried some religion classes, just because he could. Those haphazard explorations eventually led him to a nationally prominent role in medical ethics. Isaac Holeman recalled the sudden realization, as a freshman at Lewis and Clark College in Oregon, that he wasn't just consuming other people's knowledge anymore; he could start creating knowledge himself. By the time he graduated, he had the confidence and the audacity to found Medic Mobile, a company that uses smartphone services to provide better health care in rural Africa.

Right after college, I took an entry-level job at a big newspaper, copyediting minor news stories and writing headlines. My boss was a stocky, irritable man in his mid-forties who was consumed by the idea that Yale graduates enjoyed unimaginable career networks that he would never experience. Every few days, John would fulminate about the power of secret societies such as Skull and Bones. In his view, Yale's clubby elite was capable of parking any of its members, no matter how dumb or lazy, into a job that paid vastly more than his or mine. All us younger fellows stifled our smiles when these outbursts began. Yet there was something genuinely distressing in his belief that he had gone to the wrong school and that nothing he ever did could make up for this failing.

Even though some people still fixate on ranking schools' prestige, the opportunities to start anywhere—and rise high—are stronger than ever. In the summer of 2015, LinkedIn data analyst Alice Ma tracked the destinies of more than one million liberal arts majors who had graduated from colleges across the United States in the previous ten years. She found about 9 percent of them had migrated into the tech sector, often for showcase jobs at impressive companies such as Facebook, Uber, and Airbnb. The migration rate was slightly higher (9.9 percent) for graduates of elite schools in the top-twenty lists of *U.S. News and World Report* than it was for graduates of schools that didn't make the top-hundred lists (7.5 percent), but *not all that different*.

Among the schools providing especially robust pipelines into good tech-sector jobs: Western Washington University, University of South Florida, San Francisco State, Arizona State, and Temple University. All of them placed at least two hundred liberal arts graduates into tech-sector jobs during the period that Ma studied. Widen the list further, to include any college that sent at least thirty liberal arts graduates into the tech sector, and you're looking at a list of many hundreds of schools, ranging from Azusa Pacific to Western Kentucky. The data scientist's conclusion: "You don't need to attend an Ivy League school to make your liberal arts degree work for you in the long run."

If you're looking for a path into the tech-influenced sector of the economy, or if you just want a good job in any realm that will put your liberal arts education to work, here are five specific themes that can improve your odds, no matter where you start.

The Courage to Explore

Do the assigned reading. Review the study guide at least three times. Answer the prompt. Know the grading rubric and make sure you conform to it... Curriculum designers have done a lot in the past twenty years to take the exploration out of education. The fastest route to an A in many classes is to provide the answers that the system is expecting—and dodge any controversial or unresolved areas where your emerging ideas might break the rules.

College doesn't have to be that way. Freethinkers can still be found in many classrooms, and when they come in contact with one another, good things happen. Mai-Ling Garcia's academic awakening began when two professors at a community college encouraged her to aim higher. Josh Sucher found his tribe in a series of design classes after college, when he realized his dormant interest in anthropology could be revived in a big way as part of the tech sector's user-experience community. For the Dartmouth students in the previous chapter, their greatest moments of personal growth came when classics professor Paul Christesen tossed them into the deep end of the pool of knowledge—and encouraged them to find answers themselves.

How do any of us build up the courage to explore? In 2014, former Hartwick College president Richard Detweiler set out to study the difference between people who achieved major lifelong benefits from their college experience and those who didn't fare nearly so well. Being a research psychologist by training, he set up a thousand-person survey that peered into the fates of college graduates at all stages in life. His youngest respondents were in their twenties; his oldest in their sixties. Half of his survey looked at outcomes. Who had risen into leadership jobs? Who was earning at least a hundred thousand dollars a year? And who felt fundamentally satisfied with the way everything in life (family, health, peace of mind) had worked out?

With the other half of his survey, Detweiler asked respondents to recall their actual day-to-day habits during college. Who studied a lot? Who was deeply involved in extracurricular activities? Who spent a lot of time talking about social issues with friends? Who got to know classmates with radically different attitudes and backgrounds? And who got to know professors outside of class? All told, Detweiler tracked nearly a dozen important ways that his respondents' college experiences might have varied.

Data in hand, Detweiler began looking for the top performers' unique edge. The factor that caught his eye: building a close affinity with at least a few professors. About one-third of his respondents had made an extra effort to stop by for office hours, to meet for lunch—and to ask for professors' job tips, life advice, and other pointers that deepened the mentor-protégé relationship. The payoff: Students who sought out faculty mentors had a 28 percent higher chance of getting a better-than-average first job after graduation. Later on, these graduates were nearly twice as likely to end up in leadership positions. Generally, they felt more fulfilled in life. And they were more likely to be seen as mentors to others.

It sounds counterintuitive, but great mentoring and adversity often go hand in hand. After all, mentoring at its core is all about helping you overcome your doubts and frailties so that you can unlock the stronger, more capable you that's been hidden away for too long.

What mentors do is heroic, but the best mentors don't need to be textbook heroes themselves. Often it's their own zigzags and personal struggles that make them uniquely good at connecting with students. Or to make the point another way, consider the credo of Drew University's Jennifer Kohn: "My long and winding journey helps me help my students." Drew's faculty website lists Kohn as an associate professor of economics. That's part of her identity—but there's so much more. She has been a philosophy major at the University of Massachusetts, Amherst, a political campaign manager, a consumer advocate, and the senior administrator of a leading New York hospital's cardiology unit. She knows life can be full of strange, branching paths that lead from one type of career to another. That helps her see ways that students with widely scattered passions can pursue nonformulaic jobs that might unify what others regard as conflicting priorities. As a result, when Drew students aren't sure what to do next, they walk up the narrow staircase of Lewis House to Kohn's third-floor office. They chat about everything and nothing with her, trying to make all the pieces come together.

One student loved art history but kept feeling parental pressure to aim toward a job in finance. You can have both, Kohn explained. Take a seminar on Wall Street's operations—and turn your attention to the way the art market works. Full-time consultants advise people on what paintings or sculptures to buy. You could make a career in that happy junction of money and beauty. Other students have wanted to pair business and music, or business and psychology. It's hard to come up with a combination that Kohn can't tackle. She knows an endless assortment of people from her previous jobs. She's a facilitator and a doer by nature.

No matter how renowned or unappreciated your campus might be, there's someone on the faculty who wants to help you become a bolder, more confident explorer. Make the most of that opportunity. Even if you can't convert each possibility into a job or a breakthrough research project, you will come away with a greater sense of what's feasible—and a renewed desire to chart your own future.

Keep Learning After College

What can you do with a master's degree in Irish history? When Chris LaRoche was in his early thirties, he hated being asked that question. He could tell you why the Irish Uprising of 1798 failed or what Jonathan Swift really meant when writing about Ireland's politics in 1728. LaRoche still thought of himself as a thinker, probing into different cultures and the complexities of why people make the choices that they do. Unfortunately, LaRoche's dreams of becoming a history professor had fallen apart. He had lost the funding needed to pursue a PhD, and his master's degree from Trinity College wasn't much consolation. Neither was his undergraduate literature degree from the University of Connecticut.

LaRoche now works for MIT—a leap that isn't easy to make. It's worth looking closely at how he pulled it off. Like many people in this book, he migrated into a new type of work that blends a little bit of tech with a lot of the empathetic, inquisitive skills that he picked up during his liberal arts days. He taught himself some of the new skills that he needed. But he also did an unusually systematic job of sharpening up his résumé by making the most of what I'm going to call "the gray market" in academic knowledge. Instead of hurling himself into more full-time, costly, multiyear educational programs, he found ingenious ways of getting everything he needed—actual knowledge, formal certifications, and a new set of professional connections—via a much more ad hoc approach. His methods turn out to be cheaper, faster, and easy to emulate.

Formal degree programs may be pricing themselves into a zone of insane unaffordability, but more informal alternatives are rapidly filling the gap. Go online and you can take hundreds of tutorials or mini-courses from services such as Khan Academy,

LinkedIn Learning, Udacity.com, and EdX.org. Need a systematic, multi-session set of tutorials on Excel or Photoshop? For thirty-five dollars or less, the Internet will help you. Would you be better off with a six-week, face-to-face course or workshops on digital marketing or user-experience research? Organizations such as General Assembly, Thinkful, and Designlab have expanded into dozens of cities with such offerings. Even traditional universities have stepped up the role of just-in-time instruction via graduate certifications for students who don't have the time or money for an advanced degree but are willing to take a cluster of job-relevant classes in a new specialty.

Chris LaRoche took a while to find his footing. First he worked for a year as an administrative assistant for the State of Massachusetts. Then he drifted into technical writing. One of Boston's big mutual-fund groups paid him to write software documentation; so did several tech companies. For him, that was purgatory. "I'm not the world's best writer," LaRoche later told me. "And I found the work tiresome." He began doing what every disaffected office worker does: he started surfing the Internet on company time.

Goofing off has its merits. LaRoche grew interested—and then fascinated—at how some sites were beautifully easy to use, while others were tangled messes. He rejiggered his consulting contracts so that he could spend more time working on computer-usability projects and less time banging out arid, mechanical paragraphs for technical manuals. He was a self-taught man at this stage, which limited his earnings power and his ability to take a senior role on projects. But that could be fixed. Several Boston-area colleges were offering graduate certificates in the hands-on areas of the digital world that interested him. These were a bit grander than night school but a lot simpler and cheaper than pursuing another advanced degree. For eight thousand dollars, he could take eight classes and get a certificate in web design from Northeastern; for ten thousand dollars, he could take nine classes and get a certificate in user experience from Bentley University.

Step by step, LaRoche built a new professional network. After a while, he wasn't just a student at Northeastern; he did well enough in his classes that the university hired him to run some user-experience projects too. At usability conferences in the Boston area, he met his counterparts from Tufts, MIT, Boston College, and other local schools. Suddenly he was awash in peers who could share best practices and alert him to new job opportunities. To his surprise, he discovered most of them were liberal arts graduates as well. They all had cobbled together tech skills at some point in their journeys. What made them so valuable in the job market, though, was their empathy with users, insight into their experiences, and well-developed expertise in figuring out what users really wanted.

"We're trained in the methods of field research," LaRoche told me. "There's a lot of empathy in what we do. We also understand the differences between what users do and say. Just because users say one thing doesn't necessarily mean that's what they want to do."

When I spoke with LaRoche, he had become a full-time usability consultant to MIT, helping the university optimize its internal websites for faculty and students as well as its online courses aimed at learners in India, China, and other countries. That job called for him to keep a lot of different perspectives in mind, which many people find hard to do. For LaRoche, it is second nature. He had spent years in his youth trying to understand the tangled ways that Irish Anglicans, Irish Presbyterians, and Irish Catholics all reacted to the uprising of 1798. In his new job, he was harnessing those skills once again.

Move Early and Often

When Brian Anderson graduated from the University of Arizona in 1991 with a degree in psychology, he lingered in the Grand Canyon State for another eighteen months, trying to get his own business started. When that didn't work out, he decided his best opportunities would be in California. He relocated to Silicon Valley and enrolled in a master's program in organizational psychology at San Jose State University. "I had this feeling that if I could get into a hot geography, a lot of good things would happen," Anderson told me.

Ever since, Anderson's career has been on the fast track. He became one of Silicon Valley's early specialists in talent assessment and coaching, helping technically trained engineers master the managerial and interpersonal skills needed to be effective leaders. The more rapidly companies grew, the greater the need for his skills. Working for Personnel Decisions in the 1990s, Anderson opened offices in three California cities, eventually rising to be a vice president. After that, he developed a leadership-effectiveness program for another big consulting firm and did the same for Apple a few years later. Now he runs his own consulting shop, Performance Edge. Much of his advice invokes classic liberal arts virtues, he says, including the importance of "abstract thinking, judgment, and speed of learning."

What works in Silicon Valley is just as effective in similar growth hubs across the country. Seattle belongs on any opportunity seeker's list. So does Boston, Research Triangle Park in North Carolina, and the greater Washington, DC, area. Job openings there are more bountiful, average pay is higher, and labor markets often end up being so tight that employers are unusually likely to end a job interview with every candidate's favorite question: "When can you start?"

In his book *The New Geography of Jobs*, Berkeley economist Enrico Moretti explains why these regional economy booms have become so extensive—and long lasting. Growth in tech jobs is only part of the story. What's more significant is that each metro area turns into a "brain hub" that attracts clever people across many disciplines. You can see the evidence on display in the sidewalk cafés of Mountain View, California, or the antique shops of Alexandria, Virginia. These metro areas become packed with an unusually high percentage of college graduates, who cluster in the same neighborhoods for social compatibility.

Software engineers like to live near graphic designers, who enjoy mingling with architects at coffee shops. Lawyers, writers, city planners, and community activists join the mix. Theaters and art galleries spring up, providing edgy entertainment for appreciative audiences and more work for college-trained artists. Prosperity feeds on itself, to the point that a fifteen-hundred-dollar check to a moving company can become one of the best investments of your life.

When should you make a Moretti move? These relocations can pay off anywhere on the continuum between picking a college and starting your fourth or fifth job. If you live in South Carolina and are looking at college choices within three hundred miles of your home, getting into a DC-area school such as George Washington or George Mason will put you in a peer group where typical graduates earn $57,000 to $64,000 a year. Stay closer to home, and even though the cost of living will be lower, your paycheck is likely to be annoyingly smaller. Graduates of South Carolina schools with comparable reputations to GWU and GMU earn nearly 25 percent less than their northern counterparts.

In California, San Jose State is perhaps the most extreme example of what good geography can do for you. The California school isn't especially selective; it takes 63 percent of all applicants. It's rated number 39 by *U.S. News and World Report* among regional western universities. But its campus is just ten miles from Apple's headquarters. The payoff? Apple's top source of college talent, according to LinkedIn's databases, is San Jose State, with 1,494 hires. Stanford is in second place, nearly 250 hires behind.

Wait until after college, and the argument for a Moretti move is just as strong. Look at the Dartmouth graduates in the previous chapter as cases in point. Nobody stayed in Hanover, New Hampshire, even though the Dartmouth campus and surrounding town is quite beautiful. For Evan Golden, his dreams of making it as a screenwriter meant heading to Los Angeles. Environmental consultant Joe Indvik settled in Washington. Professional investor Arthur Motch opted for New York. No matter what your ambitions might be, take a moment to consider which cities are hungriest for talent like yours.

If you're especially restless right after college, that's a virtue, not a flaw. You're probably at the peak of your lifetime "freedom curve"—unencumbered by the commitments associated with raising a family or owning a home. You can make a go of it in a new city, whether that means sharing a house with friends or renting a studio apartment on your own. All the mechanics of relocation get harder after age thirty. The best opportunities to make geography work for you are available right now.

Making Audacity Pay Off

Growing up in a Mississippi cotton town, LeAnne Gault knew she had to be good at something. She just wasn't sure what. Shy, awkward, and ambitious with a jokey streak that she never could fully control, she dreamed of an acting career. When her mother squashed that idea, Gault became an English major at the University of Mississippi. She devoured the poems of Louise Glück and Sharon Olds as well as the novels of Flannery O'Connor, William Faulkner, and Eudora Welty. She hoped to become a writer herself. For the next ten years, her love of literature kept opening new doors, but when she walked through them, she found herself in situations where everything went bad in a hurry.

The first crisis came in a collegiate English class where Gault tried to defend Faulkner's *Sanctuary* as a brilliant novel, even though most scholars regard it as a hastily assembled, lurid tale written only for the money. Gault's professor scoffed. Gault argued back. The instructor cut loose with a refutation that, in Gault's words, "scared the hell out of me. I tried to hold strong, but I knew I was going to be chewed up, no matter what." Things got worse after graduation. Gault headed to Starkville, Mississippi, to try her luck at teaching eighth-grade English, with grisly results. "I did not have great classroom-management skills," Gault recalled. "I just wanted them to love literature as much as I did." No such luck. Her classroom became a seething mess of angry fourteen-year-olds with no desire to learn. After a nine-month battle to impose order, Gault left the school system, never to return.

A few years later, Gault met Fred Carl, the founder of Viking Range, at a party. His kitchen-appliance company needed an in-house writer—and Gault needed income. She had retreated into the safety of freelance journalism, writing pieces about Southern food and Southern music while raising her children. Paying the bills by writing news releases and product brochures didn't sound thrilling. But it beat being broke. When Carl asked her to submit some writing samples, she impudently e-mailed him two poems.

For once, impertinence worked. Gault had played into a useful stereotype: corporate executives' tendency to view professional writers as feisty, reckless talents, akin to moonshiners or belly dancers. As far as Carl was concerned, if Gault liked to write poetry in her spare time, so be it. She was a writer. He assigned her to create catalog copy about 4,000-BTU burners, which started out as a soul-crushing experience. But that didn't last long. The social-media revolution had begun, and Gault was about to find her voice. On her Facebook and MySpace accounts, she began bantering with musicians such as Mississippi blues legend David "Honeyboy" Edwards. She liked blues, pop, and an occasional bit of funk; performers enjoyed her friendly, sassy commentary. She struck up online friendships with chefs and food critics around the country too. The shy woman from Greenwood, Mississippi, discovered to her delight that she could say *anything* she wanted online. She was racing miles ahead of her bosses.

One afternoon, Gault decided to spice up Viking's Facebook page. It had become a little-noticed repository of corporate backgrounders about the history of Viking. Audience involvement was undetectable, but that was about to change. First Gault announced the start of National Egg Month. She shared a zany video about how to roll up an omelet and asked viewers to share their favorite recipes. Twenty-one people engaged. A few weeks later, she celebrated Maple Syrup Day. This time she got 203 likes and twenty-nine comments. Soon afterward: a contest in which Facebook visitors had a chance to win a lemon-yellow range if they just posted something clever on the site in observation of Lemonade Day.

As Gault's online banter stepped into high gear, Viking's Facebook page became an Internet sensation. Before long, it had five hundred thousand followers. Visitors loved Gault's whimsical, nutty style; her bosses appreciated the way her jokey touch helped Viking get its brand positioning right. The Mississippi company had made rapid headway selling industrial-grade ranges to wealthy suburbanites across the United States. Even people who could barely cook took pride in having three-thousand-dollar flame-throwers in their kitchens. But Viking needed to show a softer side too. To become a kitchen mainstay, Viking had to associate a good-natured sense of joy with its massive machines. The more that Gault could do to turn the company's backwoods Southern origins into a folksy competitive advantage, the better.

The balloon of Internet fame kept lifting Gault higher. She won a Shorty Award for running America's best social-commerce campaign, collecting her trophy in a New York ceremony that also honored CNN, HBO, and Major League Baseball. She went on the speaking circuit, telling audiences what made Viking's campaign work so well. When people asked how she dealt with customer complaints posted on the company's Facebook page, she avoided the corporate doublespeak that other panelists tended to use. Instead, Gault took her Mississippi drawl up a notch and replied: "We just try to get them to talk about fried chicken."

If you stand too long in the back of the line for life's rewards, it's easy to let defeatism take hold. What's inspiring about LeAnne Gault's story is that even after a long run of tough luck, she stood tall when opportunity showed up. If Viking founder Fred Carl was looking for a writer, she wanted him to know that she thought of herself as a poet—not a hack. She didn't know whether he would be offended or intrigued. Either way, she wasn't afraid to be bold.

That's the key lesson from her story, and from the other strivers' too. Calling yourself a bureaucratic ninja is eccentric, but Mai-Ling Garcia made it work. Talking up parallels between eighteenth-century Irish factionalism and modern-day user-experience research isn't the standard way of getting hired. But it's working for Chris LaRoche. We're all outsiders at some point. You break into the inner circle when you champion your strengths with as much conviction as if you were declaring, "I graduated from Harvard."

No matter where you went to school or what supposedly "useless" liberal arts degree you earned, some dimension of you deserves its own drumroll too.

Putting All the Pieces Together

When Mai-Ling Garcia arrived at Berkeley as a junior-year transfer, she struggled to fit in. Short on cash, she and her then-husband moved into an aging cottage with a leaky roof about a mile west of campus. Most days, they subsisted on bowls of Top Ramen. Her husband's military paycheck was gone; they were both students now. Each of them had secured partial scholarships, but they didn't know enough about their financial-aid options to get the maximum possible support. Neighbors took pity on the couple and shared stockpiles of frozen food. To cover expenses, Garcia took a part-time job teaching art at a grade-school recreation center in Oakland.

Finishing college can become impossible when life gets this harrowing. Partway through her second semester, Garcia began tracking down what she now refers to as "a series of odd little foundations with funky scholarships." People wanted to help her. Before long, she was attending Berkeley on a full ride. Her money problems abated. What she couldn't forget was that initial feeling of being in trouble and ill-prepared. Her travails were pulling her into sociology's most pressing issues: how vulnerable people fare in a world they don't understand, and what can be done to make their lives better.

Simultaneously, Berkeley's professors were arming Garcia with the tools that would ultimately define her career. She spent a year learning the fine points of ethnography from a Vietnam-era Marine, Martin Sanchez-Jankowski. He had earned a PhD from MIT; at Berkeley he taught students how to conduct field research. He sent Garcia into the Oakland courthouse to watch judges in action, advising her to pay close attention to the ways racial differences tinged courtroom conduct. She learned to take careful notes, to be explicit about her theories and assumptions, and to operate with a rigor that could withstand peer-review scrutiny. Instead of getting mad, she was learning how to dig deeper.

Was Garcia destined to become a researcher—or an advocate? Unsure of her future, she moved between those two roles for several years. First she conducted field research with a Marine community in Southern California, building her senior thesis around the erratic nature of support systems for warriors' families living on or near military bases. She documented bureaucratic snarls so powerfully that faculty members encouraged her to present her results to the California assembly and to the American Psychological Association.

For the next few years, Garcia tried to fix the system herself. She spent two years working at a nonprofit organization, Swords to Plowshares, that tried to untangle Veterans Administration bureaucracy. After that, three years at the Department of Labor evaluating hundreds of grant applications related to veterans' employment. She was winning many small battles, but she felt profoundly frustrated working in an environment that was behind the times technologically.

Living in the San Francisco Bay Area, Garcia constantly faced the contrast between government torpor and the private sector's giddy embrace of mobile technologies that put an incredible new power into everyone's hands. Renting a vacation home, booking a restaurant, or arguing online about a news article had never been so easy. Trying to accomplish anything in government—from reporting a pothole to changing a jury-duty date—was utterly different. American democracy remained stuck with primitive online systems that were hard to use. If the VA could work as smoothly online as Instagram, if city hall were as easy to use as Yelp, everything would be different. Instead, nothing was changing.

Could Garcia help fix government? Yes, she decided, but it would require more zigzags in her training. She needed to become a tech enabler rather than someone who merely bemoaned its failings. She started with night-school lessons in digital marketing from General Assembly.

After that, she spent eighteen months as a marketing specialist at Back to the Roots, which sold mushroom-growing kits online. It was hardly the pinnacle of Garcia's career, but the pay was good and the training even better. She was learning the fast-paced cadence of California's start-up culture—where new ideas were being tried out all the time, where "failing fast" was considered a virtue, and where raw prototypes were rapidly retooled and relaunched until a winning new product emerged. Power flows differently in such settings, and the sociologist in her needed to know how and why.

By the summer of 2014, Garcia was ready to reenter government, this time as a full-strength agitator for change. She pounced on a job ad in which the City of Oakland announced that it was seeking a bridge builder who could amp up online government services on behalf of the city's four hundred thousand residents.

How would this happen? No one knew exactly, but Garcia—and Oakland—were ready to find out.

Within a few months, Garcia became a co-manager of Oakland's Digital Front Door initiative. She and communications manager Karen Boyd pinpointed parts of city government that weren't making full use of modern online technology and coordinated teams of software engineers and department officials who could take city services to a better place.

This wasn't just an exercise in technology upgrading; it required a fundamental rethinking of the way that Oakland delivered services. Clerks handling paper records at city hall would need to let go of longtime habits in favor of instant electronic access for anyone with an Internet connection. Buffers between city workers and an impatient public would come down. The social structures of power would change. To make this transition, it certainly helped to have a digitally savvy sociologist in the house.

Over coffee one afternoon, Garcia told me excitedly about ways in which Oakland's city services were already improving and how much more progress was within sight. The technology that powers Expedia's plane-ticket sales and Instagram's photo-sharing service needn't be the exclusive preserve of profit-minded companies. It can be put to use for the public good too. Already, if street-art creators want more recognition for their work, Garcia can drum up interest on social media. If garbage is piling up and requests for timely pickups are being ignored, new digital tools let citizens visit the city's Facebook page and summon services within seconds. "It's as simple as zooming in on a map and clicking the exact location where there's a mess," Garcia explained.

Looking ahead, Garcia envisions a day when landing a municipal job becomes vastly easier, with cities' Twitter feeds posting each new opening. Other aspects of digital technology ought to help residents connect quickly with whatever part of government matters to them—whether that means signing up for summer camp or giving the mayor a piece of one's mind. Each new wave of technology redefines city life, social norms, and the ways that power flows through society. We're just beginning to recognize the opportunities before us.

Part Two

Your Opportunities

4

My Job Didn't Exist a Year Ago

Almost as soon as geologists trace the southern coast of Hawaii's Big Island, the findings become out-of-date. The reason: Eruptions from the Kilauea volcano keep pouring molten lava into the Pacific Ocean, altering the coastline. Sightseers from every continent gawk at the spectacle of Hawaii's shoreline growing by the minute. Look downward, through gaps in the rocks near the water's edge, and you can see red streams of molten rock. Look outward, toward the ocean, and you will behold huge plumes of steam where lava splashes down. Listen closely, and you will hear the hiss of escaping gases. The freshest land is steaming hot; it can't support life. Nearby, however, previous eruptions have cooled to the point that native ferns can take root. Another mile away, everything is lush and green. Tropical vines, flowers, and other vegetation have settled into timeless patterns.

Something similar happens in the topography of work. It isn't as dramatic; you can't find YouTube footage of tourists shrieking at the sight of new-job formation. But the analogy holds true in many other respects. As much as we may think the boundaries of gainful work are well fixed, they aren't. New types of jobs keep coming into existence in ways that catch us by surprise. Technology opens up fresh possibilities. So do changing social dynamics; so do evolving public priorities. Every year, a few million people choose to work in the equivalent of Hawaii's expanding coastline, making their mark on professional territory no one else has claimed before.

In the workplace, as in coastlines, the cycle keeps repeating itself. Millions of jobs barely known or inconceivable a generation or two ago have become mainstream norms. That's true in medicine (as seen in the rise of everything from hip-replacement surgery to genetic counseling); it's true in engineering (with examples ranging from mobile-app development to solar-cell design); and it's true in all kinds of fields where a liberal arts perspective can be put to use. Even big companies stretch their ambitions in unexpected ways, creating fresh jobs in uncharted areas. Governments and nonprofits do as well.

The result: Employers routinely insist they have no openings until they meet a promising candidate—like you. That's when your energy and optimism reshape the day. New ideas take center stage. Moods brighten. Suddenly, doubt turns into belief; diffidence into action. Before long, someone utters the magic phrase: "What if we tried…"

This chapter will chart half a dozen sectors where fresh adventure awaits. You've already heard in chapter 1 about the broad-based ways the labor market is evolving. Now it's time for a closer look at booming demand for project managers, designers, social-media experts, market researchers, recruiters, and fund-raisers. Opportunities are vast, with at least ten thousand jobs a year being added in each of these realms. All these fields prize the strengths that emerge from a robust liberal arts education: curiosity, discernment, adaptability, and a prepared-for-everything gusto that can turn chaos into triumph. Bring a few years of relevant experience to the interview, and you can end up earning an annual salary of more than a hundred thousand dollars. Even entry-level positions provide substantial paychecks that justify four years of college tuition. Companies as big as IBM are hiring; so are organizations as small as the Kentucky Ballet Theatre.

Toward the end of the chapter, you will get to know Bridget Connolly, an earnest global citizen in her twenties who has built her career on the outermost edge of anyone's professional map. Think of her as the first living presence on a lava outcrop still warm to the touch. It took more than a year after college graduation for her to find the right job. There's a lot to be learned from the way she went about her hunt, the pitfalls she encountered—and the special mix of hope, luck, and timing that finally paid off.

There's even more value in tracking Connolly's adventures *after* she got hired. At age twenty-three, she stepped into a remarkably big job: head of internationalization for wikiHow, a popular how-to website with global ambitions and no proven road map to make them come true. No one had held this job before. No one knew how to get things done, including—at first—Connolly herself. Yet she pressed on anyway, fine-tuning her strategy as she went along. You'll discover how she built an informal network of several hundred freelance translators and editors around the world, including a bored lawyer in South Korea and a Russian speaker marking time in a Ukrainian refugee camp. She survived run-ins with a series of swindlers. She learned how to project authority without seeming brittle while dealing with people twice her age. Eventually, she improvised her way to success.

If you've ever sat in front of a computer at eleven p.m. wondering how to complete a project due at dawn, you have tasted part of Bridget Connolly's world. If you cranked up the Notorious B.I.G.

on your headphones in the hope that painfully loud rap would inspire you to greatness, you have embraced her life hacks too. Working so close to the unknown isn't the easiest way to make a living. For anyone who craves a lifetime full of adventure and discovery, though, such jobs can be an adrenaline rush with a big payoff.

How do you find such opportunities? Most of them aren't clearly advertised. In fact, often there is no public notice whatsoever. Bosses develop hazy ideas about where they want to expand next without being able to articulate precisely what they want. It's an awkward fact of life that the best-organized employers usually aren't all that visionary—and the most visionary employers tend to be disorganized. So if you're hoping to land a job no one has ever held before, you probably will need to help create it yourself. All the same, those chaotic beginnings shouldn't distress you; they can be an advantage.

A few years ago, University of Chicago economist Steven Davis and several colleagues picked through the federal government's massive Job Openings and Labor Turnover Survey (known as JOLTS), which examines the way sixteen thousand enterprises do their hiring. To their surprise, it turned out 42 percent of all hires happen without any trace of a formal job posting in the previous month. After peeling away the cases where vacancies were filled so fast there was no end-of-the-month opening, the economists still were left with as much as one-sixth of all hires that seemed to be born out of nothing.

Davis suggests we think of those situations as "hiring by osmosis"; an individual is in the right place at the right time with the right opportunity. It's weird, from an economist's perspective, to believe people can find work without any preliminary recognition of a vacancy that needs filling. Then again, much of what happens in the world defies classic economic models.

Because these new jobs are being conjured up on the spot, employers start with an unusually elastic sense of what skills and past experience they might want. This can work to your advantage in a big way—especially if you're the unconventional candidate. Employers become much more willing to hire on the basis of passion and potential. If you've got an engaging life story and a willingness to work hard, you might be the right match. Your job interview won't even feel like a traditional interview. Instead, it will be a much more natural conversation in which a sudden sense of compatibility counts for at least as much as traditional résumé skills.

When the chemistry is right, employers make contextual leaps that play to the advantage of the classic prepared-for-everything liberal arts graduate. A hundred-and-fifty-page senior thesis? President of the LGBTQ association? A summer job in a cigar store? The more you can present your life journey as a testament to your diligence, leadership, or rapport-building talents, the closer you are to being hired. After all, what else can employers go by? Because they need someone ripe for an unusual new challenge, it's impossible to find past masters with the standard five to seven years of experience. Such people don't exist; these positions are bound to involve a leap into the unknown. As a result, employers won't slam the door on candidates with partly formed skills. Quick learners are welcome too.

In such settings, savor the sense of optimistic exploration on both sides of the interview table. If your interviewer isn't inspecting you for flaws (and looking for reasons to say no), it's much easier to make your own luck. Be open to any possibilities that get you started at an innovative organization or in a fast-growing field. Once you're in the door, it's a lot easier to find new contacts and opportunities that can lead to your next job.

So where do you find such jobs, and just how common are they? Here are six especially exciting areas of interest.

Market Research

From 2012 to 2016, the U.S. economy added 166,000 jobs in market research and marketing, fields in which overall employment leaped 30 percent. A big part of this boom can be traced to Provo, Utah, the home of Qualtrics. The company's easy-to-use software makes it possible for anyone to construct cheap, addictively popular online surveys. Banks, hotels, and car companies are huge users, eager to know what customers and employees think. Psychology professors are Qualtrics junkies, too. If you ever found yourself moving a ratings slider between one and seven to express your views, chances are you have filled out a Qualtrics survey.

A decade or two ago, when market research meant spending fifty thousand dollars or more to conduct a single survey via phone calls or face-to-face clipboard research, national appetites were limited. Today, a big online survey can be run for as little as one-hundredth of that amount. As a result, we're constantly polling one another about everything. Employee morale surveys happen weekly instead of once a year. Dentists send out surveys to find out what's regarded as a healthy smile. (Move the lever toward seven if you want to see more teeth; toward one if you don't.) The boom in online surveys is so intense that even though nobody is hiring phone-bank or clipboard researchers anymore, there's been a vast leap in opportunities for people who design online surveys, train online partners, analyze the data—and help everyone get smarter about what questions to ask.

In the summer of 2016, I visited Qualtrics just as the company was moving into its fourth headquarters within a decade. (All the other ones became too small.) I spent the better part of an afternoon chatting with recent hires who'd majored in psychology, sociology, English, or American studies in college before making their way to Qualtrics. These postgrads are breaking down the old barriers between sales and customer service, stepping into a new kind of job that makes them the embodiment of all-things-Qualtrics when it comes to dealing with major customers. While their titles are a forgettable blur of buzzwords involving "customer success" and "partner services," what they actually do is intriguing. They are detectives, menders, coaches, and counselors to the likes of Coca-Cola, Chase Bank, and other global businesses. Sometimes they fly to Atlanta on a moment's notice to solve an unforeseen issue; other times they coax Qualtrics' own engineers into building intricate new features that will satisfy a major client's cravings. The constant key to success: an ability to improvise.

"If it's predictable, I'm not doing my job," recent hire Cliff Latham told me. He earned a degree in industrial and organizational psychology from Brigham Young University–Idaho in 2013. Now he pitches Qualtrics' survey technology to a wide range of clients. There's no script for him to follow. It's up to him to find a way of connecting with Sports Authority on one major new survey; with a renowned psychology professor studying public attitudes on another. The biggest unifying theme in his conversations with clients, Latham observed, is "being intellectually curious."

Caroline Poole earned her sociology degree from Furman in 2014. At Qualtrics, she's part of an elite team of in-house consultants who help big clients construct complex surveys. "You need to be good at nonlinear thinking to solve problems," she observed. It can take as long as twenty hours to establish clients' true research goals—especially if various project participants don't see eye to eye. That's when her sociology training pays off; she's at home dealing with the sorts of organizational conflict (aka office politics) engineers can't diagnose or ameliorate.

Social-Media Experts

Viral videos. Tweet storms. Blogging in the name of "thought leadership." In social media, it's hard to say what techniques work, why they work, and whether they will keep working. Everyone is still figuring out how Facebook, Twitter, and their kin can be used to build brands and share ideas. During this transitional period, it's clear that traditional approaches to marketing, sales, and communications are being upended. As a result, organizations ranging from Google to the Kansas City Zoo have decided they need social-media managers—now!

Take a broad enough view, and annual demand for such expertise could total more than four hundred thousand openings a year. That's the tally Burning Glass Technologies came up with when the Boston labor-data firm counted job listings in which social-media skills were part of what employers wanted. Many of these opportunities still involve a lot of traditional sales, marketing, or public relations skills. They're fresh terrain in part; familiar work in others. Even so, the hiring templates of a decade ago now seem unduly strict. There's greater room for people like LeAnne Gault, the Mississippi English major whose jaunty wit and off-hours social-media experiments turned her into a brand-building genius for the Viking Range business.

What's the value of a liberal arts education in this fast-changing field? At some companies, you might need to be a friendly educator, stretching older colleagues' awareness of ways to connect with audiences. Or perhaps you want to be the inspiring-message shaper, conjuring up the phrases, photos, and videos that make people say "Wow!" in a world where so much organizational content is dull and forgettable. Don't hesitate to pitch yourself as the in-house cultural interpreter, discerning how your employer's business objectives interact with the rest of the world. If you've ever staked out an audacious position in a humanities seminar or slipped an outrageously good line into a term paper or connected with a social science professor's model of how the world works, you're on the right track.

Max Menke graduated from Pitzer College in 2010 with a bachelor's degree in political science and a smattering of everything from photography to acting classes on his transcript. "I'm not sure anything I did in college was relevant to my current job," he tells me. Then he reconsiders. Actually, Menke says, that college-fueled willingness to keep jumping into new areas has turned into his biggest asset. His time at Pitzer included a study-abroad term in China, which led to a variety of sales and teaching jobs in China after graduation, which greatly honed his ability to connect with people from other backgrounds. In 2015, Menke became a founding partner of GrowthX, a San Francisco start-up accelerator that helps young companies master the business strategies they need for success. In a typical month, he explains sales strategy and social-media tools to companies in fields ranging from shipping logistics to heart monitoring and women's makeup. Such varied work is the perfect home for an unreformed liberal arts explorer. As Menke explains, "I love switching gears."

Recruiting and Career Coaching

From 2010 to 2015, the U.S. economy created 73,000 new jobs for human resources specialists, the equivalent of a 17 percent jump in this sector's overall employment. This field has seen a whirlwind of software innovation, as new digital tools take the drudgery out of payroll, benefits, performance reviews, and the like. In most cases, this new technology ends up creating jobs, rather than destroying them. The reason: once clerical chores are automated, organizations start seeing HR as a good area to expand, because smart, imaginative people can make the entire organization run better.

Recruiting becomes a fast-moving source of company pride instead of a sluggish headache. Benefits become increasingly customized to each employee's needs. Employee training becomes more efficient, and on-the-job feedback becomes more timely and helpful. Stepped-up investments in HR pay their way. When new software tools are put to use by insightful specialists (many of whom have liberal arts backgrounds), the once-stuffy world of HR becomes much more innovative.

Mike Junge saw this transformation play out during the first fifteen years of his career. He graduated from the University of Arizona in 1999 with a bachelor's degree in creative writing. Unable to get established as a poet, he began working in a technical recruiting agency in what amounted to a broken job market. Companies spewed out dull job ads; engineers responded by submitting listless résumés. Nobody was happy with the status quo. Over the next few years, Junge used his college-honed listening skills and his eye for people's hidden hopes and motivations to improve the recruiting conversation for everyone.

First, Junge helped engineers describe their problem-solving skills in an upbeat, can-do manner. Then he tackled the boiler-plate language of most technical-job ads. Don't present a long string of adjectives as requirements, he told employers; you'll only deaden candidates' enthusiasm. Instead, take those same points and reframe them as questions. "Are you responsible and conscientious? Can you work efficiently under pressure?" Invite candidates to see themselves as winning the job because they have what it takes. That simple shift in perspective "provided a surprising edge in terms of getting good response rates," Junge told me. What looked like better writing was actually the by-product of two liberal arts mainstays—empathy and curiosity. Junge's strengths led to zestier messaging, so both job seekers and recruiters felt they were engaging with someone who understood their interests.

In 2011, Google asked Junge to join its recruiting team. His mission: to hunt for the best engineering talent anywhere in the world and to draw those candidates into Google's interviewing process.

At about the time Junge joined, LinkedIn was hitting its stride as a giant database of potential job candidates that amounted to a recruiter's best friend. Suddenly, recruiters in California who needed to find big-data experts with at least three years of Hadoop experience could bypass the laborious old routine of visiting university professors, asking about prior students, and trying to wiggle into industry conferences in hopes of meeting Hadoop-trained engineers. With a few clicks at the keyboard and some basic knowledge of the Boolean logic that underlies database searches, recruiters could find many thousands of established engineers who weren't looking for new jobs but who might be open to an approach. In Junge's words, "LinkedIn put the entire universe of talent into our hands."

The faster recruiters could find candidates, the more Google's appetite for talent grew. If the pool of Silicon Valley candidates seemed thin, why not pinpoint the thirty best Hadoop engineers in Texas and see if they wanted to move? How about considering the top fifty in Israel? No matter how many recruiters Google hired, it wanted more. By 2012, the search-engine company had nearly eight hundred people in its recruiting organization. Having established himself as a top producer at Google, in mid-2012 Junge went back to Southern California, where he is now head of talent acquisition for a financial-tech company.

Ultimately, tech companies like Google rely on their own engineers to assess each prospect's suitability via a series of interviews and coding tests. For getting the conversation started, though, there's a special role for recruiters with the unique blend of rapport and engaging communication that comes with a liberal arts education.

Fund-Raising

In 2010, full-time fund-raising was such an unusual job that federal statisticians didn't even recognize it as a stand-alone category. By 2016, the Bureau of Labor Statistics tallied 68,900 people in this line of work. Once again, assistive technology had created a flurry of new jobs. Software tools such as Raiser's Edge and CauseOS made it vastly cheaper, faster, and smoother for small organizations to go prospecting for donations than it had been. Online campaigns meant that postage, phone, and printing costs dropped to zero. Fund-raising initiatives that never happened in the old regime — because high costs would have overwhelmed the amount of money raised — suddenly became feasible and often outright attractive.

Crowdsourcing initiatives such as Kickstarter and Indiegogo open up new avenues too. Anyone wanting to make a movie, launch a product, or help out a worthy cause can go online and seek support from around the world. Early boosters can rally their friends via all the communications tools of our interconnected world. You don't have to be the American Red Cross anymore to be able to raise money effectively.

In Lexington, Kentucky, dancer Brie Lowry found she could support her professional passion—and make additional part-time income—by becoming a fund-raiser for the Kentucky Ballet Theatre. Some of her successes came via digital connection with potential donors in Florida. Others came from face-to-face contact with local Kentucky businesses such as Maker's Mark. (Who could resist an evening of "Bourbon and the Ballet"?) In essence, technology freed up time and extended her reach.

In *The Generosity Network*, longtime fund-raiser Jennifer McCrea argues that landmark donations take shape when "two people sit down together and have a deep conversation." Ideas swirl about. Bold solutions start to take shape. Consortiums form around the notion of doing something together "that might be creative, exciting, rewarding, and fun." Her model acknowledges the importance of technological tools but only to the degree that spreadsheets, donor-yield studies, and so forth make it easier for like-minded people to find one another. Writing from the perspective of a philosophy major (BA, Allegheny College, 1988) with more than twenty-five years of fund-raising experience, McCrea emphasizes the importance of creative longings that bring people together. The passion found in liberal arts majors can be infectious, making it easy to draw in partners once these grads start talking about their beloved causes.

Digital Designers

In 2003, Soleio Cuervo graduated from Duke University with a degree in music composition. Within two years, he had wiggled his way into Facebook as one of its first designers. His role: making the young social network's site appealing, clean, and easy to use. No one knew how Facebook's rapidly evolving Wall should function or what it ought to look like. That was fine with Soleio (he prefers to go by his first name only), a supremely self-assured son of Colombian immigrants. His technical skills were solid, thanks to a multiyear spree of building websites as a hobby in college. His great mark of distinction, however, grew out of his aesthetic sense. Not only did Soleio know what beautiful music should sound like, he was brimming with ideas about what great design should look like and how it could move technology forward. In this new job at Facebook, Soleio was ready to experiment.

When I first met Soleio, in 2008, he was already making a name for himself as a relentless champion of understated efficiency. Other parts of Facebook's development team kept wanting to add features; Soleio insisted that everything be as streamlined and unobtrusive as possible. Never use five words when one would suffice. Never use words if an icon could get the job done just as well. Pare everything down to its essential form. With his shaven head, booming voice, and lush eyebrows, Soleio carried himself like an artistic giant. Over time, he earned serious acclaim both inside and outside Facebook. The *Wall Street Journal* made him famous in 2011 by profiling him as the inventor of the thumbs-up "Like" button. Since then, he has set up his own venture firm, becoming a much-sought-after investor in other people's start-ups. I was amused (but not surprised) to find that he has turned his first name into a registered trademark. If you look him up on LinkedIn, you will find him listed as Soleio®.

Digital design is such a young field that you can create your own credentials to a surprising degree. Hal Wuertz, a Brown philosophy major, has recast herself as a digital design specialist. So has Brad Neal, who studied art history at the University of Illinois. Both of them now work for IBM in Austin, Texas.

All told, about sixty-seven thousand web-development and web-design jobs come open each year, according to Burning Glass Technologies. Most of these positions are treated as computer-industry jobs by the Bureau of Labor Statistics, but the truth is, digital design relies at least as much on a person's aesthetic sense as on his or her technical knowledge. Pick up a basic grounding in industry tools, such as Adobe InDesign, Pixate, Sketch, Figment, Framer, or their successors. Beyond that, show up with nerve, a few ideas, and a willingness to learn fast. *And once you get established, don't forget to trademark your own name.*

Project Managers

In late 2013, I received an invitation to come to Minneapolis and address a regional conference of something called the Project Management Institute. I assumed this must be a group of defense contractors and construction engineers. It didn't take long to realize my perceptions were painfully out of date. Yes, the notion of project management as a serious line of work in its own right can be traced back to men in hard hats who built submarines or bridges. It's a different story today. The worldwide ranks of registered PMI members have surged more than 500 percent in the past fifteen years—to 467,000. Most of that growth involves our kind of critical thinkers, the ones who bring interdisciplinary ingenuity to a new breed of projects with a high-tech twist.

Amazon hires lots of project managers. So do Google, Nestlé, Oracle, Sony, KPMG, Microsoft, American Airlines, and a never-ending list of start-ups with cute names such as Wonderful and Faith. If you take one of these jobs, you will be guiding, planning, and mediating. You will put out metaphorical fires—and perhaps a few real ones too. You will help the folks in engineering understand what the sales team wants. You will constantly use soft influence to get help from people who don't work for you. Many of these jobs go to people with specialized industry skills, but a surprising number of them don't.

When big bosses go hunting for project managers, they cherish people with the full suite of critical-thinking skills. If you can make allies, think on your feet, and learn fast, you're the sort of liberal arts graduate who should thrive in such settings. It's unlikely that your first job out of college will involve nothing but project management. Even geniuses don't mature that fast. Spend a few years figuring out how an organization works, though, and you could be looking at a long and exciting future in this field.

Just ask Bridget Connolly.

Growing up in Chester County, Pennsylvania, Connolly thought she wanted to become a diplomat. She inherited her mother's love of travel; childhood trips to Ireland, Spain, and Puerto Rico left her wanting to see more of the world on her own. As a high-school junior, she spent two weeks in a Mexican homestay in Cuernavaca as part of a Spanish-language immersion program. As a high-school senior, she wrangled her way to Australia as part of a girls' leadership conference. She leaped into high-school student government and volunteered with the Obama presidential campaign in 2008. As she discovered how politics really worked, however, her ambitions changed. Diplomacy became a distant dream; heading straight into government lost its allure. She opted for an international relations major in college, now uncertain how she might apply it.

Instead of being a means to an end, travel became an end in itself. Other classmates at Stanford dabbled in marijuana; she loaded up on anti-malaria medicines. In the spring of her junior year, she journeyed to South Africa to study whether crime rates in impoverished areas could be reduced by building social cohesion. To gather data, she plunged into a radically different culture. She learned some isiXhosa, a clicking language spoken by seven million South Africans. She and a research partner conducted sixty-two field interviews, building alliances with community guides, so they could be sure respondents were providing candid answers instead of saying whatever they thought might please foreigners. She bought headlamps and pepper spray to ensure her safety in the event of a power outage; she savored every day of the adventure.

When Connolly graduated in 2011, the U.S. economy remained on shaky ground after the financial meltdown of 2008–2009. Career-minded classmates got the jobs they wanted at such firms as Bain and Morgan Stanley. For Connolly—and many of her friends—it was a different story. Her rambling adventures weren't what big corporations wanted. She had kept busy leading learning trips for a grassroots nonprofit in Ecuador, but she didn't see a long-term future in such work. Each week, she hunted for opportunities on Craigslist, Monster.com, and other job boards. Day after day, she dispatched cover letters that began "To whom it may concern" and ended with "I look forward to hearing from you." Nothing worked.

A quiet sense of terror started to take hold. As Connolly later explained: "There's this feeling that you need to get your stuff together by the time you graduate, or you're screwed." In her first year out of college, she hadn't yet found a permanent job.

Hoping to connect anywhere, in September 2012 Connolly applied to be a creative manager at wikiHow. The job was an imperfect match; wikiHow wanted a visual whiz, and that didn't exactly play to Connolly's strengths. Even so, she sprinkled her cover letter with as much enthusiasm as she could muster. Talking up her campus photography and film projects, she pitched herself as "an artist with a bold and creative eye." What else could she do? The company sounded intriguing, and her job-hunting anxiety was mounting.

It was Connolly's good fortune to step into a company rooted in the striver's maxim "Hire for attitude; train for skill." Her interviewers didn't spend much time grilling her about her (nonexistent) design portfolio. Instead, they asked for an example of a time when she'd shown initiative. Connolly seized the moment. Without knowing whether this was what her interviewers wanted to hear, she started recounting a plucky path that led her to shoot a video documentary on the world's largest coral-reef restoration project. She and her boyfriend were vacationing in Indonesia. Other tourists were lazing on Bali's beaches—but that wasn't her style. She had a video camera with her, and she wanted to interview coastal fishermen.

The fishermen didn't speak English. She didn't speak Indonesian. So she memorized one crucial phrase: *Memberitahu kita tentang karang* ("Tell us about the coral"). Then she headed to the piers at five a.m., before the boats left. Relying on this single query, she interviewed restoration workers and fishermen, who responded in their own language. Later on, translators could create the English-language subtitles she needed.

Could wikiHow harness such raw energy? A wild idea popped into the mind of Elizabeth Douglas, the company's tightly focused president. "I know we've been talking about the visual-design job," Douglas said. "But there's this other project I want to tell you about." She dreamed of wikiHow being a global business someday. That meant translating thirty thousand or more of the site's most popular articles into Spanish, Arabic, Korean, and at least a dozen other languages. Nobody knew how to pull this off on a tight budget. Quality standards couldn't be compromised. All the same, Douglas asked, what if...

"It was as if a lightbulb went on," Douglas later recalled. Before the boss could finish explaining the internationalization project, Connolly shot back: "I definitely want to do that!" The two women started to talk about the challenges of building translation teams across the globe. It would be new territory for everyone. Connolly didn't mind. "This is what I'm passionate about," Connolly declared. "I'm a fast learner. I will put in the hours."

That week, Douglas and Connolly shook hands on the new job; wikiHow was about to hire its first international project manager. Ironically, the job hadn't existed until this twenty-three-year-old walked in the door.

For all of us who like adventure, there's nothing like the first glimpse of uncharted territory. Find such a situation, and you enjoy delicious freedom to set your own goals, choose your own methods, and write your own rulebook. In boom times, we savor the open-air thrills of being the first to discover something new; we cherish the euphoria of getting it right. If obstacles arise, at least we can battle to find solutions no one else has ever tried to find. Month by month, we gain mastery of a new discipline. We're always growing. We experience what the great dancer and choreographer Martha Graham described as the "divine dissatisfaction" of being an artist: the "blessed unrest that keeps us marching and makes us more alive than the others."

If your liberal arts education has led you everywhere (and nowhere), take heart. Your formal skill set might be just as ragged as Connolly's. No matter. If you've got enough energy, optimism, and willingness to learn, what you've already developed might suffice. In fact, you might be surprisingly well prepared for the work's newest terrain. If you need more encouragement and some specifics, consider these eight pointers from Connolly's own survival path.

The first few days will be scary. On day one, Connolly discovered she had inherited a rickety collection of translation attempts dating back nearly four years. The Spanish version consisted of eleven thousand answers to various questions, yet it lacked many of wikiHow's biggest hits. (People around the world can't get enough of wikiHow's article "How to Kiss," for example.) The Italian version had barely taken shape. A rudimentary Dutch site had been constructed, but it appeared to be abandoned. "The first thing you need to do," supervisor Chris Hadley told her, "is build out the spreadsheets that keep track of what we're doing."

Awkward! Connolly's résumé identified her as proficient at Microsoft Excel and other office-software tools. That was... optimistic. When Hadley observed her trying to manipulate an Excel spreadsheet, he winced. "Try using an IF command," Hadley advised. A few moments later: "It will go a lot faster if you use VLOOKUP." Connolly did her best to act unflustered. Each time, she replied, "Oh." Then a pause, followed by "Okay." And eventually: "Got it."

With so much to learn, Connolly relied on tenacity to pull her through. For the next few weeks, she arrived early and left late.

She kept switching her seat, pulling up a chair next to someone who could help her. Her questions were so incessant that some colleagues' patience wore thin. All the same, she kept getting better. She tried so hard that people rallied to her side. When things got tense, wikiHow president Douglas reminded everyone, "We all screw up sometimes. That's part of the culture."

You will make surprising allies. Most big jobs call for a lot of teamwork. Typically, the allies you need are one desk away or just down the hall. If not, at least they speak your language and share your culture. Befriending them is pretty straightforward. Not so in Connolly's world. She needed local-language managers—and esoteric subject experts—everywhere from Amsterdam to Bangkok. Her future hinged on building a loose-knit confederation in a hurry and keeping it moving forward.

Had college prepared her for this? Indirectly, it had. Connolly couldn't speak Dutch or Thai; she knew nothing about wikiHow topics such as how to adopt a child. But she had been well trained in how to make sense of unexpected settings—and how to connect with people profoundly unlike her. "I've ended up becoming a diplomat after all," Connolly told me. "I figure out what different people want, and what they are capable of doing. I negotiate with them. If they're older than me, I treat them with a hundred percent respect. But I'm also very clear about what we need."

Connolly's most eccentric triumph: Finding a boss for wikiHow's German-language rollout. None of wikiHow's early users in Europe seemed suitable. Then Connolly discovered Monica Miranda, a retired Swiss chief executive who had settled in Costa Rica. This time, everything clicked. Miranda's German was impeccable; her technical knowledge was vast. Best of all, she had a knack for rallying German-language speakers anywhere in the world to serve as translators. Miranda's home situation was bizarre; she lived in a tree house thirty feet off the ground. "But it had excellent Wi-Fi!" Connolly told me. "We could Skype in my morning and stay in touch by e-mail the rest of the time."

Similar recruiting triumphs played out across the globe. In Connolly's new world, mastery could be found in the most unlikely places. There was room for Namiko, Ahmad, Rosa, and Sonya.

When in doubt, improvise. Early on, Connolly concentrated on hiring translators with strong English skills. That seemed wise. As she soon discovered, though, the best answers came from translators who wrote with great accuracy and clarity in their own language. English mastery actually didn't matter so much. People with limited English but keen attention to detail could rummage through dictionaries and end up producing fine translations. Catastrophes were far likelier when wikiHow relied on people who chatted engagingly in English during Skype calls but got sloppy about metric conversions or social niceties in their own language. As Connolly wryly told me: "If you're going to tell people how to bake a cake, the batter needs to rise when you put it in the oven."

It all comes back to one of the essentials of critical thinking in the real world—being mindful of other people's perspectives. A notable moment for Connolly involved an effort to communicate in person with her South Korean translation team. "We had done fine via e-mail," Connolly recalled. When everyone finally met in Seoul, however, "We couldn't understand each other's spoken English. We just couldn't. So we typed out messages on our phones and passed them back and forth." Weird? Yes. Effective? Absolutely.

Fresh feedback will tell you what to do next. If you're a stubborn manager, you rely constantly on your own expertise. If you're a pragmatist, you soak up useful information from others, basing your decisions on many people's insights. Connolly wasn't a business major; she hadn't studied different leadership models. Even so, her international relations courses had developed her social antennae, especially when unexpected clashes arose.

In general, wikiHow avoids translating articles that would be patently offensive in different cultures. The result: nothing in Russian about marijuana oil; no articles in Arabic about how to brew your own vodka. But what about an Arabic version of the legendary article "How to Kiss a Girl for the First Time"? That was tricky. While this piece waited in the Arabic translation queue, one Egyptian man protested its inclusion. Unsure how to proceed, Connolly began paying close attention to wikiHow's community forum, where members shared pointers and gripes.

Before long, women across the Arabic-speaking world began to weigh in. *I think it's gonna be ok if we know how to kiss,* one wrote. A loftier perspective: *It is important for partners or couples.* The ultimate insight: *We are curious about this stuff.* Smiling at the responses, Connolly decided the people had spoken and wikiHow was ready to do its part to make the world a slightly happier place; anyone in Egypt, Jordan, or other Arabic-speaking countries who needed to know could at last get the answer to that burning topic: *Kayf litaqbil fatat li'awwal marr?*

There will be moments when you work inhumanly hard. For most people, Halloween is a one-evening holiday, full of momentary mischief. For Connolly, it was a nightmare that wouldn't go away. During her first autumn at wikiHow, she discovered that the company's Spanish site — supposedly the most advanced translation project — was tangled in record-keeping snarls. Translators, editors, and administrators all had different, incomplete spreadsheets of which English-language articles had already been translated, making it hard to know what should be done next. A few popular articles had been translated two or three times; other favorites were not being prioritized. Orderly growth would be impossible unless someone created a universal database to coordinate everyone's efforts.

Finish by the end of October, wikiHow president Elizabeth Douglas told Connolly. Bring everyone's information into a single system that amounted to the fundamental "source of truth." Time began to blur for Connolly. She couldn't tell whether it was sunrise, late afternoon, or one in the morning. Day or night, she would be staring at a gigantic Excel spreadsheet, trying to tame the chaos. ("How to Avoid Mean Friends"? Done. "How to Dribble a Basketball"? Not yet. "How to Measure the Height of a Horse"? Done twice — heaven knows why.)

To keep despair at bay, Connolly pumped her headphones full of the throbbing techno-pop sounds of Ratatat playing "Wildcat." When that didn't suffice, she resorted to the Notorious B.I.G. declaiming about "Mo Money, Mo Problems." Finally, after a late-night work binge, the Spanish project had found its fundamental source of truth. The next morning, Connolly walked up to Douglas and whispered the two words that had seemed unachievable just a few weeks earlier: "It's fixed."

Help will arrive. By December 2013, a year after joining wikiHow, Connolly had expanded the company's global offerings to eight languages. Why stop there? She hired a freshly minted international relations major, Allyson Edwards, to join what was now a two-person team, which gave Connolly extra resources to get wikiHow established in even more languages. All of Asia beckoned. It was time to visit new countries where wikiHow could make a mark.

On their second prospecting trip, Connolly and Edwards started in South Korea, where a small translation effort was ready to expand, and then prepared to travel onward to Thailand. Because of various airport snarls in Seoul, the two women ended up nearly a mile from their airplane's gate with only a few minutes to spare before the Bangkok flight departed. "We were running through the corridors, clutching our backpacks and duffel bags," Connolly recalled. "Allyson didn't think we were going to make it. I kept telling her: 'We're fine!' Every time we encountered a group of people in a line, I'd tell them: 'We're doing good things! We work for an educational website. Can we get through?'"

The crowds parted. Connolly and Edwards made it onto their flight with seconds to spare, laughing and high-fiving each other. They were headed to Bangkok, confident they could hire another forty-five translators before the week was over.

You're in uncharted territory; sometimes you must start over. Could wikiHow connect with the Indonesian market by using the same approach that had succeeded in most other languages? Connolly didn't see any reason to be wary, so she signed up dozens of translators and a small cadre of editors to start customizing popular articles. The translators' work might be erratic, but if so, the editors would surely catch mistakes and fix awkward wording. With everyone based in Indonesia, what could go wrong?

A few weeks later, Connolly realized her mistake. Some Indonesian translators did nothing more than shove English articles into Google Translate, producing barely intelligible clots of misaligned phrases. The Indonesian editors then declared everything was flawless. Connolly had ended up with a pool of editors who felt it wasn't appropriate to criticize others' work. Her translation teams were so dysfunctional that a do-over had become essential. She and Edwards needed to fly to Indonesia and recruit a new batch of translators and editors. This time, they steered clear of unreliable operators in the capital city, Jakarta, who hadn't lived up to their promises of careful work. Instead, the two women made a fresh start at a provincial university, three hours outside Jakarta, where the efforts of students and their mentors were much more closely aligned with her expectations.

Having taken an adventurous approach to college course work, Connolly didn't find such a workplace crisis so terrifying after all. It can seem hellish, as a college sophomore or senior, to abandon a research topic that isn't working out and to scramble to complete a term paper on a new subject with half the available time already gone. Even so, there's honor in starting over. Get on the right track, even belatedly, and progress becomes possible once more. Terror subsides. Even a hasty sprint to a B-minus—or a red-eye flight to Indonesia—beats the paralyzed anxiety of being trapped in a project destined to fail.

Eventually, it's time for the next great advantage. Some people like to sustain what's working well; others prefer the thrill of repeatedly starting something new. Toward the end of 2016, Connolly couldn't stifle the urge to begin a fresh adventure. She wanted to make documentaries again; she wanted to work in the social sector; she even wanted, perhaps, to give politics a try. She handed over control of the globalization effort to a wikiHow colleague and headed to Ecuador for a short-term research project on a traditional weaving method called ikat.

I spoke with Connolly a few weeks after she returned to the

United States, and she was savoring the opportunities to come. "I've got twenty books that I'm interested in reading," she told me. "I know how to teach myself what's needed to succeed in a new area. The project-manager skills I learned at wikiHow can be put to work in so many different areas."

5

The Problem Solvers

Hello, Pittsburgh! In October 2016, Barack Obama and thirty other speakers arrived in a city famous for its postindustrial rebirth, ready to talk about the future of innovation. The event: the White House Frontiers Conference, held on the campuses of Pittsburgh's best-known universities, Carnegie Mellon and the University of Pittsburgh. The agenda: to stretch people's minds about what the country's future could hold. The majority of the speakers: single-subject experts such as NASA's chief scientist, a robotics inventor with a thousand patents, a top neuroscientist, and half a dozen of America's brightest software experts. The brainpower in the room: immense.

To make everything fit together at this conference, White House organizers needed one more type of expert: a speaker with the courage to step back and share simple truths. Someone had to peer at artificial intelligence with the eyes of a sociologist, an ethicist, or a poet. Just as welcome, someone who could balance today's excitement over Google Maps and drone-delivered medicine with stories of how early humans harnessed fire or the way household electricity had gone from rare to commonplace in the 1930s. To create a deeper dialogue between speakers and audiences, someone ought to share a historian's insights about the ways society resists, modifies, and then accepts technological progress. The more conversational the tone of that speaker, the better.

What the Frontiers Conference needed was Tim O'Reilly.

Look up O'Reilly on Google, and it's easy to jump to the (mistaken) conclusion that this grinning, energetic man is a lifelong technologist. It's not just the fact that O'Reilly relies on static electricity to send his thinning gray hair streaming in every direction. He owns a technical publishing company whose top-selling titles include *Node.js for Embedded Systems* and *Programming iOS 10*. He runs conferences on topics such as open-source software, big data, and artificial intelligence. He serves on the board of Code for America and Maker Media, which promotes digital-age craftsmanship in schools and other settings. With a background like that, he must have been a computer science major or something similar, no?

Actually, O'Reilly's beginnings are a well-hidden surprise. As a Harvard student in the 1970s, he opted for a bachelor's in classics — and never earned any other degrees. His senior thesis was on Plato and mysticism; his favorite class focused on the writings of Samuel Johnson. Deep down, O'Reilly still thinks like a humanist. In his Pittsburgh talk, he repeatedly invoked social forces that most pure technologists didn't even see. He talked about how life improves when citizens are "willing to spend money to educate other people's children." He picked over the ways that Victorian England built social structures that reined in the nastiest effects of disruptive technology so that early apprehensions of job loss abated and living standards improved. He invited people in the room to focus on social problems that human minds can't crack but that might succumb to carefully administered doses of artificial intelligence.

When O'Reilly finished college, his finances were so pinched that he needed to borrow a suit from an older associate in order to make his first business presentation. Today, O'Reilly favors rumpled chinos and fraying print shirts, but he dresses humbly by choice. As head of a media company that employs more than five hundred people, he has netted many millions of dollars over the years by spinning off various commercial ventures. Much of that has been plowed back into his business; even so, estimates of his net worth range as high as $100 million or more. We could linger on how O'Reilly made his money, but that would be missing the point.* The reason Tim O'Reilly opens this chapter is his ability to step into the world of technology as a humanist and see things the pure technologists never notice.

In a 2005 *Wired* magazine profile, journalist Steven Levy chronicled O'Reilly's talent for picking up trends before anyone else. As Levy saw it, O'Reilly's penchant for reading incessantly, talking to everyone, and listening carefully "helped him understand the significance of the World Wide Web before there were browsers to suit it. And it led him to identify and proselytize technologies like peer-to-peer, syndication and Wi-Fi before most people had even heard of them."

Fortunately, the career quadrant that has paid off so well for O'Reilly can be your jackpot too. The next few sections will focus

---

* In 2006, O'Reilly famously declared that "money is like gas in a car—you need to pay attention to it or you'll end up on the side of the road. But a successful business or a well-lived life is not a tour of gas stations."

on the second and third elements of critical thinking that were highlighted in chapter 2: your analytical methods and your problem-solving skills. Your liberal arts education has taught you to move forward as a researcher in the face of ambiguity. You know how to make solid inferences in the face of thin or contradictory information. You know how to extract every last morsel of meaning from a difficult text. You can adapt to a changing environment; you can work effectively with minimal oversight.

Just as important, you know how to inch toward a solution that can't be reached all at once. You've written rough drafts that may be only 50 percent of the way toward success, and you haven't flinched at the struggle for improvement that lies ahead. When necessary, you have overhauled your early efforts multiple times until you came up with a winning final version. You aren't frightened of the hard issues. You know how to come at a problem from three or four different directions if no single approach is sufficient.

Step into any fast-changing field, and those critical-thinking skills will be invaluable. New technologies are transforming industries ranging from digital advertising to 3-D printing, genetic counseling, publishing, and education. Self-driving cars, military drones, hobbyists' drones, "smart" houses—the examples keep piling up. In all these arenas, it's not enough to perceive what great engineering can build. Success or failure depends on seeing the bigger picture. Huge questions remain regarding how these technologies should be applied, how the market will react, and what the risks and limits of each breakthrough might be. The hunt for answers requires people like you.

In the late 1950s, the British scientist C. P. Snow wrote a landmark essay entitled "The Two Cultures" in which he argued that intellectual leadership in Western society was being split into two camps that couldn't make sense of each other: physical scientists and literary intellectuals. Each group had a curious, distorted image of the other based on dangerous misinterpretations. People who understood the second law of thermodynamics had no idea what Shakespeare had to offer, and vice versa. "The degree of incomprehension on both sides is the kind of joke which has gone sour," Snow declared. "If the scientists have the future in their bones, then the traditional culture responds by wishing the future did not exist."

One of the saving graces of the American educational system is that it keeps trying to bridge this gap. As a nation, we ask students to spend four years getting their undergraduate degrees (Britain does it in three) because we want everyone to try classes outside their specialties. We want engineers to read a few novels; we want poets to appreciate the natural beauty of numbers and equations too. If you are a science or engineering major with a fondness for liberal arts electives, you've prepared yourself well for this bridge-building role. If you're a history or English major who doesn't panic at the sight of a few numbers or formulas, you're on track too. The growing popularity of interdisciplinary majors such as cognitive studies speaks to increased awareness on the parts of employers, students, and university faculty that graduates with multiple perspectives bring something extra to the job market. Count me in as a champion of almost any approach that helps span the two cultures.

Right now, the job market lacks universal, easy-to-understand language that captures these multidimensional skills. As a result, the best opportunities for liberal arts graduates are likely to reside in jobs with awkward, long, and opaque titles. You might be trying to get hired as a partner advocate, a business-development manager, a relationship manager, or a customer-success specialist. Each organization has its own vocabulary. Linguistic reform is needed.

For now, let's refer to these as *bridge-building jobs*. This term is simple, easy to remember, and flexible enough to cover a wide range of industries and corporate structures. It's hard to say how many of these jobs exist or how rapidly they are coming into being, but one useful starting point is the Burning Glass estimate of hybrid job openings in the U.S. economy. These positions blend some tech expertise with a considerable amount of nontechnical insight. At least 240,000 openings arise each year, according to Burning Glass's tally.

Ask individual companies how they staff these chasm-spanning jobs, and everything becomes clearer. "We'd much rather hire a passionate candidate with potential than an uninspired candidate with a sparkling résumé," says Alan Knitowski, the CEO of Phunware, an Austin, Texas, company that builds smartphone apps. His customers range from big banks and hospitals to celebrity astrologers. There's no telling what aspects of mobile technology will fascinate each potential client, or what anxieties might arise. As a result, "We hire candidates who aren't afraid of learning on the job," Knitowski adds. "They possess the initiative to find a hole and fill it."

Consider what happened when Skycatch, a California drone-software company, wanted to enter Japan a few years ago. Someone needed to go to Tokyo to lead negotiations with a promising potential partner. Skycatch's choice: Mimi Connery, a 2008 graduate of Williams College with a degree in political science. Her edge: she was a seasoned negotiator, with experience ranging from venture capital to managing the band Third Eye Blind.

She had well-honed instincts about how deals should come together and what to do when obstacles arose. Other people at Skycatch knew the technology better and could advise her as needed. The Japanese alliance depended most keenly on how well everyone could align needs and capabilities. That played to Connery's strengths. As she points out: "Williams taught me how to interact with people, and that's valuable in any industry." Connery now is launching XX Incorporated, a maker of women's products.

Again and again, it's the core liberal arts strengths that employers prize. "You're really differentiated if you understand humanities," says Bracken Darrell, chief executive of Logitech. His company started out making keyboards and computer mice; now it's trying to come up with more advanced gadgets that make virtual reality as enticing as possible. That's more than an engineering challenge; success depends on gaining a deep understanding of what satisfies people at work and play.

Connecting Different Worlds

What do we mean by blockchain?

I'm on the phone with Oliver Meeker, a 2009 graduate of Hobart College, a small liberal arts institution in upstate New York. He's working for IBM in New York City in a fascinating job that requires him to think about technology and the ways future business networks might operate. He's a sociology major who has come into this specialty by a roundabout path. I'm eager to find out what he does. If he wants to open our conversation with this simple, enigmatic question, that's fine with me.

While I'm puzzling over the answer, Meeker takes me on an

intriguing journey. Imagine how an ancient village traded, he begins. Long ago, you knew which neighbors grew your grain and where that grain came from. Trust was inherent; you didn't worry about adulterated crops. If you traded your pig for some grain, your neighbor was equally confident in the quality of your pork. If disputes arose, they could be easily resolved, since the nature of the transaction and the responsible parties were obvious. As economies grew, such small-village trust became impossible. Far-flung markets took hold, with intermediaries trying to keep everything orderly. Production efficiencies increased, but so did uncertainties about goods' origins and buyers' recourses if things went wrong. You no longer knew your ultimate trading partner.

I sense where Meeker is heading, and there's no reason to interrupt. I'm enjoying this lively, genial introduction to a new world. The next thing I know, Meeker is telling me about blockchain, the digital era's latest transformational technology. I'm wary at first, because when I hear *blockchain,* I think *Bitcoin,* and that conjures up renegade actors in the underground economy carrying out drug deals. But Meeker wants me to appreciate an entirely different context. For him (and IBM), blockchain is fundamentally about building trust that can be applied prudently in areas ranging from trade settlements for capital markets to the validation of federal quality certificates from food suppliers. As Meeker explains, "It is all about trust."

Most business-minded discussions of blockchain are highly abstract, with hard-to-grasp allusions to greater transparency and security. Meeker keeps it real. "Let's say you want to know with one hundred percent confidence that the salmon you are eating is actually organic," he says. With blockchain, uncertainties vanish. The various people and businesses along your salmon-supply chain—the fishermen, shipping company, warehouse, and retailer—have a single view of where the fish has been on its way from the ocean to your plate.

IBM and a host of other companies are working on ways to use blockchain technology in mainstream sectors such as health care and supply chains, he adds. Digital technology already has created trillions of dollars of value that can't be touched or seen. Think of credit cards, debit cards, and wire transfers. Then think of PayPal, Apple Pay, and GooglePay. The connection between abstract electronic systems and U.S. paper currency gets thinner all the time. At some point, blockchain could turn out to be the best way of exchanging goods and services, Meeker contends, thanks to the key traits he alluded to a few moments ago: immutability, security, decentralization, and transparency.

I'm fascinated but not surprised to find that IBM's blockchain team includes a sociology major with more than four years of experience in Vietnam, along with the necessary dozens of computer science majors, finance specialists, and the like. The cultural and business implications of transformational technology are huge. Somebody needs to make sure society gets it right. Meeker is one of the bridge builders that such ambitious projects require. He is a Phi Beta Kappa intellect with a disarming laugh and an upbeat personality. You wouldn't necessarily expect to find him at IBM, but there he is. When asked to introduce a start-up at billionaire Richard Branson's island resort, Meeker dressed the part, showing up in an open-necked pink oxford shirt with his sunglasses perched atop his head. Thanks to his overseas stint, Meeker recognizes the importance of always being sensitive to local contexts. There's never just one way to solve a problem, he explains, and "you always—always—need to understand your audience."

As Meeker sees it, his path to IBM makes more sense than most people realize. "Going to Hobart really pushed me to grow," he recalls. "You were pushed to argue and to think about problems from multiple perspectives." In his sophomore year, at the suggestion of one of his sociology professors, he spent a semester in Vietnam and found it life changing. Jettisoning his earlier plans to become a corporate lawyer, Meeker broke away from the American expatriate community and made dozens of Vietnamese friends. His favorite moments involved sitting on tiny plastic stools on the uneven sidewalks of Hanoi observing a fascinating ancient society deal with modernity.

At the end of his semester abroad, Meeker produced a treatise comparing the leadership styles of political revolutionaries Ho Chi Minh and Vo Nguyen Giap with that of American auto executive Lee Iacocca. After graduation, he earned a Fulbright scholarship that let him return to Vietnam to carry out research on the country's rising entrepreneurial class. Fluent in Vietnamese and eager to see more, Meeker stayed on as an analyst for a premier private equity fund, Vietnam Investments Group. Among his projects: negotiating a franchise deal that brought Dairy Queen to Vietnam.

When Meeker returned to the United States in 2013, he flirted with a job in finance but refocused his hunt when a friend said, "You've got to talk to IBM about Watson." The big computer-services company was investing heavily in Watson, its artificial intelligence initiative. Now IBM needed eclectic minds to help Watson strike up business alliances. Meeker's ability to build a career in Vietnam impressed his hiring managers. They brought him into the Watson project for two years and then encouraged him to try his luck as a business-development specialist with IBM's next big idea: blockchain.

Now Meeker works with various organizations that might harness blockchain technology with IBM's help. Being effective means mastering an unfamiliar and highly technical area, but that hasn't fazed him. "I read everything I can on blockchain," Meeker says. "It's hard work. I learned about PBFT, which is Practical Byzantine Fault Tolerance. I learned how to talk about validator nodes, e-certs, t-certs, and the list goes on. I also have to envision industry transformation, new business models, and create new business cases." Was it like learning Vietnamese? "Absolutely!"

His boss, Brigid McDermott, tells me she wants to build a solutions ecosystem that combines software engineering and sophisticated new business models and a critical mass of participants. That calls for knitting together teams of IBM specialists, with each person playing a different role. Meeker doesn't need to be the classic high-energy salesperson, she observes. He is most valuable as a team builder. In such settings, a well-traveled sociology major can be surprisingly useful.

Taking Data to Good Places

Of all the technical fields that turn out to have a big nontechnical component, statistics is in a class by itself. Working with data has stopped being a fierce test of an individual's math skills, just as modern forestry no longer depends on finding strong people to swing axes. Automation has radically redefined the human role. With the rise of software tools such as SPSS Statistics, SAS, and Microsoft Excel, technology now puts numbers at our fingertips. What becomes crucial is human guidance in terms of asking the right questions—and finding the best ways of sharing data insights with society at large. "Statistics is not math," Cornell University statistics instructor William Briggs provocatively wrote a few years ago. As Briggs observed, we've transitioned to a new era in which "statistics rightly belongs to epistemology, the philosophy of how we know what we know."

For an opportunity to see what Briggs is talking about, let's take a close look at OpenTable, which has been blending dining and data since its founding in 1999. Spend time in New York, Los Angeles, Dallas, Atlanta, or any other big city, and you are likely to use OpenTable to book a restaurant reservation online. It's quick and always available, day or night. While munching breakfast, you can reserve dinner for four, even if the staff at your favorite restaurant is hours from starting the workday. If your ideal time slot isn't available, OpenTable shows you a full run of alternatives. To date, more than *one billion* restaurant reservations have been made this way.

Unless you have a relative in the restaurant business, it's unlikely you've encountered the other half of OpenTable's business. Those billion reservations translate into a wealth of data about patrons' booking habits that can be marketed to restaurants themselves. OpenTable knows how far in advance people make Valentine's Day reservations and what percentage of those early bookings get canceled. OpenTable knows whether slow turnout on Tuesdays is typical for your city or whether your restaurant is missing out on midweek traffic that everyone else is enjoying. The data insights will jolt your confidence in how well you are running your restaurant—which makes this information hard to look at and impossible to ignore.

On any given day, at least a hundred OpenTable experts fan out across the United States, iPads in hand, so they can brief restaurateurs on countless business metrics that can affect profitability. These emissaries' backgrounds? Exactly what you would expect. Open-Table doesn't restrict itself to employing business or hospitality majors. It repeatedly hires Spanish majors, child psychology majors, English majors, and political science majors. Those are the sorts of recruits best suited to sharing properly dosed—and properly couched—nuggets of data analytics with the proud, prickly bosses at leading restaurants.

To see how this works, hop in a car with Shawna Ramona, one of OpenTable's most effective restaurant-relations managers. She paid her way through San Francisco State in the late 1990s by waitressing part-time. It took her six years to earn an English degree, but she still loves to chat about the characters in Armistead Maupin's *Tales of the City* or F. Scott Fitzgerald's *The Great Gatsby*. She likes people. She likes figuring out what makes them tick. And when she visits restaurants, she thrives on the kaleidoscopic subtleties of figuring out each character's inner story.

First stop: Town Hall, a busy San Francisco restaurant that specializes in country ham and other Southern-inspired cuisine. Ramona's iPad is loaded full of data suggesting that the restaurant isn't doing enough to attract large groups. But Town Hall's business manager, Bjorn Kock, isn't in the mood to hear about it. He's a sharp-tongued German immigrant with strong opinions about what makes his restaurant succeed. He glances at an OpenTable pie chart showing that his restaurant hardly ever seats parties of ten or more—and angrily waves it away. "Our design does not lend itself to a lot of large parties," Kock declares. Big groups take too long to finish, he explains. Their rush of orders at the same time strains the kitchen. Besides, his restaurant's long, angular layout would make big tables as unwelcome as a boulder in the midst of a stream. "Those tens!" he says with a dismissive sweep of his hand. "I don't want them in our dining room."

Ramona doesn't give up. "I see your point," she says. "But what about trying an experiment on Sundays, when traffic is lighter. You could offer one ten-seat booking at five p.m. That wouldn't strain the kitchen. It might be extra business that you wouldn't get otherwise." Kock smiles. He's been won over. "That could work," he says.

Next stop: Park Tavern, a wine bar and restaurant in San Francisco's trendy SoMa District. It's run by Anna Weinberg, who greets Ramona with a big hug and a shriek of joy. Being in Weinberg's presence is like watching a sped-up movie where characters flit across the screen faster than you can recognize them. She's sitting. She's standing. She's summoning someone to pour glasses of sparkling water. She's telling a story. She's flipping her blond ponytail back as she laughs at her own punch line. She's rearranging everyone's chairs and it's all happening faster than you can read this sentence. For Shawna Ramona, it's a wonderful show and there's no reason to interrupt.

Then comes a lull. Ramona pulls out her iPad and invites Weinberg to take a look at a giant "opportunity." In the past year, it turns out, hundreds of OpenTable users had been told that seats weren't available at Park Tavern. Ardent fans try to book tables in advance, only to discover that the restaurant offers a mere thirty-day look-ahead. Ramona puts on a sad face—and lets the implications sink in. "Fine!" Weinberg declares. "Let's do sixty days, then. We'll do it for all three of our restaurants."

Third stop: Perbacco, a traditional Italian restaurant in the heart of San Francisco's financial district. The silver-haired owner, Umberto Gibin, has spent more than forty years in the restaurant trade. Gibin never went to college; he started as a teenage waiter in Italy, learning to carve ducks at tableside. He's old-school and proud of it. Other people stare at spreadsheets to see how business is doing; he can tell just by walking up the staircase of his restaurant and taking in a hundred diners' gestures. He and Ramona sip coffee together for nearly an hour. They gossip. They reminisce. She brings up the importance of creating a mobile-friendly website—raising the subject so gently that he hardly notices the conversation has switched from his business to hers. "I'm a dinosaur when it comes to technology," Gibin protests. Still, he acknowledges that mobile matters. By the time their chat is over, Ramona has made the next generation of technology seem more inviting (and less scary) than it did before she arrived.

Within OpenTable, about a hundred and twenty people are involved in the flow of data to individual restaurants. Only fourteen of those people are data scientists. By a ratio of nearly eight to one, this expertise squad is dominated by nontechnical emissaries like Shawna Ramona. Tagging along with her, I'm fascinated to see how the data revolution touches a mainstream industry. The big surprise: Getting the numbers right is the easy part, requiring only a few people. The hardest challenges relate to human habits and hesitations. That's why only a small slice of Ramona's restaurant visits focus on the charts and graphs tucked away on her iPad. The heart of her job involves understanding each restaurateur's hopes and anxieties. As we've seen before, a tight nucleus of tech-driven innovation creates an enormous number of nontechnical jobs for the people who can build connections between what already is and what will be.

OpenTable's top performers are defined by "endless curiosity and the sense that they are fun to be around," says Andrea Johnston, the company's senior vice president in charge of sales. "They don't dominate the conversation, positioning themselves as experts," she adds. Instead, her stars "connect with all the different kinds of personalities in our industry. They become trusted consultants, whose starting point is: 'I'm here to work with you.'"

If that description resonates with the back-and-forth of a lively liberal arts class, it's hardly a coincidence. Johnston herself started out at Vassar (class of 1989), where she was an international relations major.

The Power of Plain English

Danielle Sheer earned a bachelor's degree in philosophy from George Washington University before heading to law school and embarking on a career in corporate law. Since 2009, she has been the general counsel at Carbonite, a Boston-area data-protection company. When Sheer joined the company, she felt intimidated by the constant stream of technical terms and acronyms in major meetings. She tried to be invisible during the discussions. Before long, though, she realized that a simpler, clearer style would help Carbonite's customers as well as its own specialist employees in different areas.

The payoff has been bigger than she ever expected. "By articulating complicated technical or strategic ideas in plain English, you'd be amazed at how much progress we've made solving problems," Sheer told *Fast Company* magazine. Often, Carbonite employees have been chagrined and then relieved to discover that they've been arguing over a misunderstanding of what a certain term means. In other cases, people have been racing too quickly to lock down a particular solution to a problem without rechecking assumptions to see if a faster, simpler solution might be available. "I don't believe there is one answer for anything," Sheer said. "That makes me a very unusual member of the team."

Before the rise of coding boot camps, at least a thousand liberal arts majors a year recast themselves as full-time software developers. Since the baseline year of 2010, that migration rate has probably tripled. Magazine stories often portray these nontraditional coders as refugees from failed job hunts who picked up new skills out of necessity when it turned out that their chosen majors had no professional value. But that stereotype doesn't do justice to the enduring value of a liberal arts education. One of my workplace neighbors in California, Diana Nemirovsky, earned a history degree from Colgate before taking up coding as a hobby and then as a career. "I don't use my degree to write code," Nemirovsky told me. "But I use it constantly in working with clients. It helps me be clear about what the client wants—and what I've committed to do. That has a huge positive impact on my productivity."

In jobs that straddle technical and nontechnical domains, the power of plain English is one of businesses' great open secrets. Just ask NeKelia Henderson, whose route to a well-paying, bridge-building job is highly instructive. Born in 1986, she grew up in Gwinnett County, Georgia, about thirty miles northeast of Atlanta. Her mother was an accountant; her father was a mechanic. She excelled in math as a high-school student but enjoyed English and writing classes more than anything. What should she do with those dual talents? Her parents and high-school advisers provided the standard recommendation that every academically strong teenager in a striver's family hears: become a doctor.

Mindful of everyone's advice, Henderson headed off to college as a premed at Georgia Southern University. That didn't click, so she switched to a pharmacy major. That didn't click either. After two years, she transferred to Georgia State and became an English major, minoring in Spanish. She loved the enchanting, baffling cadence of Chaucer. She became intrigued by Dante's *Inferno*. She graduated in 2009 with a 3.8 grade point average, no obvious job prospects, and two very anxious parents.

What ensued was the classic liberal arts journey: several years of quirky-job-hopping accompanied by additional training that eventually led to a happy resolution. Henderson started with a postcollege gig as a customer-service representative in a call center. "I was good at it, and I made a lot of money, but I didn't like it," she recalls. After that, a brief move to New York, where she wrote nearly one hundred blog posts for a fashion designer. (Her verdict: Exciting, but not a durable career.) She returned to the South and did a social-media internship at CNN. (The scorecard on that one: Intriguing, but still not quite a match.) She enrolled in the public relations program at Georgia State and embarked on a second bachelor's degree, eager to see what new opportunities might arise.

Right place, right time. The public relations industry was being upended and revitalized by the rise of social media. A single Tweet—effusive or caustic—could transform a corporate brand's reputation within hours. Local PR agencies were scrambling to build up data-analytics teams that could provide clients with both the insights and strategy suggestions necessary to "win" Twitter, Facebook, and the like. One of Henderson's professors pointed her toward the Atlanta office of Porter Novelli, a global agency with clients such as NASCAR, the Centers for Disease Control, and the Almond Board of California. Could Henderson tell stories with numbers? If so, this was the right job for her.

Success at last.

Two years into the job, Henderson is the new face of data in a more inclusive world: an African American woman whose reports can be as serious as a math exam or as whimsical as a blog post. Analogies come easy to her. She likens her data-minded role within the company to that of "a cook or a medic on an expedition to climb Mount Everest." It's a sly comparison, because cooks and medics aren't merely anonymous helpers on big team projects. In lumber camps, the cook is always the best poker player. In war movies, the medic's mordant wit gets us laughing in spite of ourselves. At Porter Novelli, Henderson is the jaunty one who rounds out her social-media posts with the hashtags #NumbersDontLie and #BowDownToTheData.

While numbers don't lie, they need to be interpreted—and that's where Henderson earns her keep. Porter Novelli's clients often want to enlist the paid support of a big-time social-media personality who can help generate excitement about a particular brand. In some categories, such as health care, that's easy to do. Star bloggers (or Tweeters) appreciate the extra cash and don't mind talking up a product that appeals to them anyway. In other categories, it's much harder to find the right boosters. Henderson frequently builds "influencer maps" that show the forty or so most active social-media personalities on a particular topic and give some guidance about which ones might be best suited for a client's cause.

Getting those recommendations right is an intricate test of Henderson's ability to think in multiple directions at once. Statistical packages such as Affinio, Traackr, and Little Bird can tell her right away which social-media personalities have the greatest relevance and reach on the topic in question. But figuring out which ones will be the most credible champions of a particular brand message is an art that can't be automated. Cough-medicine makers won't win many new fans by banking on a holistic-health enthusiast to carry their message. Tech companies that are looking for "wholesome rappers" to create youthful buzz about their gadgets might want to think twice. The terrain is changing so rapidly that there aren't any sure formulas yet for what will build (or destroy) brands online. When clients ask Porter Novelli for advice, it's the subjective discernment of experts like NeKelia Henderson that ultimately matters most.

"So much of what we're doing is story-telling," explains one of Henderson's bosses, Brooke Balch. "We present data to people who aren't data people. That means explaining things simply and creating trust by making other people feel smart."

Tim O'Reilly Explains It All

In the opening paragraphs of this chapter, I raced past what might be the most valuable part of Tim O'Reilly's story. In the years between his college graduation (1975) and his eye-catching appearance onstage as Barack Obama's warm-up act at the Frontiers Conference (2016), O'Reilly needed to find his path. Knowing a bit about Plato and Samuel Johnson wasn't enough to guarantee a living, let alone a significant impact in the wider world. Somehow, he found his way. What did he get right—and can we extract modern-day lessons from his experiences?

It turns out that O'Reilly's postcollege years mirror this chapter's three main points: connecting different worlds, taking technical information to good places, and the power of plain English. By mastering all three of those realms, O'Reilly didn't just secure a steady income for himself; he laid the groundwork for what has become a robust, inventive collection of media properties. Over coffee one morning, O'Reilly revisited those years with me, marveling at the way early stumbles pay off in spite of themselves.

Coming out of Harvard, O'Reilly spent his first three years writing obscure treatises for tiny audiences. He got a federal grant to translate Greek fables. He spent a year poring through the cryptic notebooks of social theorist George Simon, annotating and editing them as best he could. After that, O'Reilly embarked on a biography of Frank Herbert, author of the science-fiction classic *Dune*.

"That's where I learned to write," O'Reilly told me. By O'Reilly's account, the biography's first draft was as tangled as Herbert's own writing. The book editor, Dick Riley, kicked that version back, demanding a clearer rewrite. On the second try, O'Reilly found his voice. His topic sentences became crisp and magisterial. He turned into a patient, lucid explainer, repeatedly using entire paragraphs to introduce key concepts that would be needed in a page or so. There wasn't anything flashy about O'Reilly's writing, but it all made sense. The denser the material, the shorter O'Reilly's sentences became.

Without knowing it, O'Reilly had discovered the style that would eventually make him the king of a technical-publishing empire. All he needed was a community that cherished his skills. Fortune struck when an experienced programmer, Peter Brajer, wanted help writing technical manuals for some of Digital Equipment's lab products. The pay—forty dollars an hour—was too good for a classics graduate to turn down. O'Reilly knew so little tech jargon that at first he would take notes silently while Brajer quizzed Digital's experts, afraid that even a brief stray remark would reveal his ignorance. For someone who had labored to make sense of fragmentary Greek texts, though, nothing Digital conjured up could be any harder. After a few months of applying his close-reading skills—and cursing the opacity of Digital's vocabulary—O'Reilly was ready to create any kind of technical manual on demand.

O'Reilly's biggest insight came soon afterward. Harnessing his bridge-building skills to the commercial needs of product-pushing tech companies wasn't the best use of his talents. Instead, he realized, he should be writing for engineers and technicians who needed to *use* these tech products to get ahead in the world. He could become their champion. He could reveal clever shortcuts that would save them time. He could turn his manuals into tools of self-improvement and enrichment, paving the way to a better life for any aspiring techie who picked up an O'Reilly manual.

From the early 1980s onward, that's exactly what Tim O'Reilly—and many hundreds of editors and writers on his team—have done. Not only does O'Reilly Media explain tech to millions of people at all levels of understanding, the company's conferences and webinars have become rallying points for a sprawling, global community of people who share an interest in a particular technology. His earliest bosses saw tech publishing as a business obligation. He sees it as an uplifting crusade.

Linda Walsh, one of O'Reilly Media's earliest employees, has this image fixed in her mind: Tim O'Reilly pacing back and forth in a sparsely furnished attic with about a dozen of his employees sprawled on beanbag chairs, pillows, or whatever else they have found to sit on. O'Reilly has taped a piece of butcher paper to the wall and is jotting down titles of possible projects that everyone could work on next. "This is a seed of an idea," O'Reilly says excitedly. "Just a seed." Waving at everyone and no one, he declares: "I want to know what you think."

Add up Tim O'Reilly's impact over the years, and it's clear that the people who came to his conferences or bought his manuals have ended up making far more money from the tech boom than he has. O'Reilly says that's fine with him. "You should always create more value than you capture," he tells me. If we want to know where that aphorism originated, he can help us trace it back to Diogenes.

6

Frozen Pipes, Thawed Minds

Bess Yount is about to tell one of her favorite stories. The setting: the Berkshire Mountains of western Massachusetts on a ferociously cold Sunday morning. An overnight ice storm has taken its toll. As people start their morning routines, it's obvious something is wrong. Showers don't work. Toilets don't refill after being flushed. Pipes have frozen and kitchen sinks have seized up. Lift the faucet handle and nothing comes out except a miserable gasp of air.

It's time to call a plumber, Yount says. But who do we call?

Now Yount is hitting her stride. It doesn't matter that she is speaking on a mild spring day. It's inconsequential that we are sitting inside Facebook's luxurious headquarters in Menlo Park, California. She has set the scene so perfectly that I'm practically shivering from the cold. My mind is conjuring up the sound of sinks gone bad. I'm imagining frost on the windowpanes, the narrow hallways of an old Colonial house, and wooden floors that feel cold to the touch. I've bought into her story so completely that imagination is replacing reality. I've become one of those Massachusetts homeowners, bewildered and frightened by this frozen-pipe problem. Time has stopped. I can't think about anything else until Yount guides me toward a solution.

Fortunately, help is on the way. In Yount's story, the ice storm's damage leads us to reach for our smartphones or our laptops. We get onto Facebook to tell our friends about our problem. We want sympathy; we want companionship—and we'd like some advice about what to do. As we type our status updates, we notice a perky ad that speaks to our situation. A plumber in town is open for business, right now. Never mind that it's Sunday morning. He specializes in fixing frozen pipes; he's ready to make a house call. His phone number is right there on the ad. All we need to do is call. Then, blessedly soon, we can enjoy a warm shower, clean dishes, and all the other pleasures of running water again.

Predicament...unexpected solution...relief. You could imagine Yount telling her story at a holiday party, a church supper, or even a small political fund-raiser. By sharing her slice of Americana, she creates a genial, reassuring way of winning people's trust. If you've ever watched an effective salesperson in action, you know the power of this classic formula. Even so, it takes a master's touch to make such tales overcome a listener's doubts.

Bess Yount is one of Facebook's best storytellers. She joined the fast-growing social network in 2010, just a few weeks after earning a master's degree in sociology. Now she is part of a three-thousand-person sales and marketing team that has helped turn Facebook from a money-losing experiment to one of the world's most profitable media companies. Nobody ever asks her to write code, yet she is every bit as valuable as Facebook's widely lionized software engineers. The reason: She connects with skeptics and draws them into Facebook's fast-growing advertising ecosystem. She makes progress seem pleasant.

When I first met Yount, she worked her magic by visiting

small-business conferences in cities such as Anchorage, Sacramento, Miami, Chicago, and Sugar Hill, Texas. At each stop, she struck up conversations with people running restaurants, nail salons, two-partner law firms, dentist's offices—any kind of business, really. Many of the people she met were in their late forties or older. They came of age when newspaper ads and Yellow Pages listings provided reliable ways of promoting a small business. Now those time-tested methods were proving impotent. Newspaper readership kept plummeting; the Yellow Pages were becoming as outdated as ditto machines. (Google them!)

At some level, business owners know they must change with the times. Yet the older ones are often bewildered and defensive. They spent a lot of years mastering the ins and outs of traditional advertising. It's depressing to see the value of those old skills dwindle. Before these merchants can move from print to pixels, they need reassurance that digital technology can pay off in their worlds. They also need a safe way of mastering new skills without feeling like the slowest learner in a gossipy classroom.

Yount makes the pain go away. She's spending less time on the road now in favor of a new focus on making upbeat videos that can be shown nationwide, but her approach hasn't changed. She's constantly sharing straight-from-the-heart stories that help listeners transition to a more up-to-date way of seeing the world. The real-life story of the Pittsfield, Massachusetts, plumber and the ice storm is now paired with new narratives that showcase Latino immigrants, Oklahoma repair shops, and more. Yount isn't the sort to show off her sociology training; you won't hear her talking about "nonformal education programs" or "the facilitation model of learning." All the same, she builds her presentations with an exquisite sensitivity to the way that new beliefs take hold. The proof is in Facebook's own growth. When Yount joined the company in 2010, Facebook sold less than $100 million in advertising a year. Six years later, that number exceeded $26 billion. By selling pixels—nothing but pixels—Facebook collects four times as much ad revenue as one of traditional media's biggest conglomerates, CBS. It has taken CBS more than eighty years to amass its collection of radio stations, television stations, Internet sites, and cable-TV networks such as Showtime and the Movie Network. By contrast, Facebook was founded barely a dozen years ago. CBS enjoys an illustrious past; Facebook owns the future.

One of modern society's biggest secrets is the degree to which our date of birth defines our appetite for new technology. As science-fiction author Douglas Adams famously observed, we seldom think twice about all the wizardry invented before we were born or when we were tiny. Nuclear weapons, jet travel, diet soft drinks? Such creations are obvious and ordinary. If our grandparents marvel at such developments, we do our best to suppress a yawn. In Adams's words, such steps forward are just a natural part of the way the world works.

When we fall in love with an innovation, it's almost always something that arrives with a bang when we're between ages fifteen and thirty-five. Everyone's chronology is different, but within this continuum of inventions in the past thirty years, pick out your own delight: cell phones, Wi-Fi, digital music, the Xbox 360, the iPhone, Twitter, texting, 3-D printing, video streaming, Airbnb, virtual reality. Not only do we hail such additions as exciting and revolutionary, we might seize upon our favorite as a ticket to fame and wealth. As Adams dryly observed: "With any luck, you can make a career out of it."

Left for last in Adams's social segmentation is the way people react to everything invented after they turn thirty-five. In such situations, *it's all too late*. We already feel locked into the habits that have defined our lives. With a few exceptions, we aren't in the mood to change. Grumpiness sets in. We can't feel the magic of something new anymore. Whether we own up to it or not, we want progress to stop. Adams's trenchant putdown: anything invented after your thirtieth birthday—no matter how benign— will strike you as being "against the natural order of things."

No matter how anyone feels about it, technological progress keeps coming. The previous chapter showed how industrial-sector breakthroughs intensify demand for critical thinkers with analytic and decision-making skills. This chapter will highlight the ways that fast-moving advances in consumer technology stir up the need for critical thinkers who specialize in adjacent skills: reading the room and communicating in inspiring ways.

For change-resistant consumers, it's as if a UPS truck keeps unloading new packages (labeled TECHNOLOGY SURPRISE!) on their doorsteps faster than anyone can open them. Seventy percent of us now have broadband Internet, up from essentially zero in 2000. Americans average fifty minutes a day on Facebook, compared with just sixteen minutes a day reading newspapers, if we read them at all. We've replaced movie theaters with Netflix; department stores with Amazon; file cabinets with Dropbox. And we're just getting started.

Whether you take Douglas Adams's demarcations literally or figuratively, there's no arguing with his basic message. The big societal challenge for the modern world doesn't involve how rapidly engineers create new technology. The great point of strain involves how rapidly the skeptics and the hesitant can absorb each new wave. That's especially pressing because as the baby-boomer generation gets older, so does our overall society. We aren't making babies fast enough to keep America as youthful as it used to be. (The median age of an American is now 37.8 years, a remarkable jump from a low of 28.1 in 1970.) We've ended up with more than half of America on the cranky side of Adams's final dividing line, inclined to regard each new advance as a debasement of the natural order.

Technology by itself can't master the art of persuasion. Artificial intelligence systems can do a brilliant job of playing the intricate Japanese board game go—but they can't make you *want* to sit down for a session yourself. Tools such as Alexa, Siri, and Cortana, which are meant to make tech seem friendlier and more approachable, delight those who start out warmly disposed to digital helpers. They horrify those who fear the robots are taking over. There's a reason why the U.S. economy employs fourteen million people in sales and just four million in computer-related jobs: it's impossible to automate the highly nuanced feat of changing people's minds.

The smartest marketers and salespeople know the limits of synthetic persuasion. Automated systems such as MailChimp and HubSpot can spray us with customized e-mails, drawing inferences from our shopping habits of a month ago. Tracking cookies can chase us from website to website, showing us the same T-shirt ads no matter where we go. (Their hope: if we abandon a shopping cart on one clothing store's site, our previous interest in buying a T-shirt can be rekindled.) Yet there's a limit to the effectiveness of such brute-force techniques. Often they annoy us. Young or old, we don't like being treated as a node on someone else's vast grid of business-to-consumer selling. As Stephanie Meyer, chief marketing officer at software maker Connecture, observes: "It can't be B-to-C; it has to be B-to-human, or B-to-me."

The result: A newfound respect—even reverence—for people who tell persuasive stories. If you've come through college with that gift, take a moment to realize you possess skills that are both scarce and precious. You can reach other people in ways the algorithms can't. Your wit and warmth will help you be persuasive in one-on-one settings, your ability to read the room will serve you well in small groups, and your capacity to inspire people will enable you to succeed on an even larger scale.

If you aren't yet convinced of how valuable your strengths are, let Silicon Valley executive Santosh Jayaram put the full picture together. He is an engineer by training who worked for several years at Google before setting up a series of his own companies. A few years ago, he was prowling the Stanford campus, looking for talent to hire. But he didn't stop by the engineering school. Instead, he slipped over to the humanities quad to recruit.

Once there, Jayaram explained to Michael Malone, an adjunct writing instructor, how everything had been turned upside down. Nowadays, it didn't take a year of intense engineering to build features. Getting the code right was the easy part. Many software-based products could be assembled in a few weeks as teams of programmers outside the United States stitched together existing chunks of code. The hard part came when it was time to connect with potential users, who would either embrace this exciting idea or ignore it. To create bonds, Jayaram explained, he needed storytellers who could make the rest of the world imagine how much better life would be if they were already using this marvelous new creation. To pull off that magic trick, he said, "English majors are exactly the people I'm looking for."

Never forget how much these organizations need you. Companies historically have undervalued the importance of getting their stories right. They believed that frontline marketers or back-office technical writers were worker ants who did nothing more than fuss with the details. That belief was dubious then, and it's preposterous today. Find a fast-moving field, and your well-honed communications skills become a huge asset. You're entering the picture when the overall strategy is still in flux. Your technical colleagues and their bosses haven't found their story. They're inarticulate or mute, which terrifies them. They don't know how to connect with America's older technophobes; they probably aren't certain how to reach people young enough to be excited about new approaches. Without you, ambitious organizations are stuck. If you can be their Bess Yount, expect pay and recognition that will make you proud.

Let's examine three important ways your storytelling arts can pay off.

Striking Up a Conversation

It's crowded out there! Experts at the University of Southern California calculate that on average, each of us is exposed to seventy-four gigabytes of data a day. We're talking about fifteen and a half hours of texts, e-mails, Snapchats, Instagram pictures, YouTube videos, corporate videos, and so on, every day. Most of it is instantly forgettable.

How does this overload affect your chances of being noticed if you set out to be a blogger, journalist, podcaster, author, or any kind of message maker? Cynics may deride you for embarking on a hopeless quest. It's easy to believe we're in a world with too much information and too little attention. Even corporate "content providers" with business degrees are struggling to protect their page-view numbers and their click-through rates, and they are spending millions of dollars to optimize their offerings. The big media companies are squeezing as much value as they can from today's standard audience-engagement formulas. What hope do you have?

How can you prevail with your liberal arts degree and your appreciation of creativity for its own sake?

Don't waste energy arguing with the doubters. Just draw strength from the story of Andy Anderegg, an English major who turned the naysayers' arguments inside out, demonstrating a path to success that remains wide open today.

In the spring of 2010, Anderegg was just another English major in the American heartland, finishing a master's in fine arts from the University of Kansas. As for what lay ahead, she didn't know. Nobody in New York wanted to publish her novel. In fact, she hadn't exactly written a novel yet. She was exploring the crazy-quilt world of genre writing, in which different writing styles serve everything from celebrity memoirs to PhD dissertations.

When her own writing stalled (which happens to all writers), Anderegg would fantasize she was living in Kansas City, ninety-five miles from KU's campus. Among her indulgences: repeated visits to Groupon.com so she could savor the site's discount coupons for the big city. Such joy! If she lived in Kansas City, with Groupon's help, she could buy a pink spangled cowboy hat at Rusty Spur Couture. In fact, for twenty dollars, she could double up, thanks to a two-for-one special.

The Kansas City fantasy didn't last long, but Anderegg's enchantment with Groupon kept growing. The site's job section posted an opening for in-house writers at the company's Chicago headquarters. Starting pay: thirty-three thousand dollars a year. It wasn't great, but Anderegg hadn't expected to get rich as a writer. She could make it work for a year or two. Even though the site's edgy style would be a huge departure from scholarly writing, she was willing to give it a try. Her genre-writing training would help her deconstruct the way Groupon's writers worked their mischief. All she needed to do was pass Groupon's writing test.

The quick-witted grad student with the big glasses prevailed.

Anderegg broke into Groupon's writing lineup with a deliriously exaggerated portrayal of how much fun it could be to go bowling in Detroit. She began with an ode to the thumb: "the highest throne in the human hand castle." Bowling "celebrates the thumb," she declared. She brought that awestruck tone to the bowling alley's most mundane details. The seating: "classic orange." The ball returns: blessed with "supernatural abilities." The scorekeeping screens: "designed primarily for box jellyfish who, for the sake of fairness, direct only two of their twenty-four eyes at the pins."

Who knew bowling could be such a delightful, goofy experience? The secret, of course, was that Groupon wasn't really selling bowling; it was selling whimsy and unpredictability. Its target audience consisted of millions of people across the United States (at all points on the spectrum between sociable and lonely) who couldn't decide what to do with their time or money. Groupon became the giddy friend with a never-ending series of invitations to embark on adventures. A well-written Groupon ad could make anything sound exciting. Even more important, Groupon's sassy tone made it easy for subscribers to corral their friends without seeming needy or domineering.

What Anderegg mastered in June, she was teaching by August. With Groupon's coupon traffic growing 300 percent a year, the company constantly scrambled to hire more writers. Few people at Groupon knew how to explain the site's quirky writing style. Most job candidates couldn't master it on their own. Anderegg stepped forward with a training module that helped dozens of other English majors crack the code. She took charge of writer recruiting and training, pushing up her pay to forty-seven thousand dollars a year.

Merchants who wouldn't dream of lampooning their own offerings discovered that Groupon's wit—and a discount coupon—brought torrents of new customers to their doors. Something as ordinary as family-style salads at a Wyoming steak house could become silly and intriguing in the hands of Anderegg-trained writers. Do you want a nuclear-family salad? Or maybe an extended-family salad? Heck, summon all your courage and try a dysfunctional-family salad. *The fun never stops.*

Groupon caught the American mood perfectly, for a short time. Millions of people signed up for daily e-mails that provided giggles, discount coupons, and the promise of new adventures. Investors rushed to buy stock in Groupon, which went public in 2011. At its zenith, the company claimed an enterprise value of more than $15 billion. Eventually, Groupon's growth curve turned downward. What was hilarious in 2011 was starting to become familiar in 2014. Cost-cutting took hold, and Anderegg's writers were told to crank out e-mails much faster, even if it meant recycling last month's phrases. By the beginning of 2015, Anderegg herself had moved on.

Groupon's stumbles didn't need to be Anderegg's setbacks, which is the most important lesson from her journey. When Groupon was riding high, she earned several more promotions at the company. Within five years of graduating from Kansas, she had become the Chicago site's managing editor, at a salary of more than a hundred thousand dollars a year. When she quit, she moved to Southern California and set herself up as a well-paid consultant to other digital-media companies. Working half-time, Anderegg was able to sustain a six-figure income and still work on a collection of short stories. Not only had she become a digital-era shaman, blessed with mysterious knowledge of what made viral posts work, she also was perfectly positioned to build a consulting practice around her expertise.

Those sorts of skills will always be valuable. What's more, no employer can ever pry them away from you.

I Hear What You're Saying

Does empathy pay?

For most of the past century, the answer has been an awkward "no." We expect—and even appreciate—high levels of caring from social workers, nursing aides, kindergarten teachers, store clerks, and restaurant waitstaff. But in the United States, at least, such fields tend to pay poorly. Big earners in our society are defined by ambition and relentless priority-setting. Some are nice, some can be gruff, but they generally expect the rest of the world to adapt to *their* attitudes and priorities. Paul Piff, a University of California, Irvine, psychologist who has studied the interaction between wealth and social behavior, finds that the most affluent Americans tend to be more narcissistic, less reliant on other people, and more consumed with a feeling of entitlement.

This is a dismaying truth for anyone steeped in a liberal arts way of thinking. On college campuses, the ability to understand other people's points of view is an unquestioned virtue. Pull up a seat at any graduation ceremony, and you'll hear well-crafted tributes to the power of empathy. The best psychologists, anthropologists, political scientists, and sociologists are constantly trying to understand what makes other people tick. "Viewing the world through many lenses…is the very core of a college of arts and sciences," declared Northwestern dean Adrian Randolph in a 2016 speech. It's a sad turn of events if our society gives no consideration to the art of being considerate.

In his book *Give and Take*, Wharton management professor

Adam Grant offers a cheerier alternative. He divides the world into people who are givers, takers, or a bit of both, which he calls matchers. Many people who achieve the least, he finds, are givers whose generous natures end up being exploited by others. Yet people who accomplish the most often turn out to be givers too. They just approach the wider world with a more careful strategy. On first encounters, they err on the side of compassion. If that warmth is reciprocated, they carry on. If they are snubbed, they pull back. Grant's conclusion: generosity and empathy are winning virtues; you just need to be careful about choosing your friends.

In our tech-influenced society, empathy's rewards may be intensifying. Cutting-edge companies that hope to redefine America's habits—not just Facebook but also a host of other disrupters—can't bully their way to success. The confrontational bosses at Uber, for example, keep advertising for community managers and growth managers to join the ride-sharing business. These specialists excel at the rapport building needed to recruit drivers and keep passengers loyal, even when a particular trip turns sour. That's a challenging job. Annual pay can top eighty thousand dollars. Scan through a LinkedIn list of Uber's current community managers, and you'll see that such a job attracts people whose college backgrounds radiate empathy, including psychology majors from Swarthmore and art history majors from McGill.

Another factor that helps turn empathy into a highly marketable skill is that it's easier than ever to keep score. People's business reputations are constantly on display via Yelp, TripAdvisor, eBay, and countless other rating sites. Being known as a nice person to interact with becomes a valuable asset. Equally important, as we spend more time online absorbing information and trading gossip, banter, and jokes, we become starved for deeper emotional engagement. Emoji masquerade as sustenance for a while, but at a certain point, such digital gestures fail to satisfy. We crave real smiles and the full, five-senses delight of doing business with someone willing to view the world—for a moment—through our lens.

A few months before starting work on this book, I spent a week in California's almond country working on a *Forbes* magazine profile of Build.com. The online company sells about five hundred million dollars' worth of faucets, door handles, and other home-improvement gear annually. It's an improbably strong competitor to much larger rivals such as Amazon and Home Depot, even though it's outgunned in terms of money, prestige, and brand recognition. I wanted to find out why. The best place to hunt for answers: Build.com's sales desk, where nearly two hundred employees field calls from contractors and homeowners who need advice. The right person to study: Mary Helen Smith, a University of Nevada, Reno, English major turned salesperson.

By the time I put on headphones to listen to Smith's customer calls, her sales that day had already topped twenty-five thousand dollars, the most of anyone on the floor. Yet she didn't seem rushed or pushy. Instead, Smith drew out the details of each caller's situation with good-natured wonder, as if she were reconnecting with a longtime friend. One woman in Hawaii wanted to buy a Kohler sink but was trying to bargain down the price. Smith never said no; she just asked the woman to tell her a bit about the home-remodeling project. Each detail elicited a friendly response. "That's a great choice!" Or "You've picked a lovely color." Two minutes later, Smith booked the sale, at full list price.

Try too hard, and such cheery patter seems fake. It doesn't work; it can even backfire. In Smith's case, empathy is a central part of who she is. During a lull, I asked her to tell me about her path to Build.com. Did she absorb the liberal arts mind-set on campus or had she been headed that way from early childhood? In Smith's case, it was a bit of both. She grew up in an intensely rural stretch of eastern California, near the Nevada border. Her father ran a feed store; her mother taught high-school English. Smith was raised with a profusion of animals at home, not just her dog Stanley, but cats, ducks, and horses too. As a little girl, Smith thought she wanted to be a veterinarian.

Four years as an English major at University of Nevada, Reno, added sophistication to Smith's warmhearted nature. Her most vivid memories of college include the different ways various students reacted to the assigned texts. Studying Toni Morrison's *The Bluest Eye*, she was struck by how the women and men in the class took such different stances on issues. "I stood firm on what I believed," Smith recalled. "But I still was open to a good argument from someone else." A term abroad in Romania, a seminar picking apart Shakespeare's *Henry V* ... at each juncture, the collision of different cultures and the efforts to reconcile them left indelible impressions.

Every few minutes at Build, a bell rings to celebrate some salesperson's big order. I hadn't expected to find an unheralded intellectual crushing the sales quotas at this plumbing-supply company. The more I talked with Smith, however, the more logical her success—and her background—became. As she explained to me, part of the fun of her sales job involves decoding each caller's fears and aspirations. Each of Build's customers "is like a character in a novel. I like to gain their trust. It feels good."

All Your Friends Are Here

Every street musician knows this trick; you probably do too. If you want to earn some money playing your violin in public, it's not enough to leave an empty instrument case open in front of you in the hope that passersby will toss in a few coins. It works better if you create the appearance of a new social norm by sprinkling in an assortment of quarters, singles, and a few five-dollar bills before you start playing. That way, spectators feel an implicit obligation to contribute. They hear you, they see the illusion of prior payments — and they assume that it's right and customary for them to leave a donation too.

Arizona State psychology professor Robert Cialdini loves to cite this example as a rudimentary demonstration of the power of social proof. When we're trying to decide how to handle an unexpected situation, we gladly take cues from what everyone else is doing. If we hear laughter on the sound track of a TV show, we start laughing too. The desire to fit in is so strong that we leave donations even if we weren't amazed by the caliber of a street musician's performance; we join in the guffawing even if the comedy show's jokes weren't all that funny.

Take a more serious look at the concept of social proof, and you will find it coursing through every aspect of a liberal arts curriculum. Read *Anna Karenina*, and you can't help but be struck by how much Levin's personality unravels when he moves to Moscow. In the countryside, he is a decisive man with big ideas. In the capital city, he is a spendthrift, caught up in the artifices of trying to keep pace with a new group of high-rolling friends. Has he fundamentally changed? Or is he being swayed by the company he keeps?

Study psychology, and it won't be long before you're revisiting Solomon Asch's pioneering research related to conformity. Put a person in a roomful of opinionated strangers and then ask him if two lines are the same length or not. The truth is right in front of him, ascertainable by his own eyes. Yet his answer will be skewed by what everyone else says. If enough people assert with great confidence that two unequal lines are actually the same length, most individuals at some point will capitulate and join the crowd. Let a person write the answer in secret, so no one can mock or disagree with it, and he or she is more likely to cling to the truth.

Study current-day politics or try to make a living as a political consultant, and there's no escaping the growing power of social proof. As the Pew Research Center found in a landmark 2014 study, if a person identifies as a liberal, he or she is likely to get most news from CNN, National Public Radio, MSNBC, or the *New York Times*. If a person identifies as a conservative, Fox News is his or her most trusted source. "When it comes to getting news about politics and government, liberals and conservatives inhabit different worlds," a team of Pew analysts declared. At both ends of the political spectrum, people who discuss politics seek out like-minded individuals and unfriend or block those contacts on social media who disagree with them. Favorite opinions keep being reinforced; other points of view hardly register.

Whatever your pathway, your liberal arts classes have deepened your understanding of the ways people can be swayed by others' beliefs. By the time you graduate, you have analyzed enough situations to make your own judgments about what's authentic and what's fake; what's persuasive and what's futile; what's beneficial and what's harmful. You know social proof is much more than a five-second ploy that helps buskers win bigger tips. You appreciate the delicate ways trust is built (or destroyed) over long periods in high-stakes settings. Even so, you know how powerful it can be to declare: "All your friends are here."

If you're intrigued by social proof but want to apply it in socially minded, noncontroversial ways, consider the example of Jeff Kirschner. He is a University of Michigan creative writing major who set up Litterati, a socially minded enterprise that encourages volunteers to pick up trash. Convincing people to contribute more than a single afternoon's labor is usually a hopeless task, yet Kirschner has managed to organize sustained cleanups in San Francisco, in Stockton, California, and in a host of other cities. Many of these are ongoing projects in which volunteers regularly fan across neighborhoods to grab hold of empty cans, cigarette butts, hamburger wrappers, and the like.

Kirschner's unique edge: he arranges for each volunteer to snap a smartphone picture of every piece of litter, along with a geo-tagged location. The result: Litterati creates detailed maps of trash outbreaks that can help city officials redefine their street cleaners' routes. In San Francisco, Litterati's photos help identify cigarette butts by manufacturer—a powerful tool in ensuring that offending brands pay their fair share of cleanup costs. As technology creates immediate feedback and a shared sense of doing good, volunteers delight in being part of a posse whose group successes are tallied by the minute.

All of which brings us back to Facebook, the frozen-pipe story, and the hidden beginnings of the job that Bess Yount enjoys today. In the autumn of 2008, Facebook was just four years old. Software engineers represented the largest group of employees, and they included more than a few college friends of the company's twenty-four-year-old founder, Mark Zuckerberg. Facebook's culture back then was a raw, exuberant blend of tech zealotry and college-dorm fun; coders raced their RipStiks across carpeted halls whenever office tensions got to be too much.

At a staff meeting that autumn, someone asked Zuckerberg to

explain Facebook's approach to advertising. I was in the room at the time, and I remember how enthusiastically he talked about the way that Facebook's vast assortment of drop-down menus would let advertisers manage campaigns without anyone needing to talk to a human being. Looking to reach women ages eighteen to thirty-four? Click on a few buttons, and you've got them targeted. Prefer to focus on people who like gardening, watch horror movies, and have traveled to France? Click. Click. Click. You now hold them in the crosshairs of your advertising rifle.

At that moment, Zuckerberg thought his engineers were building such an automated marvel that traditional advertising teams would become as unnecessary as lamplighters. Good-bye, *Mad Men*–era politics! Good-bye, handshakes, expense-account meals, and the personal back-and-forth of making ad deals happen. Zuckerberg felt sure he had glimpsed the future. In advertising, at least, the road ahead was going to be a triumph of technology over humanity.

By 2010, Zuckerberg had changed his mind. Human sales teams weren't so pointless after all. The splendors of Facebook's drop-down menus turned out to be too much, too fast. First-time buyers didn't buy ads. They found the automated system too chilly and impersonal. It didn't speak to them. Facebook's regular users didn't mind all the automation in the background controlling what stories popped up in their news feeds. For them, technology was an invisible helper that made it easy to stay in touch with friends. For advertisers, though, the technology was too prominent. It felt sterile and rushed. There weren't any social preliminaries that put merchants at ease in the way that old media's ad-sales teams made it safe and pleasant to buy a magazine ad or a TV commercial.

It was time to regroup. If business managers wanted personal reassurance before buying Facebook ads, Zuckerberg and his business-savvy chief operating officer, Sheryl Sandberg, would make that happen. If businesses wanted to hear stories about similar enterprises that had bought Facebook advertising, they could make that happen too.

Today, Facebook employs thousands of people in its advertising, marketing, sales, and business-development teams. They coexist alongside the company's famous hoodie-clad engineers because they possess valuable skills that don't involve software coding. They tell stories well. They empathize with their customers. They show how potent a degree in history, English, psychology, or any other liberal arts discipline can be in a business setting. After all, these new hires know how to reassure people on the brink of trying something new. Everything is safe; your friends are already on board.

7

Ruling the World

When Stewart Butterfield was twelve, his parents sent him to the most prestigious private school they could afford. The Butterfields had spent more than a decade rambling around western Canada, including a stint on a hippie commune. The counterculture had lost its charm; remorse was setting in. Maybe their son could make up for lost time by joining the patrician world of St. Michaels University School, on the south tip of Vancouver Island. There would be squash courts, cricket fields, and dormitories carrying august Anglo-Saxon names such as Winslow and Symons. Instead of wearing dirty T-shirts, their son would embrace the preppy dress code and respectful conformity of St. Michaels. At least, that was the hope.

Stewart Butterfield wasn't about to become anyone's pawn. He started his rebellion carefully, wearing soft-collared polo shirts to classes and then, when his teachers weren't looking, slipping into a dark jacket with a mean-looking Iron Maiden logo on the back. Eager to help this newcomer settle in, school administrators invited him to lead the dinner-hour recital of the Lord's Prayer. Surely the boy would understand the importance of this trusted honor and acquit himself honorably. Instead, Butterfield and an accomplice delivered the entire prayer—"Thy kingdom come," "our daily bread," and so on—in squeaky voices that sounded like Donald Duck. Two hundred classmates howled. Teachers seethed. It was Butterfield's way of telling the world he intended to be a nonstop rule breaker his whole life.

Today Butterfield runs Slack Technologies, a San Francisco software company that private investors have valued at $3.8 billion. It is a tech-industry sensation, attracting more than three million users at organizations such as IBM, Capital One, and the Associated Press. Slack's workplace-messaging tools are a conjurer's delight. They combine the addictive pleasure of Facebook with the orderly flow of team e-mails in a way that makes it almost fun to be in contact with colleagues.

As Slack's founding chief executive, Butterfield owns several hundred million dollars of stock in the company. This giant success is the provocateur's revenge, the latest twist in a lifetime full of odd events. Butterfield is in his early forties now. He has been zigzagging from project to project for more than twenty years. It's as if his mission in life is to seize whatever new idea intrigues him, regardless of conventional expectations. When I asked what made Slack so successful, he started talking about *eudaemonia*, the ancient Greek concept of "happiness that comes from fulfilling your purpose."

It won't surprise you to know that Butterfield was a philosophy major in the mid-1990s when he attended Canada's University of Victoria. The field's intellectual rigor appealed to him; so, too, did the opportunities to twist ideas in ways only a prankster could appreciate. "It all depended on my state of mind," Butterfield recalled. "There were times when I felt this could be complete bullshit. At other times, studying philosophy provided the finest opportunities to think. I learned how to write very clearly—and how to follow an argument all the way down.

"Ninety percent of contemporary Anglo-American philosophical writings are really murky," he added. "It can be a struggle to articulate what it means. And yet, there's this wonderful, unique feeling of it all becoming clear, at least for a moment. In college, I got a great education in how to think about things. It's certainly helped me run meetings, and it's helped in many other ways as well."

As Butterfield's example shows, there's no limit to how far you can rise with a liberal arts degree, as long as you don't mind considering unconventional paths to the top. That's how it should be. Your own education doesn't mirror the orderly norms of business and engineering schools. In college, you hunted for classes that revolved around intriguing questions rather than courses that packed your brain with universally acknowledged facts and formulas. You jumped back and forth in the course catalog instead of taking Marketing 101, 102, and 103. You celebrated originality, clarity, and conviction, even if you weren't always right.

The world needs your strengths; it just needs them in unexpected places. Let the business and engineering graduates enjoy their moments of triumph at campus job fairs. They have spent four years training for this moment. If a Delaware chemical company needs a fermentation engineer for seventy-five thousand dollars a year, some engineering graduate is the perfect match. That's not you. You didn't enroll in college to become the best-trained candidate for a narrowly defined job. Instead, you are hunting for wide-open environments that need your critical-thinking capabilities. The greatest payoff for your college education is likely to be years away, perhaps in your fourth job, perhaps in your seventh. You're playing a longer game, looking for situations that reward you for being able to say "I'm an explorer," or "I'm a team builder," or "I'm someone who can make sense out of situations most people don't understand."

If you like such destinations but could use extra help in getting there, spend time with the closing chapters of this book. Chapter 12, "Telling Your Story," peels away the hidden agendas of common interviewing questions. It shows you how to convey your liberal arts strengths in ways employers will appreciate. Much of your college experience should align with the working world's requirements. Bosses and recruiting managers simply need to hear your achievements expressed in the language of commerce rather than that of the campus. Whether you're writing a résumé or preparing for an interview, the techniques explained in that section can help you make a winning impression.

Chapter 13, "Getting Paid Properly," covers the best ways of improving your earnings power, either with or without an additional round of formal education. Your first-year income after graduation needn't constrain your pay for years to come. Better days lie ahead, and a seven-step system can help you exploit these opportunities. Over time, it's often possible to overtake college counterparts who opted for vocationally oriented degrees. They snagged the bigger starting salaries; you won unique expertise that creates infinite possibilities for success.

Need proof? Consider this three-part look at lifetime-earnings trends for college graduates across ten common majors. The liberal arts team is represented by English, history, philosophy, psychology, and political science majors. Your vocationally minded counterparts are represented by peers who chose to major in accounting, civil engineering, computer science, nursing, or business management.

There's no denying that liberal arts graduates start slowly.

TYPICAL STARTING EARNINGS
Annual Earnings, 0–5 Years' Experience
(per PayScale)

Computer science	$63,500
Nursing	$57,500
Civil engineering	$57,200
Accounting	$48,300
Business management	$45,800
Philosophy	*$44,700*
Political science	*$44,300*
History	*$42,200*
English	*$40,400*
Psychology	*$38,300*

Let careers play out for a decade or two, and life gets better. If you hold a humanities or social science degree, by your thirties or early forties, you may achieve complete parity with business and nursing majors. (Catching the engineers, alas, is less likely.)

Most common majors, on average, end up earning somewhere between $60,000 and $80,000 a year.

TYPICAL MIDCAREER EARNINGS
Annual Earnings, 10–20 Years' Experience
(per PayScale)

Computer science	$111,000
Civil engineering	$96,300
Philosophy	*$84,100*
Political science and government	*$79,900*
Accounting	$77,200
Nursing	$74,100
History	*$72,600*

Business management	$72,300
English language and literature	*$68,200*
Psychology	*$62,100*

It's important to remember that annual income is hardly a complete measure of success in life. That's true regardless of whether people opt for the liberal arts or the vocational track in college. Over time, other questions often loom larger. Are you looking for ways to maximize your social impact rather than your cash income? Are you keeping your work hours manageable enough to have time for life outside the office? Are you doing right by your friends and family? Such factors make it hard to say that a small percentage difference in pay says something meaningful about how successful or unsuccessful a particular education-and-career path might be.

Still, there's nothing wrong with wanting to rise to the top of a field or earn the outsize income that comes with making an outsize contribution in some form. Within the context of this chapter, it's worth looking at the data in a different way, to see what we can learn about the highest flight paths available with each major. The place to turn: the Brookings Institution's Hamilton Project, which analyzes U.S. Census Bureau data that lets us track lifetime earnings by college majors. Zoom in on those findings, and it's possible to see how much the highest tenth of achievers, major by major, end up earning before their careers are over.

Now you can see the liberal arts in full ascent. Disciplines such as philosophy and political science turn out to be springboards for high achievers—who end up overtaking their counterparts in vocational fields such as computer science. Not every political science major will earn more than $4.8 million in his or her lifetime. But many mayors, senators, and governors do. As for history majors, the high achievers who end up running foundations, hosting television shows, or writing bestselling books reach the same economic stratosphere. Prosperity arrives in a big way for philosophy majors, too, as shown by the success of Stewart Butterfield and some of Wall Street's most accomplished investors.

HIGH ACHIEVERS' LIFETIME EARNINGS
Top Tenth by Major (Hamilton Project)

Political science and government	*$4,810,000*
History	*$3,750,000*
Accounting	$3,650,000
Philosophy	*$3,460,000*
Business management	$3,070,000
Civil engineering	$3,360,000
Computer science	$3,200,000
English	*$2,810,000*
Psychology	*$2,640,000*
Nursing	$2,160,000

The rest of this chapter will look at three proven paths by which liberal arts majors end up ruling the world (either literally or metaphorically). The first involves bountiful opportunities in the public sector and at nonprofit organizations. Government by its very nature puts the full suite of critical-thinking skills to the test. To be an effective leader, you constantly need to manage the intersection of competing forces and competing objectives.

The second big area of opportunity is the money trade, particularly specialties such as venture capital, hedge funds, and private equity. Choose one of these investment-centered domains, and you won't have twenty thousand people working for you. Instead, you will control vast sums from a small, elegant office with a few dozen staffers taking care of the details. Perhaps you will walk the same path as some of America's top venture capitalists, such as the ones who bankrolled Twitter, Uber, and LinkedIn. Alternatively, you could be part of the cluster of humanities majors whose stock-picking genius has made them unimaginably rich.

Finally, entrepreneurship is a natural home for restless minds shaped by a liberal arts education. Businesses such as Chipotle and Pinterest were started by political science majors. A background in humanities inspired the founding executives of Whole Foods Market and Salesforce. Spend four years studying the liberal arts, and you work up an appetite for tackling new areas and coming up with unexpected solutions. There's an old saying you hear from entrepreneurs: "I had to start my own company, because I couldn't work for anyone else." That's still true for free spirits like Stewart Butterfield, and the closing pages of this chapter will explore his journey in more detail.

I've found only one area of high-profile leadership where the liberal arts are underrepresented: the chief executive's chair at big corporations. Let's take a moment to see the mournful reasons why this is so before turning to cheerier alternatives.

Big Companies, Narrow Path

In 2002, Teachers Insurance picked a Yale philosophy major, Herb Allison, to be its next chief executive. Over the next few years, Allison became an oft-cited example of the ways that even the most "impractical" liberal arts degrees could lead to the top job at a giant corporation. (Teachers Insurance manages more than $400 billion in retirement assets, chiefly on behalf of university professors.) Allison was a man of wide-ranging interests with a career to match. He had spent four years in the U.S. Navy, serving briefly in Vietnam. He had worked in Tehran in the 1970s for Merrill Lynch, when U.S.-Iran relations were smoother than they are today. When Allison fell in love with an Iranian woman and wanted to marry her, her father refused to consent unless Allison started learning Farsi. Delighted by the challenge, Allison built up a thousand-word vocabulary in two weeks, thanks to diligent practice with flashcards.

When Allison retired in 2008, Teachers Insurance did not hunt for someone with an equally eclectic background to replace him. Instead, the New York institution chose Roger Ferguson, a Harvard economics graduate with a nonstop record of business-centered achievement. Ferguson had earned a PhD in economics and a law degree from Harvard. He spent the 1980s working as a corporate lawyer and a McKinsey consultant. After that, a stint as a Federal Reserve Board governor and a leadership post at Swiss Re, a major insurer. Ferguson was a trailblazer in his own right as a pioneering black executive who had scrubbed bathrooms in college to help pay Harvard tuition. When TIAA picked Ferguson, however, his personal journey wasn't highlighted. Instead, TIAA's board of directors deemed Ferguson the "ideal choice" because of his background in strategic management, financial services, and economic policy.

It's sad but true: Large companies have dialed back their willingness to put liberal arts graduates in the chief executive's seat. Corporate boards may be more cautious after the financial and economic spasms of 2000 to 2002 and 2007 to 2009. There's less of an appetite for entrusting the CEO's job to someone with an exciting, eclectic background that could lead to a lot of fresh approaches. Managerial time horizons have shrunk too. At many large, publicly traded companies, success (or survival) is all about handling the pressures imposed by quarterly earnings targets. As a result, there's more of a desire to play it safe and guard against the unexpected.

The most reliable route to the top of a big company now involves an engineering degree — and "joining a fraternity while you're at it," declares Christian Stadler, a management professor at England's Warwick Business School. He is an expert in CEO succession and the author of *Enduring Success: What We Can Learn from the History of Outstanding Corporations*. As Stadler sees it, the skew toward engineering-minded CEOs is likely to intensify as multinationals become more open to candidates who came of age in non-U.S. settings such as China, India, and Brazil. In those countries, ambitious students gravitate almost exclusively to engineering programs.

It's not that big companies don't appreciate the ingenuity, open-mindedness, sound judgment, and communications strengths of liberal arts graduates. The problem is that as organizations get more complex, there's a tendency to keep the most creative minds one or two levels below the CEO's job. Corporate boards prefer to play it safe with the top job, picking candidates who steadily climbed the company ladder via traditional roles. Three-quarters of all Fortune 100 CEOs come from operations; 32 percent have at least some experience in finance. With those priorities, it's no wonder that engineering and business majors fare best in the race to the top.

For a long time, the executive-search firm Spencer Stuart analyzed the educational backgrounds of every CEO working at one of the five hundred leading U.S. companies. In 1999, about 15 percent of these bosses had liberal arts backgrounds. In 2008, the liberal arts presence had dropped to 6 percent. By contrast, engineering majors in 2008 held 22 percent, while the next three most common majors, economics (16 percent), finance (13 percent), and accounting (9 percent), together accounted for more than a third of the sample. It would be nice if Spencer Stuart had even fresher data, but the firm halted such studies after 2008. Clients weren't interested in the results anymore. Pedigree had become a settled issue.

Ask corporate boards how they pick CEOs, and the answers are likely to focus on pedigree-neutral factors such as leadership skills, strategic clarity, and a proven record of success in recent jobs. Directors rarely acknowledge a deep, explicit interest in candidates' long-ago academic choices. Even so, today's most-favored career trajectories at the twenty largest U.S. companies keep adhering to the same patterns. At eight companies, including ExxonMobil, Microsoft, Procter & Gamble, and Verizon, an engineering degree is the path to the top. At another eight, including Walmart, Coca-Cola, AT&T, and Oracle, the CEO holds a business or economics degree. Only one full-strength representative of the liberal arts appears in this top-twenty list: history major Brian Moynihan, who runs Bank of America. (The CEO of JPMorgan Chase, Jamie Dimon, holds a dual degree in economics and psychology.) Even the ultimate renegade company, Apple, is playing it safe now. With the death of founding CEO Steve Jobs in 2011, the company no longer is run by a Reed College dropout extolling the importance of liberal arts thinking in high-tech settings. The big boss at Apple now is Tim Cook, an Auburn-trained industrial engineer.

Such trends can feed on themselves for a long time. Current and past CEOs tend to be directors of one another's companies. While corporate boards are responding to pressure to increase gender and racial diversity, they aren't facing major calls to bring in directors with nontraditional educational backgrounds. As a result, boards full of business and engineering majors are likely to keep picking CEOs with business and engineering backgrounds. Without the right connections, liberal arts graduates find it harder to break into the club.

At some point, all this might change. In the meantime, if you want to soar with a liberal arts degree, plenty of other pathways await.

What the Social Sector Admires

Justin Davis graduated from the University of Maine in 2014 with a degree in political science. Alix Rudzinski majored in the same field, graduating from Assumption College in 2015. Both work full-time in Washington, DC, now, and there's nothing glamorous about their duties as staff assistants. They answer phones, they do a little document research, and sometimes they make coffee for their bosses. Their annual salaries: less than twenty-nine thousand dollars.

Don't feel sorry for them.

In politics, traditional career escalators operate as efficiently as ever. Entry-level jobs may be low paid and include a lot of menial work, but the opportunities for advancement are bountiful. The average congressional staff assistant stays in the job for just 1.9 years. Look alert, make friends, and become known as a doer. It won't take long for better jobs to emerge.

The path upward is especially obvious for strivers like Davis and Rudzinski because their boss, Maine senator Susan Collins, got started in Washington as a congressional staff assistant herself. She had just graduated from St. Lawrence University in 1975 with a degree in government. Maine's junior senator at the time, William Cohen, needed extra help in his office. She took the job, low pay and all. She put up with a group house and a spending budget so tiny that she couldn't afford more than sandwiches for dinner. That penury didn't last long. By 1981 she was a staff director for a powerful subcommittee and eventually a candidate for statewide office herself.

What worked well in the 1980s works even better today. Your liberal arts education provides you with excellent instincts for the give-and-take of modern-day politics. You can make sense of voting blocs; you can understand angry constituents' real issues beneath the furious insults that are hurled your way. You know how to persuade people and perhaps even inspire them too. In Collins's own words, a liberal arts education "enables you to cite both Plato and Spider-Man in the same speech."

What's more, you enjoy every college student's familiarity with blogs, podcasts, Tweet storms, social-media campaigns, sentiment analyzers, and all the other tools of modern digital communications. For older bosses, it's all a mystery. As a result, when openings for press secretaries and directors of communications arise, it's often a staffer in her or his twenties who is seen as the ideal pick. In the days of black-and-white films, political press secretaries were grizzled old newspaper reporters. Now, the press secretary is more likely to be a newcomer such as Christopher Knight, a 2013 political science major from Stonehill College who deals with the media for Senator Collins.

No one knows what specific achievements in coming decades could propel someone to the highest levels of government. Public tastes keep changing. In different eras, people have prized everything from military service to union activism. That fluidity plays to your liberal arts strengths. Historical records show that during every period from the 1960s onward, a substantial number of U.S. senators and representatives with college educations earned liberal arts degrees. This ability to improvise never goes out of style; it helps you stay in command amid ever-changing norms.

In philanthropy, too, a liberal arts degree turns out to be the best credential for making it to the top. People with humanities or social science degrees run eight of the twelve largest foundations, including the Ford Foundation (government and communications); the Getty Trust and the MacArthur Foundation (history); the Hewlett Foundation and the Lilly Endowment (religious studies); and the Moore Foundation and the Mellon Foundation (psychology).

These leaders are the sorts of explorers that we've met in earlier chapters; they take a semester off from college, switch majors, work in warehouses after graduation for a stretch to get their priorities sorted out, teach in universities...and then let their own curiosity guide them through a lot of different jobs. In fact, I've just given you the condensed bio of James Cuno, the Willamette history major who now serves as the J. Paul Getty Trust's chief executive. As Cuno observes, there is no proven master plan for getting to be a foundation head. If anything, boards are looking for people who have lived on both sides of the income divide. It's crucial to understand the world from different perspectives, to know what it's like to be poor as well as prosperous.

Conquering the Stock Market

Liberal arts degrees on Wall Street? You won't find such credentials everywhere; much of the financial sector is staffed by people who loved money as little children and went on to earn a bachelor's degree in economics or finance so they could chase riches as briskly as possible. All the same, there's an island of diversity when it comes to people who excel as professional investors. A surprisingly large number of these money managers hold humanities degrees, most commonly in philosophy.

Consider George Soros, who studied philosophy at the London School of Economics before building an investment fortune that *Forbes* magazine estimates at $24.9 billion. In books such as *The Alchemy of Finance,* Soros argues that his entire life has been an exploration of the interplay between thinking and reality, with successful trading strategies emerging as a happy by-product. His favorite zone of exploration: the ways crowd mentalities can take hold and briefly distort reality before eventually disintegrating. By exploiting this dynamic, which he calls "the principle of reflexivity," he has made billions trading oil stocks, betting against the British pound, and so on. Investment successes made him famous, but in Soros's words, "the abstract came first."

The two biggest mutual-fund companies in the United States, Vanguard and Fidelity, are both run by people with strong liberal arts backgrounds. Vanguard CEO Bill McNabb was a government major at Dartmouth, and Fidelity CEO Abigail Johnson studied art history at Hobart and William Smith. Both of them earned MBAs a few years after graduating from college; they can hold their own just fine in meetings focused on the usual business metrics. Still, both acknowledge in media interviews that their companies' biggest opportunities call for a curious, open-minded perspective that isn't bounded by what's on today's spreadsheet. "Don't assume that the answers are out there in the form of somebody else already doing something," Johnson told Forbes.com in 2013. "Sometimes they are. But you have to think beyond that. The right answer for you and your organization might not be something that's been done before."

Large-scale investing is where the cerebral types hang out. Professional investors read incessantly. They join organizations such as the Council on Foreign Relations, partly because they want geopolitical insights that could help them make money and partly for the impractical reason that it's *interesting* to ponder China's future. A disproportionate number end up as college trustees, allowing them to reconnect with academia. (Being willing to advise a school's endowment managers helps too.) Even the hunt for bargain stocks is conducted in quasi-academic fashion, in conferences packed with leading New York money managers who deliver heavily footnoted lectures to one another.

One of America's most combative (and successful) investors is Carl Icahn, a bearded, voluble man famous for buying stakes in underperforming companies and then pressing for strategic shakeups. Executives resist, he hectors them, and before long, they usually capitulate. While working as a *Wall Street Journal* reporter in the early 1990s, I talked with Icahn half a dozen times in the midst of these controversies. Each time, I was struck by his eagerness to analyze both sides' positions. Our phone calls wouldn't end until he had explained why he was right, why management disagreed, what the other side was missing, and why he expected his views to prevail. He managed to be both strident and professorial.

Long before those exchanges, Icahn was a Princeton philosophy major, writing his senior thesis on "The Empiricist Criterion of Meaning." I tracked down a copy of the eighty-page tract, and it reveals early signs of his famously argumentative style. How do we know sugar dissolves in water? college student Icahn asks. We run an experiment. How do we know a typewriter won't dissolve in water? We infer it, based on our existing knowledge of water and metals. Experiments, inferences...he dances back and forth between the two, developing his theories. Only at the end does Icahn betray his reasons for pursuing philosophical questions so keenly. Experts haven't fully defined *meaning*, the college senior contends, but they are drawing close. It's as if we live in a city that "suddenly finds itself in possession of a great homogenous mixture of gold and sand. If the gold could be separated from the sand, it would prove a great deal more valuable."

Ever since, philosopher Icahn has been pushing away the sand so he can amass a seventeen-billion-dollar fortune with what remains.

On the West Coast, humanities majors opt for a different type of investing: bankrolling start-ups via venture capital. Each year, *Forbes* magazine highlights the top one hundred venture capitalists in its Midas List, and a surprising share of them have nontechnical, nonbusiness backgrounds. Among them is Matt Cohler, a Yale music major. Another is Peter Fenton, a 1994 Stanford graduate with a bachelor's degree in philosophy. Both work at Benchmark Capital, a firm renowned for being an early investor in eBay, Instagram, Snapchat, and Twitter. Ask each about his investment approach, and the answers pay homage to the central concepts of critical thinking. They're comfortable working through a lot of ambiguity. They look for executives with a strong desire to learn and an ability to attract outstanding people.

Enter venture capital with a liberal arts background, Fenton points out, and you "ask questions that are by nature expansive." Often that means stretching beyond product and engineering technicalities, he says, in favor of seeking essential insights about people and businesses most likely to rise to greatness.

LinkedIn's best-known founder, Reid Hoffman, now doubles as a venture capitalist with Greylock Partners. He earned his Stanford degree in symbolic systems, an interdisciplinary blend of psychology, linguistics, and philosophy with computer science and statistics. Being schooled in so many disciplines at once has proven hugely helpful, Hoffman says. Instead of focusing on companies that solve narrow problems, Hoffman concentrates on something much more ambitious: "improving human ecosystems through tech finance and entrepreneurship."

Press ahead in any liberal arts discipline, and at some point you will encounter giant ideas in conflict. Those Hegelian tensions make investing both exasperating and intoxicating to liberal arts majors, contends Dan O'Keefe, a Northwestern philosophy graduate who now runs mutual funds for Artisan Partners in Milwaukee. To be a great investor, O'Keefe explains, "you need two almost-incompatible traits—or at least ones that create extreme tension. You need extreme conviction you can step into the market, regardless of what everyone else thinks, and develop unique ideas that will make money. But you also need an incredible amount of humility. You must be open to new information, even if it could be overtaking all your earlier work."

Building Greatness from Scratch

We've all heard this refrain: Engineers and computer science majors know how to start companies. Some are so brilliant they can drop out of college and create companies like Facebook, Spotify, or Microsoft that are worth billions. Business majors know how to launch start-ups too. They use their college years to get highly focused training in identifying markets, creating business plans, wooing customers, and achieving profitability. But *liberal arts majors?* What can they possibly know about starting companies that endure?

They don't get mad; they get even. Liberal arts graduates shred their own stereotype every day. For full-fledged proof, just take a look at *Inc.* magazine's annual ranking of the five thousand fastest-growing start-ups in the United States. You'll see what people with degrees in psychology, philosophy, and studio art are capable of creating. You'll encounter thriving start-ups in fields ranging from business services to talent agencies, organic juices, and party planning. And in nearly a third of the most successful start-ups, you will find liberal arts graduates are part of the founding team.

People with liberal arts backgrounds have a knack for "starting a business which is driven by ideas and doesn't require lots of capital," says Robert Sprung, a seasoned venture capitalist. A perfect example involves Globalization Partners, which is one of *Inc.* magazine's ten fastest-growing companies. It provides tools and contacts to help thousands of U.S. companies expand into countries ranging from Peru to Singapore. Its founder, Nicole Sahin, originally planned to become an anthropologist after studying humanities at Maryville College in St. Louis. After extended fieldwork in Colombia's highlands, however, "I realized I didn't want to keep visiting one village for the rest of my life," Sahin told me.

It took Sahin more than a decade to settle on her business ambitions, with many detours along the way. (She set up a school in Cambodia at one point; she spent enough time in the Philippines to gain local-language competency, and so on.) When she finally did form her own company, in 2014, her haphazard ramblings had graced her with an invaluable network of contacts around the world. Spin the globe, pick a country at random, and Sahin knew someone who could act as a sales agent there. Differences in local business customs didn't faze her; in fact, she relished the chance to build cultural bridges. "It's like applied anthropology, every day," she told me.

"Liberal arts graduates know how to sell their products," said Patrick Chung, a Silicon Valley venture capitalist. "They're good at helping customers think about the world differently." A case in point: Paint Nite, which organizes painting parties in bars and restaurants that are suitable for everything from corporate off-sites to bachelorette parties. In *Inc.*'s 2016 rankings, it's the second-fastest-growing company in the United States, far ahead of half a dozen other companies trying similar ideas. What's Paint Nite's edge? Everyone else focuses on signing franchise deals with bars willing to pay top dollar. Paint Nite instead builds a network of likable artists/hosts who stage events wherever they want. Credit Paint Nite co-founder Sean McGrail (a psychology major at George Washington) with winning instincts about his customers' desires.

Two more traits belong in the liberal arts arsenal, even if they aren't talked about as much as others. One is the temerity to imagine yourself succeeding on a giant scale—ruling the world, if you will. Let the business and engineering grads stress about increasing operating margins by two percentage points. They belong at big companies, grinding ahead on a predictable path. The secret dialogue inside your head is much bolder, reflecting the big ideas and open horizons of your college days. If you're John Mackey, the University of Texas philosophy student who founded Whole Foods Market in 1978, you become obsessed with something called conscious capitalism, in which businesses serve all major stakeholders—including customers, employees, communities, and the environment—instead of fixating solely on what's best for shareholders. You imagine yourself adding a fourth great virtue to Plato's triad. Skeptics' doubts hardly matter. You have been chasing giant ideas since your student days, and there's no reason to stop. Why should you? In Mackey's case, you end up running the world's premier organic grocer, with more than fourteen billion dollars a year in sales.

Rounding out the list of liberal arts virtues for entrepreneurs:

an endless desire to get better. Entrenched businesses are notorious for reaching a certain level of performance and then deciding such a showing is both satisfactory and sufficient. (You can see the results in everything from toothpaste to airlines. Past a certain point, it's just more of the same.) By contrast, the best start-up founders never settle. They see themselves as constant learners, forever dissatisfied with the current version of their offerings, always eager to keep improving. Humility and ambition fuse together in a way that invites comparison to the heady spirit of discovery on a college campus. "We're always experimenting with features," says Ben Silbermann, the political science major who started Pinterest in 2009. His company's themed photo pages now attract more than 110 million monthly users, yet to Silbermann, "this is still an early product."

To see how all four of these traits interact, let's take a closer look at Stewart Butterfield's career. For the past two decades, his fascination with philosophy has inspired him to create elaborate online worlds. He and a few friends spent years developing these "infinite games," convinced they were tapping into something profound about the ways societies build culture. Butterfield's projects seldom caught on with the public, but each failure contained the first stirrings of a future success.

The sheer intricacy of these projects repeatedly forced Butterfield and his developers to develop game-playing shortcuts — which found new life as wildly popular business tools. Everything happened by accident. In 2004, Butterfield woke up from a fevered dream, convinced a digital-imaging tool inside GameNeverEnding could become a business in its own right. He had stumbled onto the basis for creating Flickr, a wildly popular photo-sharing service that Butterfield later sold to Yahoo for twenty-five million dollars. Luck struck a second time, in 2013, when an internal chat tool that engineers used to share ideas while working on Butterfield's Glitch game became the basis of his biggest business success: Slack.

Between those two triumphs, Butterfield discovered he simply could not work for a big company. He spent three years inside Yahoo trying to shepherd Flickr's continued growth for his new corporate masters. It didn't work. There were too many rules, too many meetings, and too many business targets tied to short-term performance. There wasn't any room to make Flickr into the best possible service it could be, especially if it would take a year or two for the benefits to show up in any financial metrics. In 2008, he decided to quit. On his way out, he wrote an allegorical e-mail that never said a bad word about Yahoo but presented a wry, surreal glimpse of his frustrations, couched in the metaphor of how a simple tinsmith would feel in such a situation.

"As you know, tin is in my blood," Butterfield's memo began.

For generations my family has worked with this most useful of metals. When I joined Yahoo back in '21, it was a sheet-tin concern of great momentum, growth, and innovation. I knew it was the place for me.... Since the late 80s, as the general manufacturing, oil exploration and refining, logistics and hotel and casino divisions rose to prominence, I have felt somewhat sidelined. By the time of the Internet revolution and our expansion into Web Sites, I have been cast adrift. I tried to roll with the times, but nary a sheet of tin has rolled off our own production lines in over 30 years.... Please accept my resignation.... I will be spending more time with my family, tending to my small but growing alpaca herd and, of course, getting back to working with tin, my first love.

Butterfield's e-mail delighted Silicon Valley. The silliness about tin and alpacas was a handy façade; the rogue philosopher was quietly getting ready to build another business—his way. This time, the big breakthrough happened inside a Butterfield-created game company called Glitch. The game itself never thrived, but everyone working on the project loved a slick online-messaging tool. Use it, and a tiny online window alerts you to just the right amount of detail about what your colleagues are doing. No torrents of spam messages, no risk of being isolated or out of the loop. Suddenly something as basic as rounding up half a dozen people for the three o'clock meeting didn't need to be such a chore. Glitch was destined to perish, but the messaging tool—named Slack in 2013—was a keeper.

Part of Slack's edge came from a sassy automated buddy providing usage hints and guidance as needed. Its name: Slackbot. Its mission: to make even the briefest interaction with Slack seem fun and efficient. Early on, anyone who typed in *Hey, Slackbot,* could get replies ranging from *Hello* to *'Ssup* and *Hay is for horses.* Get snarled in Slack's system and you would be told: *We've seen this clear up with a restart of Slack, a solution we suggest to you now only with great regret and self-loathing.*

Within twenty-four hours of a private rollout in August 2013, Slack had eight thousand users. By mid-2016, that number had grown to three million. The snarky middle-schooler who refused to say the Lord's Prayer properly (and then became the rebellious corporate executive who pretended to be a tinsmith) had turned into a very successful CEO. Now Butterfield prospered by knowing when to be silly in a world that took itself too seriously. Maybe he hadn't needed to evolve at all. Perhaps success just meant finding the right setting for a personality that never changed.

When the jokes subside, Butterfield's ambitions emerge. In

fact, he possesses all the temerity you'd expect from a liberal arts major building his own company. In a 2014 interview with Toronto's *Globe and Mail* newspaper, Butterfield declared his goal was to establish Slack as dominant in communication as Microsoft Windows was in software. Never mind the giant size disparity between the two companies; he dreamed of being a unified hub for everyone.

Is he there yet? Not at all. When I met with him in 2015, he talked about the importance of craftsmanship and about how much Slack's success depends on getting a never-ending list of tiny details right. In a mordant moment of self-reflection, Butterfield told another journalist: "I feel that what we have right now is just a giant piece of shit. It's just terrible, and we should be humiliated that we offer this to the public."

Ask Butterfield about Slack's users, and a more compassionate side emerges. Their problems are his problems, and he's committed to being as sympathetic and helpful as possible. Tech companies have been thrashing around for more than a decade trying to get smart about knowledge-sharing within organizations. It's a murky, messy area, because it's far more than a software challenge. It's also a test of human dynamics, Butterfield explains, particularly "the ability to interpret people who aren't necessarily great at articulating what they want." The more Slack can decode hazily expressed preferences, he knows, the more valuable its software becomes.

In 2008, Butterfield returned to his alma mater, the University of Victoria, to give a talk as a distinguished alumnus. He was jokey at the outset, promising to explain "how to make a fortune in applied philosophy." Quite quickly, though, he turned serious.

"Entrepreneurism is a good avenue for exercising the kinds of things you learn with a humanities degree," Butterfield declared.

"If you have a good background in what it is to be human, an understanding of life, culture and society, it gives you a good perspective on starting a business, instead of an education purely in business. You can always pick up how to read a balance sheet and how to figure out profit and loss. It's harder to pick up the other stuff on the fly."

Part Three

Your Allies

8

Employers That Get It

Dark skirt, black heels, two well-rehearsed examples ready to go.
During her senior year at the University of Chicago, Sonia Vora
marched through this campus-interviewing routine about a dozen
times. That's how you landed a job in financial services, she
thought. You auditioned for big banks and investment firms, trials
where even the opening handshake was a test of whether you'd fit
in. Success depended on how closely you resembled the ideal
apprentice: someone ready to embrace the long hours, rapid
tempo, and endless pressure of Wall Street.

Near the end of Vora's job hunt in the winter of 2014, though,
the pattern broke.

For the first time, Vora didn't need to deliver a canned pitch
about econometrics or the merits of investing in specific stocks.
Instead, her interview included the offbeat question "What led
you to minor in philosophy?" She described the thrill of breaking
down an argument and questioning the logic underlying certain
claims. At last, Vora could take the conversation beyond earnings
estimates and compound-growth rates. She needn't hide her fascination with Nietzsche or her decision in college to write a

twenty-page paper on his concept of the double will. In the course of her interview cycle with this unusual outfit, the recruiters told her, essentially, *If you work at our firm, you'll have a lot of careers here. We want to see what sort of intellectual curiosity you have.*

When a job offer ensued, Vora agreed to join Morningstar, a Chicago investment firm where philosophy minors are welcome. The company was started in 1984 by Joe Mansueto, a UChicago graduate who thought the world needed better analyses of mutual funds. Early on, Mansueto ran a four-person operation out of his apartment, doing much of the work himself. Today, Morningstar employs more than four thousand people in twenty-seven countries and is the showcase tenant in a downtown Chicago skyscraper. Mutual-fund research remains at the core of Morningstar's business, but the firm has expanded into half a dozen related areas.

Morningstar likes to hire liberal arts graduates with a wide range of backgrounds — people who studied Degas paintings or Chilean literature in college, for example. The Chicago company makes room for people who picked up a PhD in religious studies before deciding they didn't want to be ministers. As long as you're curious, energetic, and eager to take on the next challenge, Morningstar is refreshingly open-minded about whatever domain inspires you. Since its founding in the late 1980s, Morningstar has thrived by hiring liberal arts graduates who embody the best of critical thinking.

Such corporate cultures don't happen by accident. In the course of researching this book, I studied about two dozen havens for liberal arts majors. They span a wide variety of industries and range from start-ups like Etsy and Slack to corporate mainstays such as IBM and McKinsey. For good measure, the list includes nonprofits such as Teach for America and government agencies such as the State Department. It even includes iconoclasts such as Enterprise Rent-a-Car and McMaster-Carr, the industrial-supply company. All together, these enterprises fit into ten major categories, which we will examine shortly.

All these companies share a belief that business success hinges on the central elements of a liberal arts education: wanting to work on the frontier, being able to find insights, choosing the right approach, reading the room, and inspiring others. These companies seek a workforce that stretches beyond the formal disciplines of business and engineering. They want people like you.

Yes, it may take a little longer to train you in the particular ways of your new employer if you've spent the past few years reading Balzac instead of balance sheets or if the term *conversion rate* makes you think of religious sects instead of sales prospects. No matter; liberal arts–friendly employers understand. They realize you are able to master new material in a hurry. When such companies hire you, they believe your inquiring nature will soon result in valuable contributions.

Morningstar makes such aspirational hires all the time. Jim Murphy joined in 2008 after exploring Central Asian foreign policy at the University of Colorado. When he started out in phone sales at the company's Chicago headquarters, he wondered why the firm had bothered hiring an international relations major like him. A few months later, Murphy won a transfer to London in a new job all about face-to-face selling. Voilà! British clients liked chatting with an American who knew the difference between Whitehall and a white paper. "I could go to the pub without being the dumb American," Murphy told me. "That gave me credibility."

Emory Zink joined Morningstar in 2015 after stints as an English teacher in rural France and Gainesville, Florida. There's some finance in her background too: an MBA at age twenty-eight and a stint creating thought-leadership pieces for a pension-consulting company. She still defines herself by her college pursuits at Indiana University (BA in French and comparative literature), though, and that's fine with Morningstar. In her job as a bond-fund analyst, Zink enjoys the freedom to create zesty videos about her findings. No talking-head tedium for her; on camera, she explains everything with an educator's clarity and verve. When I asked her to cite a favorite author, she instantly replied: "I love Nabokov! Who doesn't?" Giggling at her own wit, she added: "I can say that around here. It's one of the things I love about this place."

If you're wondering why companies such as Morningstar dare stretch the usual hiring boundaries, there's a simple answer. These employers have been recruiting wide-ranging generalists for a long time, with good results. As a result, they have grown comfortable with the (big) opportunities and (not-so-big) risks of bringing liberal arts recruits into the mix. Teach for America is famously willing to cast a wide net when it hires fresh-out-of-college graduates to become instructors in challenging school districts. That boldness has its controversial side, and not every TFA placement succeeds. Even so, TFA's champions argue that the successes outweigh the stumbles. This charge-ahead mentality can be traced back to TFA founder Wendy Kopp, who launched the enterprise in her senior year at Princeton. She was a sociology major who saw a need and dared imagine how it could be addressed.

McKinsey, the buttoned-down management consulting firm, has traveled this path too. Its appreciation of impractical majors has grown since Kara Carter, a University of Virginia anthropology graduate, joined the consulting firm in the 1990s. Carter spent seven years as co-leader of the partnership's vast health-care practice before leaving in late 2016 to become chief impact officer at the California Health Care Foundation. Her success makes it a lot easier for McKinsey to invite other anthropology majors into the firm. By LinkedIn's tally, the eleven-thousand-employee consulting firm now employs two hundred and seventy of them.

Inside many companies, the best advocates for your candidacy are likely to be the top bosses, people far too senior to fret about your week-one productivity. Just ask Bridget Connolly, the international relations major who landed a job as wikiHow's globalization manager at age twenty-three. Her offer didn't take shape during her first interview with her eventual boss. It emerged, out of the blue, in a wide-ranging conversation with the company's president. Such moments of serendipity get likelier as you and your liberal arts background command higher-level attention. After all, senior executives are paid to think about strategic opportunities. Their horizons extend beyond this month's needs. They are more likely to appreciate how widely you've traveled, how many new ideas you've wrestled with, and how ingeniously you've come at the world's major challenges.

If you're interviewing at Morningstar, an hour with John Rekenthaler would fit the bill perfectly. The burly man with thick glasses and a fondness for blunt language joined the company in 1988 as employee number eighteen. He holds a bachelor's degree in English from the University of Pennsylvania and two advanced degrees from UChicago; today he is vice president for research. When I asked why Morningstar liked liberal arts graduates, Rekenthaler responded with rapid-fire reasons that resonate with all we've discussed so far. "Liberal arts graduates are comfortable with ambiguity," he told me. "You can give them something that isn't fully shaped and tell them: 'Go figure it out.' And they do so. That's not true with other disciplines. Second, liberal arts graduates are good at weighing evidence and setting priorities. They can evaluate things. Third, liberal arts graduates have a sense of context and history. That's important for investors. You need an ability to step back and look at the context."

Every June, when Morningstar's latest batch of college talent reports for work, company founder Joe Mansueto takes an hour to welcome these sixty-or-so new employees...and to share some thoughts about *why* his enterprise is put together the way it is. I slipped into the back of a large conference room to watch one of these sessions, curious to see what else he might reveal about the company's intense connection to the liberal arts community. Are Morningstar's values so idiosyncratic they don't apply to any other company? Or is Morningstar a useful model for how other enterprises can take a fresh look at how they hire? Here's what emerged.

At the outset, Mansueto does not dazzle. He's a small, wiry man with thinning brown hair, big, twinkling eyes, and a slightly goofy grin. Dressed in rumpled chinos and a pale blue polo shirt, he looks more like a motel clerk than the man in charge. It's hard to comprehend that this genial, unassuming fellow is worth more than two billion dollars. Even Mansueto seems faintly amused by the realization he's become... *important.*

Then Mansueto starts talking. His face lights up. He comes across as remarkably happy and serenely confident in the strategies underlying his business. "We hire smart, hard-working, curious, creative, and passionate people," he declares. "My message is to engage. There's a lot to take advantage of here. Lots of opportunities for stretch projects." The founder pauses for a moment, then races through a chart of Morningstar's many, many lines of business. Project names and business statistics are dripping off the chart in all directions. Mansueto shrugs. "People may say: 'You're trying to do too many things.' But to my view, it's a great strength."

As the boss's presentation concludes, someone asks Mansueto how Morningstar ended up with its unusual name. Mansueto smiles. He gets a slightly dreamy look on his face. In his mind's eye, he is eighteen again. It's a cold December afternoon. He's curled up in a chair in UChicago's Regenstein Library, working on his assignments. Even though it's well short of dinnertime, the sun has begun to set.

"It was my first year at UChicago," he recalls. "I was reading *Walden*. I had so many questions about the book. I was inspired by the way Thoreau wrote it. I wanted so much to see how he would finish it. I got to his final line: 'There is more day to dawn. The sun is but a morning star.' I thought: *What the hell does that mean?* And then I realized he was saying even something that has been around as long as the sun is still in its infancy. What I took away is that no matter where you are, you still have a bright future."

Literature. Optimism. A first stirring of a business that now employs four thousand people. Who says liberal arts values can't translate into a great career? Think of these ten types of businesses as places where your chances will be especially good.

Start-Ups in a Hurry

If you like working on the frontier, seek employers that share your addiction to what's new and unexplored. In boom times, venture capitalists pump fifty billion dollars a year into newly minted companies hoping to accomplish something remarkable. News sites such as TechCrunch and VentureWire tell you who is raising money; publications such as *Inc.* and *Fast Company* tell you which businesses are growing fast; free online directories such as Crunchbase make it easy for you to sort by industry or geography.

It won't take you long to create a substantial list of start-ups that sound enticing. Earlier chapters in this book have highlighted businesses such as Paint Nite, which transforms the way we party; Qualtrics, which puts high-powered survey tools in everyone's hands; and Slack, which promises a faster, easier, and more enjoyable way of handling routine workplace communication. Those companies (and many other pioneers, such as Airbnb, Uber, and Snap) repeatedly turn to people with liberal arts backgrounds for selling, marketing, or designing new services. At Slack, someone needed to ensure that Slackbot, the company's jaunty yet kind-hearted digital assistant, got its banter just right. The answer: Anna Pickard, a dramaturgy major whose previous paying jobs ranged from online cat impersonations to blogging for the *Guardian*.

As satisfying as it is to create a list of desirable start-ups, getting noticed will be the hard part. Most of these companies operate on such rapid internal clocks that their hiring processes can be an incomprehensible blur. Don't expect to find their representatives waiting patiently at a campus job fair, hoping you will stop by. Don't count on them reading your résumé if you send it in unsolicited. Don't look for them to offer interview sign-up lists — a month in advance — at your career center. To win a full-time job or even a seasonal internship, you need to demonstrate your resourcefulness.

In the e-book *Becoming a Rare Find*, I talk about ways of winning an employer's attention when a traditional résumé submission is likely to be useless. Hunt for intermediaries (like alumni, professors, or family friends) who can make introductions for you. See if you can wrangle a get-acquainted conversation even if there aren't any job openings at the moment. Make the most of non-weird opportunities to meet in person, such as industry conferences. Strike up rapport with customer-service representatives, administrative assistants, or other people who may not be power-ful in their own right but who can put in a good word for you—if your interactions with them warrant their doing so. Finally, imag-ine what you could do at the start-up right away, if you got hired. Then propose this idea as the basis for bringing you on board as an intern. As Forbes.com careers columnist Liz Ryan points out, most hiring happens because companies need fresh talent to address a "pain point" in the business. If you can find that pain point and propose a solution, you've taken a big step forward.

Bear in mind that start-ups are notorious for long hours and less-than-ideal pay. Many fail; others never become as successful as their founders hoped. Even so, the explorer's spirit can carry a small young enterprise remarkably far. That's what venture capi-talists are counting on when they bankroll unproven young com-panies. Most of that money is meant to be spent on the best possible way of improving these start-ups' chances: hiring fresh talent like you.

Putting Tech into Action

Can big companies thrive on the frontier of change too? That's seldom what they do best. Inertia takes hold when companies get larger and older. It's easier to extend time-tested successes instead of mustering the courage required for fresh starts in unfamiliar markets. Even so, there are exceptions. If you want to work on the frontier while savoring the security, perks, and resources of a big company, take a close look at enterprises determined to have it both ways: business-service firms with a high-tech twist.

This cohort consists of companies such as IBM, Hewlett-Packard Enterprises, Deloitte, PricewaterhouseCoopers, Accen-ture, Ernst and Young, and KPMG. Some started out as computer makers; others began as accounting firms. Either way, all now specialize in helping corporate clients install new technologies that make everything run better. Go to work for one of these companies, and you'll spend three months in Atlanta, do another stint in Houston, and perhaps even get some rotations in London, Beijing, or Buenos Aires. You'll get good at scoping out problems, drawing up solutions, and working around the clock to make everything fit into place.

Does that sound like a good match for your liberal arts education? Everything clicks when you realize the secret to keeping these giant implementation squads on the road, year after year. The only way to sustain such a business is to champion whatever new technology needs to be adopted in a hurry. Buzzwords keep changing. *Software as a service* gives way to *Mobile first* gives way to *Machine Learning* and so on. Top executives at these companies can't predict what they will be installing five years from now. They know they need adaptable, resilient minds that can get up-to-date on the next breakthrough technology, again and again—as many times as it takes.

If you've got a background in history, political science, linguistics, or even archaeology, your mind is wired the right way for such work. Think of Oliver Meeker, the sociology major who turned into a blockchain evangelist for IBM. He didn't earn that position because he knew more about the intricacies of blockchain software than IBM's engineers. IBM prizes him because he masters new concepts quickly—and explains them lucidly. Generalists like him rotate from project to project, summoning up the perfect blend of analogies, historical context, and acronym-free exposition to make clients feel smart too.

Similarly, Deloitte has been widening its hiring sights the past few years to look beyond the four core disciplines of science, technology, engineering, and math that make up the STEM fields. Now, says the company's chief information officer, Larry Quinlan, Deloitte prefers STEAM, in which A stands for the arts.

CACI International, a Virginia defense-sector contractor that specializes in tech implementation, has at least 270 English majors, 150 history majors, and 30 philosophy majors on its payroll, according to LinkedIn. True, those liberal arts degrees aren't nearly as common as the engineering backgrounds that define the bulk of CACI's twenty-thousand-person workforce. Still, if you're an ardent reader, regardless of your degree, your passion for books can strengthen your candidacy. Need proof? Take a look at these three interview points, which have become part of CACI's standard protocol for certain job candidates.

- Do you consider yourself a good writer? Outside of school, what other kind of writing have you done, and for how long?
- List three ideas that interest you. Elaborate on the first idea you listed.
- Identify two items you read recently that you found interesting.

Find yourself in the midst of such an interview, and you've got a lot of room to win recognition for all of the supposedly impractical aspects of your college education.

The Financial Elite

You're alarmingly well read, with a keenly developed aesthetic sense. You enjoy a spirited intellectual argument for its own sake. You've got the kinds of grades that could win you a spot in an elite law or medical school, but you decided to pursue your greatest

curiosities in college rather than focusing on a traditional preprofessional program. Having earned an honors degree in something
highly impractical, you want a high-paying job that lets you think.
Where do you turn?

For ambitious liberal arts graduates, the high end of the investment business is the natural place to look. If you're interested in
hedge funds (a lucrative type of investment partnership), organizations such as Structured Portfolio Management appreciate people like you. Similar opportunities abound at leading mutual-fund
companies such as Fidelity, Vanguard, Capital Group, and Dodge
and Cox.

Many of these organizations — as noted in chapter 7 — are run
by people who dashed through college decades ago in much the
same fashion that you did. As undergraduates, they concentrated
on philosophy, art history, or other nonvocational subjects that
fascinated them. They knew (or hoped!) there would be ample
time later on to transfer their intellectual skills to investing. Your
choice of a similar major doesn't guarantee you a job, but it should
earn you a fair hearing.

At Fidelity, seventy-two employees have a big dose of art history in their backgrounds, either as their undergraduate majors or
as the centerpiece of a prior job, according to LinkedIn data.
(You'll remember that Fidelity's CEO, Abigail Johnson, was an
art history major herself.) You can find them working as graphic
designers, software engineers, stock-plan consultants, equity
research associates, and directors of talent acquisition. A few
haven't even needed to repurpose their art history skills; they
work full-time as part of Fidelity's corporate art department.

Show up at Fidelity with an English degree, and you won't be
alone. By LinkedIn's tally, the company's 45,000 employees include
1,138 with BAs in English. (By comparison, finance majors clock

in at 1,186; economics majors total 1,145.) The numbers for other liberal arts mainstays are surprisingly sturdy too: Spanish, 449; history, 438; political science, 433; psychology, 368; French, 251; social studies, 221; creative writing, 150; sociology, 140; philosophy, 129.

Sometimes, it's hard to break into the financial elite with a liberal arts background. In that case, you'll need to make an extra-strong impression in three areas, says Brian DeChesare, a onetime investment banker who provides advice to all comers via his *Mergers and Inquisitions* blog. First, DeChesare says, establish that "you can do math, and in fact, you're quite good at it." Second, explain that you've been nursing along a side interest in finance that's been growing rapidly. Finally, come up with some spark that ties together some aspect of finance with the analytical skills you've honed through your liberal arts course work.

In other cases, the financial elite is expecting you. Top-tier hedge funds, according to reports on Glassdoor.com, routinely spice up job interviews with questions such as *Should police departments have access to firearms?*, *What do you think about grades?*, and *Is the existence of terrorist organizations like ISIS inevitable?* These queries arise in free-ranging group debates that feel more like college seminars than conventional job interviews. You need to make sure your voice is heard, but you don't "win" the argument by shouting louder than anyone else. You succeed by building on other people's answers too. Bonus points if you can bring to light hidden assumptions and treacherous definitions. Get hired, and you will be expected to tackle similarly complex, nuanced questions, as long as they have clear investment implications. If you're hunting for investment insights about Alphabet/Google, that calls for a point of view about the future of online advertising — which then invites you to reflect on how the human desire to be informed and entertained will evolve over the next five to ten years. Puzzle over the investment case for oil stocks, paper mills, or restaurants, and it won't take long to stretch your mind in equally elastic ways.

Nobody comes up with the right answer in every situation. All the same, your bosses will pay you a lot of money if you possess the analytical acuity to be right 65 percent of the time instead of being no better than a coin flipper.

The Problem Solvers

Nordstrom needs to save money. The elegant department store is facing a profit-margin squeeze, and its top executives have decided to target store-cleaning expenses as a prime area for savings. You've been tasked with finding a way to cut costs by 50 percent without ruining Nordstrom's appeal to customers. What do you do?

Work at a management-consulting firm such as McKinsey, Bain, or Boston Consulting Group, and such problems will become your daily obsessions. Should Starbucks sell ice cream? Should a concert hall lower ticket prices or raise them if it wants to boost overall revenue? Business predicaments keep coming your way as fast as you can handle them. You and your colleagues are the outside experts who are summoned when big companies (and an assortment of other clients) aren't sure what to do.

If you are a liberal arts major, you have come across something like this before, no? Major in anything from classics to sociology, and your most memorable academic experiences are likely to involve deep explorations of murky subjects. You're not frightened of incomplete information, haphazardly organized material, and provisional hypotheses that collapse on themselves as you dig deeper into the situation. (Annoyed, perhaps, but that's different.)

Consulting firms go out of their way to find people like you. Back in the days of wing-tip shoes and narrow ties, the top-tier consultants did most of their recruiting at Ivy League schools or a small cadre of similarly elite institutions. Now Bain recruiters can be found at more than a dozen state universities, including Colorado, Florida, Virginia, and Wisconsin. Recruiters don't camp out solely at the business school; they make time to meet with liberal arts majors too. After all, you already know how to define the objective, set up analytical frameworks, gather information—and then embark on a hunt for the right solution.

Opportunities for liberal arts graduates aren't limited to the traditional Big Three strategy consultants cited at the top of this section. Other names worth keeping in mind include A. T. Kearney, Bridgespan, Eagle Hill, Protiviti, Kurt Salmon, Censeo, and Innosight.

Save a moment's consideration for ReD Associates, a Danish consulting boutique with a sizable New York office. One of its co-founders, Christian Madsbjerg, draws frequently and quite publicly from the writings of philosopher Martin Heidegger as he advises some of the world's largest beverage, sporting-goods, and electronics companies about what to do next. ReD's consulting team is loaded with people who majored in anthropology, urban studies, or international relations. When I asked Madsbjerg why, he lauded liberal arts training as invaluable for "synthesizing complex sets of data into decisions."

Storytellers with Numbers

What can you do with a geography major from the University of Vermont, or a psychology degree from Montclair State, or a fine-arts concentration from the University of Miami? For that matter, let's add in a double major from the University of Washington in industrial engineering paired with painting and drawing. No matter what you studied, you will be welcome in the booming new field of data visualization if you can turn numbers into eye-catching charts, infographics, and full-fledged stories.

If you've mastered the craftsmanship that makes a powerful story ring true, you are halfway there. If you are comfortable with Excel and regard statistics as "the good side" of math, you enjoy all the foundational skills you need. Corporate managers in every industry are picking up books like Cole Nussbaumer Knaflic's *Storytelling with Data* and saying: "We should be doing this!" Influential business-school professors such as Stanford's Jennifer Aaker are championing data-based narratives as a way to "resonate with audiences on both an intellectual and emotional level." Purists may still be trying to write the great American novel, but if you want an easier path to fame and glory, why not set out to create the great American infographic?

Think of yourself as a chef in a high-end kitchen, seasoning your central ingredients (words and numbers) with visual garnishes that bring excitement and clarity to your message. Arrows link your ideas; quote bubbles lighten the mood; cartoons stir people's emotions. You're exploring a new communications form that hasn't been fully defined yet. Your best work is energetic without being chaotic; your biggest hits may be seen by millions of people. Entertainment companies such as Comcast and Netflix want your skills; so do media companies such as Thomson Reuters, Bloomberg, and the *New York Times*. If you bring the imagination and "good eye" that a liberal arts education can instill, you don't need a PhD in applied mathematics to become part of a productive team in this fast-growing field. Arrive with the standard amount of statistics necessary to get a degree in psychology or other research-intensive social sciences, and you can be a credible candidate for many, many data-related jobs.

Chapter 5 highlighted the ways that advertising and public relations firms such as Porter Novelli are hiring liberal arts majors to extend their data teams' storytelling power. Make the rounds of other industry leaders such as FCB Group, TBWA, Ogilvy, and Group M, and you will find many more openings. Widen your list to include e-mail marketing, and companies such as MailChimp, HubSpot, and the Creative Group may catch your eye.

Finally, take note of companies like OpenTable, which deploys battalions of customer-relationship specialists to deliver a blend of business metrics and bonhomie. You will find something similar at companies such as Zillow (local real estate prices), Medallia (customer-service rankings), and PayScale (job-specific salary data). Raw data is everywhere. All these numbers become valuable only if someone like you can sift through sentiment scores, revenue trends, demographic changes, et cetera—and clear out the clutter. Draw users' attention to the trends that matter most, and your audience will be grateful.

Media Companies

Is anyone in media still hiring? Limit your focus to traditional print publications, TV stations, and book publishers, and the answer is depressingly downbeat. Advertising revenue has dried up. Budgets keep shrinking. Even if editors or producers want to hire you, they seldom have the money to offer you a solid starting salary and a full-time job. Ramble through Wikipedia biographies, and you can find long-gone reminders of the days when aspiring writers could master their craft—and make the segue from college to career—by joining the staffs of big-city newspapers willing to hire just about anyone. It worked for Ray Bradbury. It worked for Susan Faludi. For most of us, though, that path has gone the way of carbon paper and rotary-dial phones.

Define *media* more broadly, and your opportunities haven't diminished at all. Get to know Bloomberg News, which was built by founding editor Matthew Winkler (BA, history, Kenyon College) and more recently has been led by John Micklethwait (BA, history, Oxford University). Its core audience consists of bankers and brokers paying $24,000 a year for Bloomberg terminals that provide up-to-the-minute financial news, so it's unlikely that you will be covering the White House or joining the Paris bureau for your first job. Make peace with the company's somewhat regimented culture, and opportunities keep getting better. You will find plenty of liberal arts majors at Bloomberg who thrive on beats that range from investigative reporting to the arts and education.

Digital-media companies grow amazingly rapidly when everything is going right, but they can shrink or vanish in a matter of months if luck turns against them. It's the nature of their business. Game-changing shifts in reader or advertising tastes typically take a decade or more to play out in traditional media; they can happen in one-tenth the time online. As a result, don't expect to spend thirty years with a single employer. Vox, BuzzFeed, Vice Media, *Huffington Post*, and *Business Insider* all were hiring briskly in 2016; their destinies a decade from now are bound to diverge. Keep updating your skills and stay connected with people who can alert you to the next big opportunity if and when you need to make a switch. For a more detailed look at how to sustain a stable career in an unstable industry, see chapter 13, "Getting Paid Properly."

Start-Up with a Soul

What's the social responsibility of a business? A half century ago, free-market economist Milton Friedman famously dismissed that question as misguided and outright destructive. In his view, a company has only one responsibility: "to use its resources and engage in activities designed to increase its profits." That's it. No need to get involved in social initiatives unless they help the bottom line, either right away or at some point in the future. If the previous four sentences leave you sputtering with indignation, consider working for the kind of company that takes a wider view. Your best prospect: what we might term a *start-up with a soul*.

Remember Etsy, the online crafts marketplace that figured prominently in chapter 1? Its CEO, Chad Dickerson, started out as an English major at Duke University. There, former instructor Trent Hill remembers Dickerson as someone who was "interested in finding ways to make capitalism more humane." Etsy tries to make good on that goal, positioning itself as a way for artisan creators to reach customers around the world without needing big ad budgets or manufacturing facilities to be competitive. Even though Etsy's listing rules have morphed a bit over the years, upsetting some early merchants, the site still sees its role as supporting a "people-powered economy." More than 1.5 million merchants sell everything from candles to jewelry on Etsy; many of them are parents taking care of small children at home who gain a toehold in the economy through Etsy's services.

If you're looking for a path into the world of social entrepreneuring (in which businesses explicitly work with "double bottom lines" that include nonfinancial goals as well as traditional business metrics), here are three good ways to broaden your contacts.

The simplest: read *Fast Company* magazine, which covers this sector with tremendous verve. The most ambitious: attend the annual Skoll World Forum, a gathering of social entrepreneurs that's sponsored by eBay co-founder Jeff Skoll through his Skoll Foundation. The craftiest: Follow the Skoll community on Twitter via @SkollFoundation and #SkollWF. Reach out to people making headway in areas that matter to you.

Ambassadors to the World

How do you feel about books? This is not a trick question. It's a sincere effort to find people who keep widening their knowledge by reading incessantly. Never mind what harsh words might have been hurled your way in eighth grade. Your moment has arrived. You needn't hide your secret fondness for the college classes with the *longest* reading lists. A big, prestigious employer wants people like you. It's the U.S. State Department—particularly its fifteen-thousand-strong Foreign Service branch.

Go to work in a U.S. embassy, and you'll need to know a bit about everything. The American system of government, the host country's system of government, the right way to eat a meal, the reasons why the Treaty of 1612 is still contentious. Every spring, State representatives fan out across the United States visiting many dozens of college campuses, looking for "adventurous, adaptable problem-solvers." (Those are the State Department's exact words, plucked from the first page of its careers website.) Getting hired is a drawn-out, competitive process that requires you to excel at standardized hiring exams and in-person interviews while also passing a background check. You'll want to get full details from State recruiters or the agency's website. Before you start that quest, though, let's savor two parts of the hiring routine that are deliciously tilted in favor of the well-read generalist.

Where else can you ace the entrance exam by knowing whether a stray quote should be attributed to Willa Cather or F. Scott Fitzgerald, whether a certain bit of computer mischief is phishing or a denial of service, or whether the illegal drug trade is worst in Holland, China, or the United States? At last, your tendency to pick up bits of knowledge anywhere you find them is a virtue, not a flaw. In the State Department's own words, you should be "well-informed and knowledgeable across many disciplines." The right way to achieve that status: "a solid education and a personal life-habit of reading, learning and expanding one's understanding of the world."

No matter how much you have read already, State's recruiters want to entice you with even more possibilities. Thus, a Suggested Reading List packed with sixty-eight books from every section of a big campus library's stacks is part of the application. Devour as many as you dare; in the Foreign Service, they all are appreciated. You'll be pointed toward geopolitical classics such as *Why Nations Fail*; *Guns, Germs, and Steel*; *Russia Since 1980*; and *China Goes Global*. Make time for some sociology, psychology, and behavioral economics, too, in the form of *Immigration Stories, Blink,* and *Psychology and Life*. And be mindful that living abroad will stretch your sense of cultural norms; get a head start with books such as *Kiss, Bow, or Shake Hands*.

You won't find such ardor for liberal arts values in other government jobs, but even low-key respect for your educational background can help your career hunt. Think of the Commerce Department, the Veterans Administration, the Department of Education, and congressional staffs as some of the government realms where your college choices and strengths can be appreciated.

Nonprofits That Inspire

Each year, Teach for America recruits more than four thousand college seniors, most of whom end up teaching in some of America's most challenging school districts. At its best, TFA provides an extraordinary opportunity to change young people's lives for the better. About a third of TFA recruits stay in teaching for the long haul. For the rest, it's a springboard for everything from school leadership to medical school to creating a start-up.

Organizations such as TFA, AmeriCorps, and the Peace Corps accept graduates with any major, which makes them an intriguing choice if you aren't sure how to put your liberal arts degree to work. Starting pay isn't going to make your McKinsey-bound colleagues envious, but if your experience goes well, you will be able to say, "I'm not in it for the money," with 100 percent conviction. Bear in mind that each recruit's experience is different. Even in a job that should be inspiring, you may come across angry parents, unruly students, broken desks, and a bureaucracy that seems to do everything except let you teach in peace. If you can find a way to prevail, you will be an unstoppable force for years to come. Try Idealist.org for an up-to-date listing of opportunities.

The Iconoclasts

At the start of this chapter came the observation that liberal arts–friendly cultures don't happen by accident. One of the most essential nutrients is a willingness to hire for potential and train for skill, typically through yearlong rotational programs. Spend a few months in sales, do a stint in customer service, take on a project for the HR department...and before long, you've figured out your new employer's way of doing things. You've also gained specific skills that make you a valuable employee to a particular department. You're set up for success as measured both by your near-term effectiveness and your long-term potential for promotions.

A lot of big, publicly traded companies have dismantled such management-training programs over the past thirty years. They become natural targets during cost-cutting crusades, when managers' time horizons shrink. As such programs vanish, the entry path for people with an "impractical" major grows narrower. At thriving private companies, though, it's easier for management to focus on the long term — and to keep such programs running.

One renowned haven for liberal arts graduates is McMaster-Carr, a Midwestern logistics and supply-chain company largely owned and managed by the Delaney family of suburban Chicago. McMaster recruits from liberal arts schools such as Vassar and Davidson; it seeks out people with high GPAs, and it's famously willing to consider language, ethics, and anthropology majors along with the usual finance and engineering graduates. Make sure that McMaster-Carr's long hours and intense focus on business objectives agree with you; the demanding culture isn't for everyone. Still, take heart from the story of Emily Rapport, a Davidson English major who migrated into technical training at the company and is now a software developer. When she asked managers why they were willing to take a chance on her, they replied: "You can teach people to code, but you can't teach people to learn."

Another distinctive hub for liberal arts graduates: Enterprise Rent-a-Car. The St. Louis company hires about ten thousand college graduates a year, making it one of the largest U.S. recruiters of campus talent. People who stay after its one-year management-development program stand a good chance of running a branch office or becoming a corporate manager; people who move on find that their Enterprise time translates into highly marketable skills in project management, budgeting, or sales.

About one-third of Enterprise's college hires are liberal arts graduates without a business focus. "We're not specific to major, campus or GPA," explains Marie Artim, Enterprise's vice president for talent acquisition. "We focus more on the soft skills. We are looking for someone with customer service and empathy, communication skills, work ethic and flexibility." If you can multitask well and have a knack for teamwork, even better.

9

Your Alumni Connection

"You're too impulsive." "You're scattered." Throughout college, Kaori Freda had been hearing such scoldings from well-meaning adults. Six months after graduation, it was impossible to argue with them. She wasn't holding down a respectable corporate job. She wasn't even circulating her résumé or scanning employers' websites for opportunities. Instead, she was standing on a pier in Tokyo, about to board a ferry that would take her more than six hundred miles south, to the Ogasawara archipelago.

After twenty-five hours on the open seas, her boat docked at Chichijima, a remote Pacific island one-tenth the size of Martha's Vineyard. Its population: a mere fifteen hundred souls. There, Freda began working part-time at an eco-lodge in exchange for room and board. She expected to stay for the better part of a year. This would be a great chance for her to explore her Japanese heritage. (Her mother was born in Japan; her father was an American of European origin.) During the mornings, she would feed the chickens and wash the lodge's floors by hand. In the afternoons, she could explore coral reefs, steep cliffs, and beautiful beaches.

Admit it. Somewhere deep within our ids, we all harbor a

momentary fantasy of running away from responsibility and loitering on a Pacific island for as long as we dare. Even so, we keep such dangerous thoughts under tight control. We've got bills to pay, deadlines to meet, and family expectations to uphold. Responsible people don't take such exotic sabbaticals until their careers are secure, if ever. As respected author Jeff Selingo puts it in his book *There Is Life After College*, "The longer wanderers drift through their twenties, the harder it becomes to catch up."

Or maybe times are changing. Kaori Freda opens this chapter because she found a way to enjoy her escape—and land a great job too. She didn't hurt her career prospects one bit by spending seven months in the Ogasawara Islands. Instead, this Reed College graduate (BA in studio arts, 2015) qualified herself for new work at Nike and an Oregon start-up while experiencing life on her island.

Freda's success is part of a liberating new direction that's shaking up the way people find good jobs. No matter where you start—even somewhere as outlandish as Freda's termite-infested hut—you are closer than ever to a network of career allies. It's remarkable what you can accomplish with a laptop, a Wi-Fi connection, and a willingness to ask for help. Get enough people pulling for you, and the bumpier parts of your résumé stop being so ruinous to your future. You can win fresh hearings on the basis of your greatest strengths rather than being forever penalized for your stumbles. Thanks to Skype, WhatsApp, and the like, you can build career connections with a speed and ease that earlier generations couldn't have imagined. It's as if you are stretching spider silk between the world you currently live in and the one you want to join.

Your greatest allies: thousands of alumni from your college

who can help you at each stage of your hunt. No matter where you are or what job you might be seeking, these partners are more approachable than ever. Alumni understand what little-known fields are booming, who is hiring, where you can get an interview, and, the most important skill of all, *how* to get a job. They know what insiders' secrets will help you make a strong impression. Whether you're hanging out on a Pacific atoll or marking time in a coffee shop in Perth Amboy, you've got allies. You just need to take the initiative and get comfortable with seeking out new acquaintances.

To connect with alumni who can help you, start with software tools such as Graduway, Switchboard, and CampusTap, or simply make energetic use of LinkedIn. Directory searches will help you identify alumni who are working in the industries and geographies that intrigue you. Reach out to Jessica in banking or Arturo in design with a short e-mail or message describing your common background. Propose a twenty-minute get-acquainted call in which alums can share insights about what their industry is like and how you can become the strongest possible candidate to get hired. Keep the note short and focused but inject just enough details to make the message feel personal. Most alumni want to help. They are especially eager to help students who come across as likable and authentic. If your first call goes well, don't hesitate to propose follow-ups that can include an in-person meeting, a quick review of your résumé, or introductions to other people who can help you. Even if only one in five e-mails leads to a useful conversation, you're opening doors.

Often the most helpful alumni graduated just a few years before you and thus are early enough in their careers to remain keenly plugged into entry-level hiring. You need not bite your nails about

204 • YOU CAN DO ANYTHING

whether a famous alumnus trustee has time for you. You'll fare just as well—probably better—with someone from the class of 2011 or 2015.

In Freda's case, her journey to a better job started with an overseas hunt for personal meaning. After graduating from Reed, Freda wanted to explore her Japanese roots. She bought a one-way ticket to Tokyo and vowed to live on a hundred dollars a month, covering living expenses via whatever ad hoc internships she could find. Family visits in Nagasaki went well; a stint in a Japanese kindergarten didn't.

When Freda heard that a remote island resort, Eco-Village Pelan, would offer free room and board to volunteers willing to help with chores, she decided it sounded perfect. "This is the place where my heart and soul will blossom," she wrote on her blog. Once she arrived, she found the islands as enchanting as she'd hoped. She made friends with kayak instructors; she donned snorkeling gear and chased baby octopuses in the warm, shallow water. She became close friends with her host family, teaching their little girl how to paint.

As for her obligatory chores...well, that got complicated. "I liked feeding the chickens," she told me a few months later. That had the purity of simple manual labor with an obvious reward. Tidying up the self-composting toilets was nastier, yet it took only a few minutes and could be seen as stoic service. What her hosts needed most, however, was extensive help on the construction of a goat shed. Nobody used bulldozers or backhoes for such tasks. Instead, everyone shoveled dirt by hand, week after week after week.

"I got tired of digging ditches," Freda said. Her hands blistered. Her skin got sunburned. The work was monotonous, and she found herself plunged into the despair of anyone approaching a major construction project for the first time. The more you do, the more you realize the unacknowledged vastness of what lies ahead. Each week, it's easy to believe that you're not making any progress at all; in fact, you feel like you're actually slipping backward. Meanwhile, she was getting calls and e-mails from her father, urging her to rejoin the responsible world. It wasn't clear what to do next, and the private dialogue inside her head was getting complicated. *Is this why you went to college? Really? How many more ditches do you want to dig?* Acting on a thin hope, Freda used her eco-lodge's Wi-Fi connection one evening to hunt for job openings at a U.S. company that intrigued her: Nike. As a freshman at Reed, she had met a few Nike employees at a networking event sponsored by her school's career center. She'd stayed in touch ever since. Now, browsing Nike's website, she saw an opening for a tech analyst at the company's Oregon headquarters.

That position turned out to have been filled, but other opportunities arose. Nike might need a resident artist or a short-term specialist working on security breaches and software automation. She was on the hunt.

Her contact couldn't make the final decision to hire her, but he could encourage Nike colleagues to interview her via Skype and reach their own conclusions. She should know, however, that these would be tough interviews. If she came across as unprofessional or poorly prepared, Nike would kick her application aside. It would take about a week to get the interviews scheduled. Did she want to proceed? Yes, she wrote back.

"I really wanted the job," Freda later told me. She needed interviewing tips, fast. No one on her island could help her, but with a single online request, she could become visible to as many as

twelve thousand Reed alumni. She logged on to Switchboardhq
.com, a student-and-alumni career networking site. There, she
posted a three-paragraph plea that concluded: "If you've ever
worked for Nike in any capacity and know what they like from
interviewees, please get in touch. I could use all the guidance I
can get."

A few hours later, tips began streaming in. A member of Reed's
class of 2009 replied: "My former boss is good friends with someone who is well-placed at Nike. I'll ask him about putting you in
touch." The next day, a member of the class of 1991 messaged her:
"Get in touch. I have a contact who might have some insight." All
told, 195 people saw Freda's query. At least a dozen engaged via
Skype, e-mail, or message boards.

Each exchange brought a deeper understanding of the big-
company norms that seem so obvious once you know them and so
mysterious when you don't. One responder explained how to
sound excited about Nike without seeming fawning. Another
helped her bone up on technical issues, such as the different capabilities of Adobe Illustrator and Photoshop, so she wouldn't be
tongue-tied if interviewers wanted to probe her design skills. A
third shared tips about the best ways of navigating the company's
bureaucracy and internal politics.

Could Freda convey a proper professional tone from her island
retreat? She looked around her cabin and saw ugly termite trails
on the floors and walls. They had to be concealed! With a white
sheet borrowed from her host family, she transformed the background into a serene backdrop that approximated a conference-
room wall. Then she rearranged her lights until the webcam's
video image made it seem as if she were settled into a mainstream
office.

Her Nike interlocutors never caught on. "We had a great interview," Freda told me. Six days after the anxious Reed graduate had posted her call for assistance online, she broadcast a triumphant update. "Reedies never fail to amaze me," she wrote in an online forum. "I've received awesome advice and overwhelming community support. I'm excited to share that I will be working at Nike headquarters with an incredible team, one of whom is a Reedie and a longtime Nike expert." A few weeks later, she boarded the Ogasawara-to-Tokyo ferry, the first stage in a triumphant return to the United States.

Even though her Nike project work lasted for only part of 2016, future employers now saw her in a different light. She had migrated into the eminently hirable pool of people with big-company experience and a bachelor's degree from a well-known college. Shortly after wrapping up at Nike, she joined an Oregon start-up specializing in office-productivity tools — a job well suited to her explorer's taste. At the start-up, Accompany, she is part of a customer advocacy team, researching the ways Americans get their work done, and how that can be improved.

There's a bit of Kaori Freda in all of us. According to Bureau of Labor Statistics data, college graduates do the most job-hopping between ages twenty-two and twenty-eight (5.8 jobs on average). The comparable figures for people with associates' degrees or only a high-school education: 5.2 and 4.7. When you collect your diploma, you don't yet know what kinds of jobs you do best, what type of work satisfies you the most, or where the best career opportunities reside. You need to experiment. Only after a few years of poking around does everything become well aligned. That's how you eventually settle into a winning career. No matter what your parents tell you, the great advantage of a college education isn't long-term stability; it's flexibility.

The past chapters have been packed with testaments to the

effectiveness of the meanderer's path. Create your own luck, and the opportunities for a productive, satisfying career after a bumpy start are vastly better than most people realize. That's true whether you want to join IBM's blockchain team or become the sassy voice of Viking Range's social-media initiatives. At the start of the postgrad job hunt, however, it's all a mystery. You don't know how anything will turn out. Partway along the zigzag to success, it's easy to veer off track and never make it back. What if that temporary job pouring coffee or doing office chores never leads to anything better?

Being in the midst of the great postcollege job hunt can be as scary (or thrilling) as rafting your way along a class IV river. When things go well, you're blessed with an intuitive feel for where the current will take you next. When boulders loom, you change course or bounce off them, using momentary obstacles to achieve your necessary course correction. Getting splashed doesn't bother you; each burst of cold spray passes quickly. The whole experience makes you feel incredibly alive. You're moving fast— and about to move even faster.

The rafting metaphor applies to bad experiences too. When everything goes badly, you slam into the rocks and end up over-whelmed by a solid wall of water to the point that you can barely breathe. In the worst case, you're thrown out of your raft. Before long, all you can do is struggle for survival. You've got nothing in common anymore with the happy adventurers in the other rafts. They're roaring in triumph while you're careening helplessly through rapids with no ability to control your path. All you can do is spit out water and strain for shore before rocks or undercurrents do you in.

It helps to have a guide. Here are three powerful ways that alumni connections can improve your odds of a winning career.

Defining Your Search

Every college has at least a few alumni like Polly Washburn. She's a 1990 graduate of Oberlin College (BA in law and society) who never totally left. Even though she's been out of college for more than twenty-five years, memories of undergraduate life remain a huge part of her identity. She organizes her class reunions; she serves as a trustee of the Ohio college's alumni association. Washburn is living in Denver now, but her alma mater remains dear. On weekends, you may see her wearing an Oberlin sweatshirt. You can spot her on the highway in the Versa hatchback with the Oberlin sticker.

As Washburn explained to me: "I started out as a bookworm in a large high school in Baltimore. Everything changed in college. I had much more of a social life. I became president of our dorm. I started to feel confident about myself." The farther she races ahead in life, the more of a debt she feels to the college that made it all possible. As she put it, "I'm so grateful for my liberal arts education. It's allowed me to fit in everywhere."

Traditionally, colleges regard such hyperloyal alumni as feedstock for each new fund-raising campaign. Graduate from college, and you'll soon be bombarded with opportunities to be a friend ($250) of your alma mater, a patron ($1,000), or perhaps even a benefactor ($10,000). The more you give, the more you will be wooed by the development office. You will be invited to dine with the deans; you will get mailings that tell you about the most successful students' achievements. Unless you break out of this cocoon, you will forget how bewildering it is for many seniors to contemplate life after college. You will become part of the campus elite, with only the haziest awareness of the jitters and self-doubts that leave some students too scared to know where to begin. That's unfortunate, and it's starting to change.

Private colleges such as Oberlin, Reed, Mount Holyoke, and Amherst now realize that their most valuable alumni aren't always the ones writing the biggest checks. With the college-to-career pathway for liberal arts graduates in constant upheaval, even the most progressive career-services departments can't solve every student's needs. Tapping into alumni's unique expertise becomes essential. Make the rounds at public universities, and you can find a similar awakening at schools such as Michigan, Minnesota, and New York's Binghamton University.

Oberlin, for example, has drawn more than eighteen hundred students and alumni into an online community that invites current undergraduates to ask for whatever help they need while alums offer whatever resources they feel like sharing. Matches happen dozens of times each month. One notable service promotes face-to-face chats with alums across the country in a format known as Coffee and Conversation. Suppose you are an Oberlin student spending a few weeks in New Orleans, Boston, St. Louis, or any one of a host of other cities, either for an internship or a family visit. You needn't be alone. You've got a standing invitation to network with a well-connected alum.

Polly Washburn started the Coffee and Conversation program in 2015. At first, she expected current students would be most interested in her vast network of job-related contacts. She's enjoyed seven distinct careers since leaving Oberlin, and in each one, she's made hundreds—perhaps thousands—of useful acquaintances. Since graduation, she has tried everything from legal research to newspapering, nonprofit fund-raising, television production, public relations, independent filmmaking, and web development. Now she works for the *Denver Post* as a digital producer. "If you tell me what you're interested in," Washburn says, "I probably know someone."

For all the splendor of Washburn's network, her greatest value involves something more fundamental. She knows that the meanderer's path can work. That's an unexpected—and sometimes shocking—insight for students to hear. She's the living, breathing antidote to society's constant urgings that college graduates steer themselves toward the safest, most predictable jobs that can be found.

Horizons widen. Life becomes full of a wider range of possibilities.

Because alumni like Washburn keep making it up as they go along, they provide a realistic sense of what's challenging—and what to do about it. Spend an hour with Washburn, and you will gain reassurance that you needn't find a perfect first job in order to enjoy an exciting life. She knows when to stick with a stormy job and when to move on. She also knows what it's like to chase success with one-tenth the amount of money you might want. In 2009, she set out to make a low-budget film about life on a Canadian farm in the 1850s. She scrounged for old lumber in order to create a weathered barn on the cheap; she got lots of advice about how far you could stretch a dollar before it was time to give up.

Could alumni provide this same sort of mind-stretching guidance about career possibilities even if it weren't so easy to establish connections online? Yes, to some extent, but everything would be harder and less egalitarian. Without Skype, e-mail, or chat, people would be reliant on whatever mingling did (or didn't) happen at campus reunions, corporate retreats, private clubs, and shared vacation spots. They'd be back in a stratified world where the most successful and best-connected people took care of their own—and everyone else was stuck on the wrong side of the moat.

Nearly twenty years ago, Mara Zepeda, the daughter of an immigrant painter, left her family home in New Mexico and headed to college in Oregon. She graduated from Reed College in 2002 with a degree in Russian and a great deal of uncertainty about what lay ahead. Over the next decade, she found work in higher education, radio journalism, and professional calligraphy. She built her own network of career advisers as briskly as she could. When she posted a list on her website (MaraZepeda.com) of all these allies from New Mexico, Reed, and beyond, her list totaled more than two hundred names.

On vacation in Italy in 2012, Zepeda finally realized the unifying theme to her eclectic jobs and her ever-growing circle of friends—she was unusually good at connecting people and making them glad to be part of her circle. Perhaps she could create a specialized social network that would allow thousands of alumni to help one another's careers. Zepeda couldn't engineer such a site herself, but that was an easy problem to solve. After a few e-mail exchanges with friends, she connected with Reed alum Sean Lerner, who lived eight time zones away. He listened to her animated, almost breathless pitch—and then delivered the perfect techie reply. "Yeah, that sounds interesting. I'm not doing anything too exciting this evening. I could get started on it."

A few months later, the two of them launched Switchboard, a software service that makes it easy for students and alumni to connect. Since then, Zepeda has been pitching her services to colleges across the country. I first met her at a trade show in Chicago, where she was striking up conversations with career-services specialists who might want to install Switchboard. We talked about her early work with Reed and Oberlin as well as her success in introducing

Switchboard to more than a dozen other schools, including Williams, Denison, and Kenyon. When I asked Zepeda why she and Lerner built this service, she had a deliciously simple answer: "It's something that we wish had existed when we were students."

Opening the Door

As a political science major at Binghamton University, Kevin Greer dreamed of becoming an influential global analyst, working in Washington, DC. That's a tough path to pursue, no matter where you go to college. In Greer's situation, the odds of success grew even steeper. Attend a public university in upstate New York, ten hours by train from the nation's capital, and nobody expects you to become the Henry Kissinger of your generation. You're an outsider even if you graduate summa cum laude. People in government don't see you as a player. Nobody rushes to help make your dream come true.

Undeterred, Greer headed to Washington anyway in 2012, right after college graduation. What he discovered in his first month nearly sank him. "The jobs I wanted required five to seven years of experience," Greer ruefully explained to me. "I hadn't done the kinds of internships you needed to have on your résumé." His new peer group consisted of well-connected graduates of more famous schools, who had been cycling in and out of Washington's summer-internship scene since they were college freshmen. They had worked on Capitol Hill; they had spent time at leading think tanks; they had badged in at well-known government agencies. On Greer's bio, a single stint as a congressional intern was surrounded by many college summers sitting in a toll collector's booth counting quarters at Jones Beach, on the southern shore of Long Island.

In Greer's words: "I needed to broaden my experience in a hurry."

Four years later, Greer returned—via Skype—to the Binghamton campus with a proud story to share. He had caught on with the State Department in a big way. For the past two years, he had been working full-time as part of the executive secretariat staff, traveling with Secretary of State John Kerry on various overseas missions. He got to see world leaders up close; he helped sort out the planning details needed to make each trip as successful as possible. Some of his work was cerebral, some of it was menial, but with that much proximity to power, before age thirty, he had made it onto State's fast track.

If Greer had wanted to, he could have turned his entire hour-long Skype session with Binghamton students into a personal brag-a-thon. That wasn't what his audience craved, though. The thirty or so students on the other end of the Skype connection were trying to sort out their own career options. They had a distant, hazy sense of the State Department as a fascinating place to work. They knew that senior-level jobs were enviably exciting. What baffled everyone in the audience were the mechanics of turning a Binghamton degree into a storybook career. How did you get your first few internships? Who helped you along? What job-hunting rituals were a waste of time? How could you gain experience when nobody was hiring you? The more Greer could take people through the crucial, scrappy, mundane details of getting a foot in the door, the better.

After all, career guides and employer websites may explain how your journey into the workforce is supposed to proceed, but they don't tell you how to improvise your way to success if your first few attempts come up empty. There's usually a hidden path or an alternate route somewhere. Your liberal arts training makes you temperamentally well suited to such approaches. You just need an inkling of how it's done. The right place to look for insiders' tips: alums who have made such transitions and can explain in vivid detail how you, too, can pull it off.

Since starting in 2014, Binghamton's career-services director, Kelli Smith, has been building such bridges as fast as possible. Weeks after taking office, she told a campus journalist: "It's clear we have a significant number of successful alumni with incredible loyalty to their alma mater, who are willing to help our current students." Her vow: to make the most of that resource. As she explained to me, with nineteen thousand students to serve, her twelve-person department can't do everything. As a result, she keeps looking for ways to turn career support into everyone's priority, including alumni's and faculty's.

Each February, more than five hundred Binghamton students head to New York City to be part of a carefully structured series of twenty-two visits with alumni working at well-known organizations that are in the midst of their hiring cycles. The students who want jobs at such businesses as Bloomberg, Morgan Stanley, and Ziff Davis learn how to make the best possible applications. As for the ones who are simply curious about what banking or city government might be like, they come away with hands-on knowledge.

Meanwhile, Binghamton brings high-achieving alumni to campus more than twenty times a year for in-person talks or Skype sessions. All these talks occur as part of a program called Cool Connections, Hot Alumni. Within three weeks of Kevin Greer's appearance, Binghamton students also heard from a sociology major who had risen to become president of the Sierra Club, a history major with a rich career in community service, and an English major who cohosted a morning television show for ABC.

Opening speeches are kept short; the core of each session involves the back-and-forth of students' questions and practitioners' insights.

In Greer's case, the best parts of his story involve his scrappy, two-year struggle to establish even the tiniest toehold in Washington's power structure. Ostensibly, he was in Washington to learn Persian and pursue a master's degree in conflict resolution at Georgetown University. Even before classes started, though, he embarked on a nonstop hunt for useful job experience of any kind, paid or unpaid.

For him, the crucial goal was finding work at the State Department, no matter how transient or low-paying it might be. "I applied for a bunch of different positions," he told me. "It's hard to tell from some of the job listings what's involved, but that didn't bother me. You apply for as many positions as you can, as fast as you can." Rejections didn't faze him; neither did an inability to evoke a response.

"Every interview has the potential to turn into a job," Greer kept telling himself. "You never know who's looking for what." Eventually so many copies of his résumé were in play that they achieved the diplomatic equivalent of geosynchronous orbit, circulating on their own within the department's Foggy Bottom offices.

One afternoon, Greer got the call he'd been awaiting. State's Office of Cuban Affairs needed someone to help file paperwork for six weeks. Could he start right away? "I'm pretty sure I never interviewed for that job," Greer told me, with a chuckle. He didn't speak Spanish, and the job didn't pay much. Even so, he said, "Yes!" A few months later, more work in a different section. He befriended any State employees he could find, including an HR specialist who promised to keep an eye out for anything good. A little later, he locked into the opportunity that he really wanted: a chance to join the executive secretariat staff.

Simultaneously, Greer kept looking to nurture his emerging Persian-language skills. In his first year at Georgetown, he applied for a two-month scholarship to study Persian in Tajikistan—and was thrilled to be chosen. After he got back, he coaxed his Georgetown professors into picking him as a teaching assistant for beginner and intermediate Persian classes. Next step, a part-time, unpaid gig helping Foreigncy.us, a language-learning start-up, build out its Persian-language section.

Why stop there? The University of Arizona had custody of some beautiful NASA images of Mars that had already been captioned in English, and as a gesture of international friendship, an effort was afoot to translate these captions into dozens of other languages. Greer got word Arizona needed a volunteer to carry out the Persian translations. Mastering Persian terms for English words such as *rock formation* seemed highly obscure. Even so, Greer said yes. The more versatile his Persian skills, the stronger his candidacy for future jobs. Two years out of graduate school, he might be moving so rapidly on a different track that he wouldn't need Persian after all. Or perhaps another career twist might call on his language skills in a big way. If so, he would be ready.

Greer's ultimate advice for any liberal arts graduate trying to break into a highly competitive field: "Be an advocate for yourself. There's a fine line between being annoying and persistent." A lot of his success has come from operating just a few inches on the good side of that line. As Greer pointed out: "No one else cares about your next job as much as you do."

Go around to other schools such as Colgate, Clark, and Vassar, and you will find similar efforts to make alumni connections a much bigger part of career services. That's especially true in fields such as the creative arts, political policy, and nonprofit advocacy. There, the most interesting organizations often employ fewer than two hundred and fifty people, and they don't have the time or money to send recruiters to massive campus job fairs. Yet niche companies hire college graduates too, especially if candidates show up at the right time and are exquisitely attuned to such businesses' needs at that moment. All it takes is a word to the wise from alumni to make those connections happen.

At Clark, for example, graduates of the university's renowned theater-arts program have wrestled for decades with the challenges of getting connected to big urban job markets. (Theater jobs are scarce in Clark's hometown of Worcester, Massachusetts.) With Clark's alumni online, it's much easier for theater graduates to find that first small gig in the big city that can rapidly lead to something better.

"If the Metropolitan Opera needs an assistant wig maker for a new production, that's exactly the kind of situation that's right for one of our graduates," says Michelle Bata, an associate dean at Clark who oversees career-related initiatives. Such projects may last only a few months and pay modestly. They aren't likely to be advertised extensively. Yet they represent the classic first step on the ladder, creating the name recognition and contacts that soon lead to bigger assignments. As career counselor Liz Ryan once observed, good jobs in many fields often start with a "brief consulting contract." Once employers discover how well you can solve their most pressing problem at that moment, it doesn't take long for them to come up with more enduring work that needs your attention too. Negotiate well, and you are on the road to higher pay and higher prestige.

Making the Journey Smoother

When Evelyn Perez-Landron wrapped up her junior year at Mount Holyoke College, it seemed as if her overseas adventures were finished. She had completed six months of intensive French study in the Mediterranean university town of Montpellier. She was running low on cash. It was time for the French and international relations double major to return home to Boston and get started on whatever summer job she could find. Never mind that wealthier classmates might spend the summer traveling for the fun of it or doing volunteer work in far-flung communities. She couldn't act as if money didn't matter.

But Perez-Landron wasn't ready to go home yet. Partway through the spring, alumni connections in Montpellier had won her an introduction to Yasmine El Baggari, a globally active entrepreneur who grew up in Morocco. Making the most of this new opportunity, Perez-Landron asked about the possibility of working in this French-speaking North African country for the summer. The answer was encouraging. A start-up incubator and a Girls in Tech program in Casablanca (Morocco's capital city) could each use a summer intern. Perez-Landron could look forward to plenty of work in Morocco, but no salary. Was she willing to be a volunteer?

A few years ago, Perez-Landron would have been stuck. Like most schools, Mount Holyoke helped students find paid and unpaid internships, but it didn't sweeten the terms of any engagement. Starting in 2012, however, Mount Holyoke alumni and parents began underwriting as many as four hundred internship stipends a year. This new initiative has opened the door for students like Perez-Landron to take advantage of career-boosting opportunities they might otherwise have had to refuse.

The Moroccan summer turned out to be everything Perez-Landron had hoped for. She helped Girls in Tech prepare for its formal launch; she also served as a junior analyst at New Work Lab, assisting with grant proposals and creating a database of the incubator's participants and contacts. In Morocco's multilingual environment, her French was strong enough for business settings, while her Spanish came in handy in some marketplaces. She picked up enough Arabic to be able to hail a taxi and indicate her destination.

Mount Holyoke's stipend of $4,500 stretched far enough to ensure a safe, exciting summer. Through Airbnb, Perez-Landron found a host family that took her in on affordable terms. Generous exchange rates meant that meals out seldom cost more than eight dollars. When everything seemed too jarring, Mount Holyoke alumni in the United States and Europe were just a Skype call away. They encouraged her to think of cabdrivers as potential allies; they primed her on haggling rules for outdoor markets. "No matter where in the world I went," Perez-Landron later explained, "Mount Holyoke was with me."

When Perez-Landron returned to campus for her senior year, she found even more benefits from her Moroccan summer. Talking with Mount Holyoke alumnae that she knew, she discovered one woman at Accenture, the global consulting firm, was combining her professional goals with a personal interest in helping emerging economies. Would Perez-Landron be interested in an opportunity to do the same? Yes, indeed. An introduction to the right people at Accenture soon followed, as did interviews and a full-time job after graduation.

The broader lesson of her story: Alumni aren't just job boards cloaked in human bodies. They can improve your college-to-career migration in all sorts of indirect ways too. That's especially important in your first few years out of college. When you're trying out different cities and jobs, everything is new, and the risk of getting it wrong feels greatest. You haven't yet found your rightful role in the workplace. In fact, you're likely to feel very vulnerable at some point. If an alum can help you regroup quickly, you sweep aside much of the risk associated with a zigzagging start.

Let's go through a few common situations.

If you want to explore a new direction without looking foolish, a well-connected alumna like Ashley Introne can be your trusted guide. She's a 2011 Drew University graduate (BA in economics and French) who has thrived as a human resources specialist. She knows the banking and advertising sectors extremely well, and her network of business contacts extends into many other industries. Each year, about fifty Drew students or recent graduates seek her out for advice—either individually or in groups—and she tries to oblige in each case. If you're completely at sea, she will take you through a short list of questions to help you determine whether you're better suited for start-ups or big-company life. If you're unhappy in your current job and want some quiet advice about what to try next, she can help there too.

As Introne explained to me: "I have a knack for understanding what it is that people really want, even if they're having a hard time saying so." She's too early in her career to be one of Drew's biggest financial donors. In terms of career impact on current students, though, she's a standout.

Alumni can be remarkably helpful, too, in helping you be at your best in a job interview, especially if you're picking up signals that your dream employer's routines are a bit out of the ordinary. In the opening pages of this chapter, Kaori Freda made nimble use of Reed-based expertise on Nike's hiring habits. Similarly, University of Portland graduates frequently ask April Dennis for her insights about accounting-firm interviews. The reason: she has conducted more than a thousand interviews on behalf of KPMG, the accounting firm that has employed her for most of the past decade. Think of those sessions as the equivalent of a musician's master class. You won't just be learning how to play the standard notes. You will be getting advice about how to come up with your own distinctive phrasing so that you can meet all the usual checklist requirements and still come across as you.

Dennis's specialty: Figuring out how people with unconventional backgrounds can tell a personal story, whether it be about growing crops or working in the Peace Corps, while also shaping those experiences in ways that make accounting firms say: "We should hire you!" Even something as mundane as growing bell peppers becomes a winning anecdote once Dennis gets you to recount how much your seeds, water, and fertilizer cost and how much money you made from the crop. As she explained to me: "There's a cost-benefit analysis story right there. I just help students discover strengths they didn't even know they had."

If you need help with life's little things, alumni can come through in a surprising variety of ways. Hoping to visit an unfamiliar city to carry out a short job hunt? At Pitzer College, alumni in places ranging from Hamburg, Germany, to Austin, Texas, have been known to offer short-term lodging, free of charge. Dispirited by life's setbacks? The odds are good an alum is willing to take you out for a nice dinner and a pep talk to help you get back in the game. Embarrassed about your tattered college wardrobe? Pragmatic alums will take you clothes shopping; generous ones may lend you something stylish from their own closets. Trust me, I know; I've been there. (Jacob Young, if you're reading this, I'm really sorry about getting your foulard tie wrinkled.)

If you need help with life's biggest challenges, alumni can steer you to safe ground. At Amherst College, career-services specialists have come to realize that Latino and African American students want easier ways to connect with alumni of color. Everyone's job hunt is different, observed Emily Griffen, director of the college's career center. She has introduced a new version of Amherst's online alumni portal that allows students and grads to find counterparts with the same social or racial identity. That makes it easier for students to ask blunt questions — and get real answers — about opportunities and rough spots in the job hunt, as well as how welcoming or aloof a particular employer might be once job offers are made.

A few years ago, Amherst tried to create full-fledged versions of online mentoring in which alumni and students would pair up for a long-running series of conversations. "Actually, we found out that this was overkill," Griffen told me. If you're starting a job hunt, you don't always need to come back to the same person for more advice. As a result, Amherst now offers a single, thirty-minute Quick Conversation so that students and alumni can exchange a few ideas without being roped together for months. Participation on both ends of this process has surged. Sometimes, less is more.

Even with all these initiatives in play, alumni connections remain a greatly underutilized resource. In the spring of 2016, the National Association of Colleges and Employers (NACE) asked 5,013 graduating seniors across the United States to share their experiences about fourteen types of job-hunting resources. Only 46 percent of seniors said they had direct dealings with alumni. (By contrast, 94 percent had visited an employer website, and at least 60 percent had chatted with friends, sought out parents' advice, or attended a job fair.) Interacting with alumni ranked a modest tenth on NACE's list, according to frequency of use.

In terms of actual usefulness, though, alumni rocketed into fourth place—ahead of traditional mainstays such as job fairs, career-center visits, and spending time with employer representatives on campus. The only categories that ranked higher: employer websites, friends, and campus faculty.

10

What Your Campus Can Do

Ask college presidents to list the top priorities for their institutions, and the quality of undergraduate career services ranks—according to a mischievous saying—"somewhere below parking." If you are frustrated about the limited amount of on-campus career guidance offered to you or if you're feeling guilty about not making good use of the services that *were* available, you aren't alone. In December 2016, a Gallup-Purdue survey of eleven thousand college grads found only 52 percent had visited their career centers during their campus days. Of that group, about half felt the advice they received was either "not at all helpful" or only "somewhat helpful."

There's no reason such shortcomings need to continue. Over the years, I've seen universities build exciting new academic departments, ranging from cognitive science to astrobiology, on the strength of a few scholars' zeal. I've seen the quality of dining-hall meals go from dismal to surprisingly tasty. I've seen women's sports programs overcome decades of neglect, emerging as thrilling centerpieces of campus pride that fill big stadiums and win television contracts. The people who run colleges and universities are builders by nature. They like to think big, and their next worthy challenge is right in front of them.

What if campus leaders channeled their creative energies into liberal arts career readiness in ways that paired well with the open-ended spirit of academic discovery? Imagine a campus where you could savor great literature, immerse yourself in social sciences fieldwork, and still build credibility in the job sectors that intrigued you. Call it a critical thinker's nirvana. Let's dream a bit.

When you arrive on this campus, you discover the classic freshman seminar has been redefined in a way that's both mind-stretching and good for your eventual career. If you sign up for a class on Perception, Illusion, and Technology, you might start in humanists' territory, exploring the philosophical underpinnings of imagined existence. Before long, you leap into the engineer's world, discovering how today's most advanced virtual-reality systems work. Co-teaching would become the norm, as professors from different disciplines combined forces to help you see complex issues from different vantage points.

When you declare your major, you don't just click a few buttons on a web page. Instead, you become an invited guest at a celebratory dinner where you are surrounded by people who share your academic focus. This is the perfect moment to mingle with your professors, collecting advice about how to put this new specialty to work. Even better, you will be seated at a table with several alumni who are eager to offer career advice and networking support.

If you are partway through college and don't yet have a coherent job-market strategy, your campus understands your predicament. For decades, people like you have been tagged as laggards who "visit the career center too late" and "don't return for follow-up visits." Better options have arrived. As a sophomore or junior, you and other liberal arts majors are invited (or perhaps even *required*) to delve into career strategies in the same highly structured classroom setting where so much other learning takes place.

Sign up for classes such as Taking Initiative or Exploring the World of Work and get ready for a semester-long run of coaching, exploratory exercises, group projects, and solo tasks, with a letter grade at the end. No matter how chaotic everything seems at first, you will start taking charge of your destiny as these one-credit academic classes play out. Because you take these courses a year or two before graduation, you'll have plenty of time to act on your new knowledge before being cast into the wider world.

When you do visit the career-development center, expect another happy surprise. You won't necessarily start by creating a résumé and booking thirty-minute interview slots with whatever giant companies are coming to campus. That is a winning approach for people with tightly defined vocational majors, but it isn't necessarily right for you. In this new environment, you and a liberal arts–focused counselor will huddle for a reassuring and energizing conversation about *you*.

Think about the opportunities described in chapter 4, "My Job Didn't Exist a Year Ago." Thousands of openings arise every week for liberal arts graduates with the enthusiasm and temperament to prevail in uncharted domains. You can start preparing for those moments by chatting with a counselor about your own likes, strengths, and values. Those conversations help determine the workplace settings where you should thrive. Just as important, you master the art of telling your story in ways that make employers say, "We should hire you," even if they don't have an immediate opening posted. What seems like a free-form chat is actually an astute way of pinpointing fit while preserving flexibility about the exact industry or job title where a match might occur.

Once that groundwork is completed, you will be encouraged to spend 60 percent of your time networking and only 10 percent sending out applications. Again, that isn't how the business and chemistry majors do it—but it's right for you. You and your new allies may invent the right job in the course of getting to know one another. Making new acquaintances can shade into job talks so smoothly that it's often possible to be hired without ever putting in a formal application.

Need a part-time job on campus? Traditionally each academic department takes care of its own, which leaves liberal arts majors in a bad place. You may end up scraping plates in the cafeteria while biology majors sharpen their résumés (and get paid) as lab assistants. In our new world, that caste system disappears. When the business school needs undergraduates to help with digital marketing, it welcomes English majors. In fact, a sizable percentage of stepping-stone jobs are explicitly set aside for humanities students, because your campus wants you to be career-ready too.

Looking for a summer internship that will add some sparkle to your résumé? You're in luck. Your college is committed to helping each student find a summer job that's much more than a job. Alumni and career counselors have identified organizations, big and small, that want summer interns like you. If you have something unique in mind, your counselors will help you create a job that didn't exist until you made it happen.

Finally, if you came to college without a cushion of family wealth or contacts to help you along, in this new world, your campus wants to open doors for you too. The liberal arts track is too powerful—and too necessary for our society—to be seen as an elitist luxury. If family finances are tight, expect stipends that let you accept the most valuable internships, regardless of what they pay. If you run into postgraduation stumbles, count on your campus to keep sharing job leads and networking opportunities for many years after you graduate. Whether you're the daughter of Haitian immigrants or the son of Iowa farmers who never went to college, expect your campus to help you build a diverse network that's uniquely right for you.

Does such a campus exist?

The answer is tantalizing. We're far from establishing this entire approach as standard fare on major campuses. Yet each individual element is already in place—and succeeding—somewhere. Some of the innovations cited above can be found within the colleges of arts and sciences at giant public universities such as Alabama, Arizona State, Indiana, Ohio State, Rutgers, San Jose State, and Wisconsin. Other breakthrough programs are being piloted by smaller private universities such as Clark, Colgate, Stanford, and Wake Forest. Still other initiatives are already happening at innovative liberal arts colleges across the country.

The essential elements needed to connect a liberal arts education to career success are right in front of us. Their effectiveness has been proven. What remains is to embrace these best practices more widely so today's rare excellence becomes tomorrow's common good.

Academia, of course, is famous for convening panels of experts who survey the state of liberal arts education every decade or two without doing much about the problems. Right now, good intentions are abundant. Decisive action is what's in short supply. I've spent time puzzling over the reasons why some campuses mobilize fast on behalf of liberal arts graduates' job prospects while others remain stuck at the hand-wringing stage. Typically, the following four factors make the difference.

When the President Gets Involved

In his 2011 State of the University speech, Wake Forest president Nathan Hatch raced through his usual updates (faculty salaries, new dorms, et cetera). He explained that he was preoccupied by "a major crisis that, in the last five years, has confronted recent college graduates, particularly liberal arts students." The overall job market had fallen apart in the 2007–2009 recession. For many students at his North Carolina campus, it wasn't getting better. In Hatch's words, "A Wake Forest degree is no longer an automatic ticket to a fulfilling professional position. Our graduates today are coming of age in an economy that can easily crush even the best and the brightest."

To fight back, Hatch embarked on a multiyear effort to beef up Wake Forest's career-development office. At times, his zeal mirrors a college president's response when the football team stinks and everyone is tired of losing. (You know the drill: *Pay whatever it takes to hire a mighty new coach who is a proven winner, build a new stadium, triple the budget,* and so on.) The early years of this turnaround campaign were nicely described in a 2013 *New York Times* feature that showcased Hatch's success in recruiting Stanford Business School's career-development chief, Andy Chan, to take over a similar job at Wake Forest. The campus's rapidly expanding career-development office, housed in an elegant new building, looked like a winner. Whether it could live up to appearances would take longer to tell.

Six years later, it's fascinating to look at the career-friendly initiatives that have sprung up at Wake Forest, nurtured by the belief that this is what the president wants. On most campuses, career-development teams struggle for visibility. Typically, they report to a vice president of student affairs, who in turn may have trouble getting the president's ear. As a result, promising ideas that need buy-in from other parts of the university tend to die slow deaths. That's not Hatch's approach — and it's not Chan's constant frustration. The two men have set up a direct reporting arrangement that makes it easy to race forward in dozens of ways. Among the notable initiatives:

- **Academic credit for career classes.** Such offerings didn't exist at Wake Forest until the 2011–2012 academic year. Now there are five of them, ranging from Counseling 120 (Personal Framework for Career Exploration) to Counseling 360 (Professional and Life Skills).
- **Visiting the big cities.** A decade ago, Wake Forest students who wanted to explore high-prestige careers in New York, Washington, DC, and other job hubs needed to set up exploratory interviews on their own. College-sponsored group expeditions are common now. The North Carolina school runs four highly organized Treks each year, providing hundreds of students with access to renowned employers ranging from Calvin Klein to the Brookings Institution and Google. Campus schedules have been adjusted so that trips and breaks align; trips and exams dodge each other.
- **Interdisciplinary classes.** Turf-protecting is a way of life in academia, and that can impede efforts to create classes that blend liberal arts thinking and practical managerial applications. At Wake Forest, the barriers to collaboration across different schools have come down. Business-school instructors and liberal arts professors reach accords about how to label courses, design the curriculum, and set up cross-listings. That way, students in different programs can make progress toward their majors. As a result, dual-track courses have come to life

for topics such as High Performance Teams and Design Thinking and Innovation Leadership Through Communication.

Can we see a tangible payoff in Wake Forest's initiatives as measured by comprehensive annual surveys of graduates' first destinations after college? Yes, we can. Many schools survey recent graduates about six months after commencement and ask them: "What are you doing now?" Such surveys count respondents as having achieved a successful first destination if they are either working or heading to graduate school. The fates of alums who haven't found work and aren't pursuing additional education are recorded too—assuming they choose to reply.

For reasonably selective liberal arts programs, it's common to see published success rates of 95 percent or higher among those students who send in responses. What's unclear is the fate of recent graduates who don't respond. Most schools make some effort to re-contact students who didn't respond at first, but typically one-fifth or more of recent graduates remain silent. Make some pessimistic (or realistic) assumptions about the nonresponders' situations, and it's likely that about 85 percent of all recent graduates end up with first destinations that can be deemed successful.

When Wake Forest started publishing comprehensive first-destination surveys in 2012, its results were solid but not extraordinary. About one-fifth of graduates didn't respond; of those who did, 95 percent were either working or in graduate school. Ever since, however, Wake Forest's scores have been climbing. For the class of 2015, 98 percent achieved successful first destinations within six months of graduating. Meanwhile, the nonresponse rate has shrunk to barely a tenth of the graduating class. In his 2016 State of the University speech, Wake Forest president Hatch indicated he wasn't fearful anymore of a crisis that could crush students' hopes. Instead, he said he wanted his school "to become the best at preparation for life after college."

Presidents, deans, and provosts at many other schools are pushing ahead in similar ways. Staff expansions at career centers are an important step forward; they permit more personalized support for each student. Fund-raising campaigns that create big, cheery new career-services buildings in the center of campus make a difference too. After all, fifty years of campus construction has created state-of-the-art libraries that promote studying, first-rate labs for the sciences, and world-class training facilities for competitive sports teams. Don't job seekers deserve decent settings too?

At Brigham Young University, thirty thousand undergraduates compete each year for choice internships. A decade ago, BYU's dean of humanities, John Rosenberg, became concerned that humanities majors weren't faring well in this hunt. "We needed to do more to help students build a bridge from academia to their first job without vocationalizing their majors," Rosenberg told me. As a result, he and his colleagues launched Humanities Plus, a wide-ranging initiative that showed students majoring in linguistics, English, arts, and other humanities fields how to connect with a wide range of internships.

"We decided to learn everything we could from the business school," Rosenberg recalled. "They were extraordinarily collegial. They allowed our students to participate in their internship programs." Now English majors gravitate to corporate projects where strong writers are needed. Linguistics majors help translate business websites into different languages. Career-related conversations happen much earlier in humanities students' time at BYU. The payoff includes showcase internships at organizations ranging from the European Parliament to the Shakespeare Birthplace Trust.

Overall, 25 percent of BYU's humanities majors now graduate with career-relevant internships on their résumés, up from 5 percent before the Humanities Plus program began. When top administrators get involved, such changes happen.

It's also intriguing to see campuses trying harder to recruit high-energy career experts to run these nice new centers. As one Midwestern college president confided to an executive recruiter: "Getting the right career-center chief may be the most important hire that I make during my time in office." Campus presidents like to recruit. They have a long history of wooing brilliant professors away from other schools to build up a national reputation for leadership in a field. It's about time that this team-building energy was redirected toward helping students' job-market prospects too.

Artists Are Not Accountants

When Eilis Wasserman was earning her master's degree in education from the University of Dayton in 2013, she embarked on a provocative research study of undergraduate attitudes toward career counseling. Overall, she found most students felt they were getting effective advice. Humanities majors, however, didn't feel well served at all. As they saw it, campus centers were optimized for providing technical advice to students with career-oriented majors. The system lacked the patience, ingenuity, and resources to help students with supposedly impractical majors.

Wasserman's study exposes an open secret: If you're a biology major hoping to join Johnson and Johnson or a finance major with ambitions of working at Visa, the traditional career-center model is well tailored for you. Big companies that want you will visit campus regularly for job fairs or specially designed recruiting sessions. Your point of contact will be a full-time campus recruiter from these organizations, someone trained to regard résumés as the appropriate starting point. Your career counselors know the drill. They will gladly shine up your résumé, helping to prove you took the right classes and mastered the right skills.

For many liberal arts majors, this formula fails. Your greatest strengths might come through in conversations, not in résumé bullet points. The careers you're targeting might not align well with the job-fair model either. Perhaps you hope to connect with a nonprofit or smaller employer that isn't inclined to pay three thousand dollars for the privilege of setting up a table at a campus event. Or maybe your breakthrough moment will be more non-traditional; you strike up a connection with a big company's free-spirited manager, someone who doesn't visit campuses or read résumés for a living.

Bottom line, you know you've got a great story to tell. You realize that artists aren't accountants. But there mightn't be anyone at the traditional job fairs who wants to hear it.

Indiana University understands your situation. Like many big state universities, Indiana operates multiple career centers on its main campus so engineering majors can get the advice that works best for them while liberal arts majors in the College of Arts and Sciences can follow a different path. Instead of grudgingly acknowl-edging that students in the humanities and social sciences like to consider a lot of possibilities before deciding on their career choices, Indiana embraces the questioning spirit.

"We prepare the explorers and the constantly curious, those whose dreams won't fit into a one-size-fits-all degree," Indiana's Walter Center for Career Achievement declares on its website home page. If you're starting out a career hunt without a fully formed plan in mind, the Walter Center hosts a flurry of Discover events, inviting you to chat up alumni and employers in whatever field momentarily intrigues you. If you're starting to narrow your choices, Indiana offers ten career clusters—such as media, government, or education—where you can mingle in person or online with what might be your crowd. If you change your mind and want to try a different cluster, that's fine too.

Indiana advises liberal arts undergraduates to spend only 10 percent of their career-minded energy actually applying for jobs. That is a shockingly low number for people with vocational majors. It makes sense, however, in many fields where hiring happens by word of mouth or personal chemistry. Indiana's career counselors know that; they advise liberal arts undergraduates to steer 60 percent of their job-hunting energies into connecting with people who could be helpful. (Save another 30 percent for researching specific opportunities.)

You'll hear similar advice at the University of Texas. "Talk to as many people in your field of interest as possible," says Tatem Oldham, assistant director of Texas's College of Liberal Arts. Or, as one of the campus's career coaches, Amira Sounny-Slitine, advises, "Be the author of your own story. Don't let other people tell you what you can or cannot do with your degree. Set goals, reach them, and then do it again."

Telling your own story well is an acquired art—every bit as important as getting your résumé in shape. In the late 1990s, *Fast Company* magazine created an enormous stir by extolling "the Brand Called You." Nobody knew then whether it was possible to champion yourself without coming across as annoyingly narcissistic or arrogant. It's still possible to do a bad job of telling your own story, but there's now much greater understanding of what's involved in doing it well. When employers openly ask for candidates who are "comfortable and charismatic" (remember that phrase from chapter 2?), there's every reason for your college to help you master this increasingly important part of the job hunt.

Iowa State gets it. Its College of Liberal Arts and Sciences offers workshops such as Tips to Build Your Personal Brand and Get Hired. So does the University of Wisconsin, Madison, with numerous offerings including a for-credit class called Taking Initiative, in which one of the stated goals is to help students become really good at giving a two-minute "elevator speech" about their backgrounds, strengths, and ambitions. The University of Illinois is on board, too, with a career-readiness program that begins by helping you identify the four central elements of your story: what you like doing, your strengths, your values, and your purpose. As Illinois's career counselors observe, being able to explain yourself on a fundamental level "is what makes you unique and the right fit for an opportunity."

Critical Thinking's Newest Guises

Lee Franklin is trying something different this afternoon. The Yale-educated philosophy professor has been lecturing on Plato and Aristotle for more than a decade, winning campus teaching awards for his trouble. "I know what's effective," he tells me as we chat in his small, ground-floor office at Pennsylvania's Franklin and Marshall College. In recent years, though, Franklin has worried students aren't engaging with the material as deeply as he would like. Instead, they absorb his lectures with the passive wonder of pedestrians watching a jet plane fly overhead. They look up...they follow this high-speed performance as it traverses their line of sight...and then, when everything is done, they resume regular activities without much change.

Rather than stick with the status quo, Franklin is overhauling his signature class, putting students in charge. Ten minutes into an hourlong class, Franklin poses the day's big question: "What can you learn from a shadow of a vase?" Then he stops talking. For the next twenty minutes, it's incumbent on his students to attack this Platonic mystery as boldly as they can.

In the back of the room, a noisy, confident spirit of discovery takes hold. "You'd know someone was making the shadow," one freshman observes. "You couldn't figure out the vase's size," another remarks. They realize Franklin wants them to start with literal observations and then build out a deeper understanding of the distortions and limitations of indirectly received knowledge. Speakers interrupt each other constantly. They regroup and weave various insights together. They are excited and having fun. At a different table in the front of the room, torpor sets in. "You know it's not a car," one student observes. The others nod. An awkward silence ensues. No one can think of anything else to say.

"This is still very experimental," Franklin tells me after the class is over. "It takes us twice as long, or occasionally even five times as long, to cover everything that would be in a single lecture. But when I started teaching this way last year, by the end of the term, students had improved in ways that hadn't ever happened in any other class of mine. They were grappling with Aristotle's most challenging writing. We teach this way in graduate school, and there's no reason we shouldn't be doing this now."

When new classes and new teaching approaches take root, they generally need to be justified on purely academic grounds. That said, some simple adjustments can strengthen students' career readiness without weakening an institution's academic rigor, and in such situations, there's no reason intellectual purists should resist. Here are four areas in the twin causes of career readiness and academic innovation that are especially harmonious. They bear out the notion that critical thinking renews itself via constant experimentation.

More discussions, fewer lectures. Lee Franklin's bold teaching experiment is being echoed on many other campuses, and that's good news for liberal arts majors with career ambitions outside academia. Employers want college graduates who know how to work in teams, and even long-established schools such as Williams College are responding quickly. "I want to produce graduates who can work effectively in that environment," says Williams president Adam Falk. It's harder to decide who gets an A, B, or C when most work is done in teams, Falk acknowledges, but that doesn't bother him. "If the cost of collaboration is giving everyone an A, that's okay," he contends. Another prominent example is the Minerva Project, an organization that operates seven college campuses around the world. It is forsaking traditional lectures entirely, boasting in its marketing material that "every class is a small seminar designed to keep you actively engaged."

New majors and programs. Fifteen years ago, the boundaries separating psychology, neuroscience, philosophy, computer science, and linguistics were inarguable. Now, all these disciplines converge in ways that have led to the rise of cognitive science. How do we think? What influences affect our thoughts? At more than forty U.S. schools, ranging from Caltech to Vassar, undergraduates now can wrestle with such questions via boundary-breaking programs in cognitive science. We don't need to guess about the value of this interdisciplinary approach blending engineering, physical sciences, and liberal arts perspectives in the labor market. In job ads, employers such as IBM, Amazon, and Los Angeles County are explicitly asking for candidates with training in cognitive science.

On a smaller scale, schools such as Clark University and the University of Oregon have been overhauling freshman seminars so that students can apply their emerging critical-thinking skills to immediate, real-world problems.

I spent a fascinating afternoon in October of 2016 watching Clark president David Angel teach a seminar about the inner workings of a modern university. His school has worked hard in recent years to make its 1960s-era main library into a friendlier place, and Angel turned that campaign into an impressive series of teaching moments. Some students became field researchers, taking notes on the ways their peers used the library at different times. Others became historians, learning about the reasons why Clark opted for a brutalist design when the library was built— and exploring the university's later decision to ameliorate the sight of so much concrete. The result: a chance to sharpen up everything from research skills to debating practices in a feisty room.

Greater roles for digital tools. When Alicia Ellis, a literature professor at Colby College, assigns challenging novels such as Michelle Cliff's *No Telephone to Heaven*, she asks students to use Pinterest as a repository for photos and articles that highlight aspects of the book's journey through Jamaica and personal identity. Students who aren't sure what to make of the book as a whole can start collecting fragments that relate to specific passages or chapters. Class discussions become livelier, mastery of the material increases, and a useful new note-taking habit sets in. Nobody authorized her to turn Pinterest into a modern improvement on index cards, but that's fine—nobody needed to. Her off-label use is a fine reminder that even simple campus routines can become proving grounds for nimbler learning habits that can help out in the workplace too.

Society's Difference Makers

During his freshman year at Rutgers University–Newark, Dyllan Brown-Bramble was the student nobody noticed. Even though he earned strong grades in his psychology major, he minimized his time on the New Jersey campus. Commuting from his parents' home eight miles away, he usually arrived at Rutgers just a few minutes before his ten a.m. classes started. Once his afternoon lectures or seminars were done, he retreated to parking lot B and revved up his 2003 Sentra. By 3:50 p.m., he was gone.

He kept quiet about his family heritage too. Both his parents had grown up in Dominica. His father ran a small construction business; his mother managed a tourism office in New York City. Privately, he was quite proud of them, but it seemed pointless to explain his Caribbean origins to strangers. People always reacted inappropriately. Some imagined him to be the son of dirt-poor refugees struggling to rise above a shabby past. Others cast him as a superhero immigrant: "an astrophysicist who could fly." There wasn't any room for him to be himself: articulate, opinionated, and tired of fighting other people's stereotypes.

In the autumn of 2015, partway through sophomore year, a campus flyer caught his eye. It urged students at Rutgers-Newark to enroll in small evening workshops called the Braven Career Accelerator. "I knew I was supposed to be networking in college," Brown-Bramble later told me. "I thought, okay, here's a chance to do something."

Suddenly, Rutgers became a lot more compelling. For nine weeks, Brown-Bramble and four other students of color became evening allies. They met in an empty classroom on Tuesdays at six to construct LinkedIn profiles and practice mock interviews. They picked up tips about local internships, aided by a volunteer coach whose life and background were much like theirs. They knit together as a group, discussing each person's weekly highs and lows while encouraging one another to keep trying for internships and better grades. "We had a saying," Brown-Bramble recalled. "If one of us succeeds, all of us succeed."

At Rutgers-Newark, 63 percent of the undergraduate population is Latino, Asian, or black. Within the Career Accelerator program, minority participation is even higher. In the spring term of 2016, when Brown-Bramble participated in the program, the volunteer coaches all came from minority backgrounds too. Among the coaches: Josmar Tejeda, who had graduated from the New Jersey Institute of Technology five years earlier with an architecture degree. Since then, Tejeda had worked at everything from social-media jobs to being an asbestos inspector. As the coach for Brown-Bramble's group, Tejeda combined relentless optimism with an acknowledgment that getting ahead wasn't easy.

"Keep it real," Tejeda kept telling his students as they talked through case studies and their own goals. Everyone did so. That feeling of being the only black or Latino person in the room? The awkwardness of always being asked, "Where are you from?" The strains of always trying to be the "model minority"? Familiar territory for everyone.

"It was liberating," Brown-Bramble told me. Surrounded by sympathetic peers, Brown-Bramble discovered new ways to share his heritage in job interviews. Yes, some of his Caribbean relatives had arrived in the United States not knowing how to fill out basic government forms. Yes, as a boy he had needed to help them. But that was all right. In fact, it was a hidden strength. "I could create a culture story that worked for me," Brown-Bramble said. "I know a lot about another culture. I can relate to people with different backgrounds. There's nothing about me that I have to rise above."

Take a close look at the college-major choices of students from underrepresented backgrounds, and you will find something surprising. Some 33 percent of first-generation college students choose a liberal arts major, according to a 2016 nationwide survey, compared with a national average of 30 percent. Psychology, in particular, exercises its strongest pull on undergraduates with lower-than-average family incomes. Each major is its own story, and English majors do tend to come from wealthier families. In general, though, if you've been told that a liberal arts education is a luxury only students from well-entrenched families can afford, you've been misinformed.

For college and university leaders, the liberal arts' appeal across the socioeconomic spectrum is both exciting and daunting. As Dan Porterfield, the president of Pennsylvania's Franklin and Marshall College, points out, first-generation students "may come to college thinking: 'I want to be a doctor. I want to help people.' Then they discover anthropology, earth sciences, and many other new fields. They start to fall in love with the idea of being a writer or an entrepreneur. They realize: 'I just didn't have a broad enough vision of how to be a difference maker in society.'"

If you are a striver choosing the liberal arts, one key element to college and career success is likely to be missing: well-connected relatives who can tell you what classes to take or how to win a choice summer internship. As a result, if you are a first-generation college student, your odds of graduating on time are slimmer, and your ability to find good first jobs (without extra support) is impaired.

Can colleges offset these deficiencies? They are trying. Initiatives such as the University of Washington's Husky 100 program or Michigan State's Citizen Scholars program provide clever ways of recognizing a few extraordinary students from austere backgrounds and providing them with an extra lift. Fundamentally, though, colleges run into one of two problems. Large public universities generally lack the money or staff resources to provide the intensive, one-on-one advisory sessions that open opportunities fastest for students from underrepresented backgrounds. Elite private schools aren't short of resources, but their campus cultures tend to be so far removed from the realities of first-generation students' lives that even well-intentioned initiatives can seem clumsy.

To close these gaps, a handful of colleges are teaming up with nonprofits that specialize in building career-readiness programs for students most in need of extra support. One such group, America Needs You, assists hundreds of students at schools such as City University of New York, DePaul, and the University of Illinois–Chicago. It targets "high-achieving, low-income, first-generation college students" with two-year programs that include twenty-eight full-day workshops and 220 hours of one-on-one mentoring.

I asked Shirley Collado, the executive vice chancellor of Rutgers-Newark, what defines the best of these career-readiness programs. "The power of the cohort," she replied. When students settle into small groups with trustworthy peers, candor takes hold. The sterile dynamic of large lectures and solo homework assignments gives way to something more collaborative—and more intimate. As seatmates and coaches provide mutual support, motivation soars. "You build social capital where it didn't exist before," Collado explained.

Strapped for cash and talent, Rutgers-Newark can't run its Career Accelerator programs on its own. But a fast-growing nonprofit, Braven, can. The nonprofit's founder, Aimée Eubanks Davis, is a former Teach for America executive. She set up Braven when she grew frustrated that many of the children taught in TFA classrooms had done well enough academically to head off to college but didn't thrive later, when they tried to make the transition from college to meaningful careers. Eubanks Davis's goal: to teach the skills and create the support networks that help such students make the most of their potential.

Braven, which began operations in 2014, has already reached about four hundred students at Rutgers-Newark and San Jose State. It mixes liberal arts students with vocational majors in each cohort, the theory being that all can learn from one another. Scaling up the Career Accelerator program to reach thousands of students nationwide is the next step. The pool of volunteer coaches will increase rapidly, Eubanks Davis says, if Braven can develop strong partnerships with employers that supply the coaches. Funding is surging, as employers in Newark and Silicon Valley help underwrite costs in the belief that Braven's Career Accelerators can help improve their own job-applicant pools.

Meanwhile, early graduates of Braven's program are showing signs of becoming the difference makers that such programs aim to create. By early 2017, Rutgers-Newark's Dyllan Brown-Bramble had lined up three internships at various social-media companies. His grade point average had climbed to 3.93. He began mapping out plans to get a law degree, work in corporate law for a few years to pay off his student loans—and then set up his own law firm, specializing in start-up formation. "I'd like to help other entrepreneurs do things in Newark," he said.

He's not invisible on campus anymore either. For the closing ceremony of the spring 2016 cycle of Career Accelerators, Brown-Bramble was picked to introduce Newark's chancellor. He was petrified at first. Then, after two evenings of rehearsals in the school's Starbucks lounge, Brown-Bramble delivered his talk. He kept his voice strong, just the way coach Josmar Tejeda told him. When the audience broke into applause at the end, Brown-Bramble later confided, "It felt good. I could imagine doing this again."

11

Prepared Forever

When David Risher graduated from Princeton (BA, comparative literature, 1987), he picked a literary quote to serve as his yearbook epigram. His choice came from Marlow, the introspective narrator in Joseph Conrad's *Heart of Darkness:* "I don't like work—no man does—but what I like is *in* the work—the chance to find yourself."

Not too many people approach Conrad's harrowing novella as a source of self-help insights, but inspiration can come from the strangest of places.

Let's seize hold of Risher's unusual starting point and see where it takes us. The impact of this quote resides in the final five words: seeing work as "the chance to find yourself." Implicitly, this means transcending the economist's view of work as a habitual exchange of labor for money. Yes, work provides paychecks, which translate into food, shelter, clothing, and modern-day luxuries. But something bigger is in play too. Work's full significance touches on entirely different factors—simultaneously more ethereal and more essential.

Work is how you establish your identity. It's how you enhance your sense of self when life is going well; how you redefine yourself when you're feeling restless; and how you redeem your identity when fate has treated you cruelly. In the "tough love" self-esteem workshops of Joseph Conrad, when the sense of self has fallen apart, there's only one thing for us to do. Get back to work, and find ourselves anew.

Never mind the opening of the Conrad quote and its perfunctory insistence that work is inherently unlikable. In the decades since Conrad set down his fountain pen, work has been transformed—at least for college graduates—into something safer, more comfortable, and more sustaining for the human spirit.

Until now, this book has focused most often on the career choices people make in the final stages of college and in the first few years after graduation. The Conrad quote nudges us into provocative new territory, with its implied insistence that work *always* becomes the crucible in which identity is created, melted down—and created again. Perhaps the process doesn't stop when a person turns thirty.

Instead, Conrad invites us to see each new job as beginning a fresh chapter in our never-ending quest to define who we are. We're always Josh Sucher, stringing Internet cables across a floor and wondering what comes next. We never stop being Bridget Connolly, listening to Ratatat on her headphones near midnight and trying to meet the toughest deadline of her life. We're forever Oliver Meeker, returning from Vietnam and hoping his past journeys have helped him develop enough ingenuity to master this new language called blockchain. By implication, the spirit of exploration that carried us out of college and into our first few jobs must be a crucial part of our forties, fifties, and beyond.

I'm going to spend the rest of this chapter exploring the full implications of the roads we choose in college. I'll start with what liberal arts educators hope is true, followed by the results of a comprehensive study of the ways we Americans relate to our jobs. After that, a series of life stories that speak to the long-term trajectories a liberal arts background can create. At the end, I will share the full—and quite remarkable—story of David Risher, the Princeton graduate who brought Joseph Conrad's epigram into the conversation in the first place.

If you were born in 1990 or later, think of this chapter as reassurance that a strong grounding in the humanities or social sciences doesn't have an expiration date. Not only have you gained strengths that help you win good internships at age nineteen and intriguing full-time jobs soon after graduation, you also possess critical-thinking strengths that will help you thrive in decades to come, no matter what social and economic transformations lie ahead.

If you've been out of college for a long time, think of this chapter as a nuanced look at how to relaunch your career at any point. Optimists end up being refreshingly happy with their ever-evolving choices; even the wariest people achieve a calmness that helps them deal with life's ups and downs. Shrug off the ways advancing age brings gray hair and aching joints to your cohort; it's still possible to stay in touch with the explorer's spirit that has defined this book.

When university deans, provosts, and presidents talk about the liberal arts' impact on life, it's natural for them to take the conversation back to ancient Rome. Where did we get the term *liberal arts?* The right place to look is in the first century B.C., when Cicero positioned the *artes quae libero sunt dignae* (arts worthy of a free man) as being markedly different from the *artes serviles* (the servile arts of lower-class tradespeople). The elitist nature of Cicero's distinction makes us squirm today, but we still cherish the implication that the liberal arts train us to take full advantage of our freedom, helping us be the most thoughtful, engaged citizens we can be.

A similar etymological argument is in play when we look at the word *humanities*. It derives from the Latin term *humanitas*, which, as writer Michael Lind points out, is meant to evoke "the higher, uniquely human faculties of the mind." Practical disciplines can prepare people for next month's work; the humanities are meant to prepare us for eternity.

Such antecedents help educational leaders position the liberal arts curriculum as an asset that brings rewards long past graduation day or the hunt for the first few jobs. It's reassuring to hear George Forsythe, the president of Westminster College, define a liberal arts education as "the path to a lifetime of genuine success and fulfillment." It's inspiring to hear Marvin Krislov, the president of Oberlin, portray liberal arts values as the foundation for "a more fulfilling life." And it's enormously satisfying to visit the Internet's home pages of liberal arts programs at schools as diverse as Youngstown State, Holy Cross, and the University of Texas. Such upbeat messages are expressed in a hundred variants. Get a liberal arts education, and you can expect all the benefits of "lifelong learning," "a sense of wonder," and "active engagement in the world."

The skeptic within me wonders, though, if liberal arts' biggest boosters are selling too hard. As a newspaper reporter, I have met people in the most unlikely professions—from actuaries to feedlot operators—who keep gaining new insights from their jobs. People strain too hard if they claim that studying the humanities and social sciences is the only way to understand the world and how one fits into it. Other paths may prove worthwhile too. Can we portray liberal arts training as measurably better than the alternatives?

Yes, we can.

In 2014, a joint polling initiative by the Gallup Organization and Purdue University asked 29,560 college graduates of all ages how they felt about their jobs. About 40 percent said they were enthusiastic about what they did for a living and emotionally connected to their jobs. (That's noticeably higher than the 32 percent score for Americans across all levels of education.) Curious to learn more, researchers hunted for statistically significant differences between graduates of big universities and small colleges, and between alumni of highly selective schools and those that take almost everyone. None of those sorting methods uncovered a schism in respondents' sense of fulfillment, but a different segmentation did.

Within the Gallup-Purdue survey, 41 percent of the humanities, arts, and social science majors said they felt fully engaged by their jobs. By contrast, science majors clocked in at a slightly lower 38 percent; business majors at 37 percent. That isn't a gigantic gap, but it isn't a rounding error either. What the researchers' data shows is that a liberal arts degree provides at least a slightly better chance of long-term fulfillment in your job. "What I like is *in* the work—the chance to find yourself."

Ask people what makes a great job so satisfying, bestselling author Daniel Pink writes in his book *Drive: The Surprising Truth About What Motivates Us,* and you will find the most powerful responses tie back to three intrinsic rewards: autonomy, mastery, and purpose. Many of the examples that he cites turn out to be—surprise!—fields where liberal arts graduates predominate. Whether you are a writer, a musician, a business leader, or a social activist, you know how to find rewards in what you do. You are driven by a desire to control your life, learn about your world, and accomplish something that endures. Instead of obsessing about other people's notions of success, you possess the confidence to build your own norms and stay true to them.

Autonomy, mastery, and *purpose.* Those terms can guide us in a deeper exploration of Conrad's fundamental theorem of work. Pink's taxonomy also fits in nicely with this book's five-part dissection of critical thinking. Each line of argument converges on the same essential truths.

• As we extend our careers into our forties and beyond, living on the frontier becomes less about staking out terrain that no one else has ever claimed before and more about creating the freedom to define work our way. We become more willing to ply our trades in proven territory, as long as we enjoy the flexibility and trust that are embodied by **autonomy.**

• Analyzing complex situations and finding the right solutions stop being two distinct skills. They fuse into something new, called **mastery.**

• Reading the room and inspiring people stop being talents that we share unhesitatingly. We become less likely to tolerate mismatches between an organization's objectives and our private values. Instead, we look for clarity of **purpose.**

Let's take a closer look at how these principles have played out in five people's lives.

Autonomy

On a drizzly October weekend, Abe Dane is guiding me through a *Candide*-style tour of his work history. As far as I can tell, he is on his sixth career. Or perhaps his seventh. Way back when, he graduated from Pennsylvania's Haverford College (BA, English,

1984) with scattered interests in British romantic poetry, the philosophy of science, and the writings of the Brontë sisters. He lacked any clear career plans. After a series of stops in New York and Boston, he eventually settled in Providence, Rhode Island, where he and his wife own a big, bohemian house. It's late afternoon, and I'm chatting in the kitchen with Dane as he tries to get dinner ready.

Nothing in this kitchen fits into normal middle-class life. Elegant flourishes abound, including the giant copper-bottom skillet in which Abe is conjuring up a creamy version of sliced potatoes and sautéed spinach. Chaos abounds too. The Danes have decided to eat by candlelight, even though they don't seem to own any candleholders. In an effort to help, I try to jam two long green tapers into wine bottles. Then I notice that neither candle has a visible wick. This doesn't surprise anyone. We improvise a solution by squeezing half-burned matches into the tips of the candles, creating makeshift wicks. And why not? That's how the Danes roll.

In about an hour, we will start discussing the serious stuff, including Dane's current job as president of Tizra, a software company that specializes in getting educational and professional publications online. Since 2006, Dane and co-founder David Durand have built Tizra carefully, with notable achievements that include digitizing the complete papers of Albert Einstein. Eventually, Dane will tell me how he invented this high-profile job that provides all the autonomy (and purpose) he could want.

But we're not there yet. First Dane wants to take me back to his awkward beginnings after college. "My self-esteem was all over the map," he recalls. "I was so infatuated with my literary heroes that the only goal I could think of was someday to fill a couple feet of library-shelf space. On the other hand, I was supporting myself with yard work and living in a shared house with a bunch of friends. I'd eat most of my meals at bars' happy hours. Thank God for Beer and Fear nights at pubs. If you played it right, you could pay a dollar to get in. They'd screen a bunch of horror movies. I'd hover at the buffet table and hog the free hot dogs."

After eighteen months of aimlessness, Dane signed on as an editorial assistant at a newsletter company. He fetched coffee. He wrote news capsules about corporate governance. He tried free-lancing for more exciting publications and got a few pieces pub-lished. When *Popular Mechanics* offered him an editorial assistant job, he jumped. A few months later, his new boss quit. Suddenly Dane was the interim science and technology editor. Making the most of the magazine's gee-whiz culture, Dane drew up a long list of cool things that he wanted to report on. Could he ride in a jet fighter? Could he travel through ocean waters in a submarine? His editors said yes every time. He began to build a writing portfolio.

In 1993, Dane won a yearlong sabbatical to join an MIT pro-gram for science journalists. He headed to Cambridge, Massa-chusetts, thinking he would bone up on systems engineering. Then he discovered the Internet was coming alive. "It was all that students were talking about," Dane recalls. "I was about thirty and they were nineteen, but I was learning a ton from them." When he returned to *Popular Mechanics*, he built a tiny website at home so he could pitch his boss on the idea of putting the publica-tion online. "The magazine's computers couldn't run a web browser," he says, so he went home, got his big old 486 computer, hailed a taxi, and lugged the machine into the office.

A few months later, Dane took charge of a magazine-website initiative for parent company Hearst Corporation. His salary doubled to $100,000. For a year or two, he was a big-league player in New York's media scene. No longer confined to *Popular Mechanics'* embryonic site, he helped build online versions of mass-readership titles such as *Good Housekeeping* and *Redbook*. As those projects took off, however, Hearst's bosses decided to put editors with more subject expertise in charge. Dane was shunted aside. Now he needed to find something else.

During his time at Hearst, Dane found his professional destiny. He discovered he was good at getting editorial teams, marketing teams, and information-technology teams working together. And he was ready to cut loose from the big offices, high prestige, and shrinking fortunes of old media. Getting involved with scrappy new projects and rethinking everything from first principles delighted him, even if his new staffs and budgets were far smaller. "It felt great to do something that wasn't in decline," he explains, adding that it was as exciting as flying in an F-15.

All he needed was the right project.

This proved surprisingly difficult. In 1997, Dane and his brother Mike created E-Prints, a digital e-commerce company for professional photographers. They won 390 clients and filed patent applications for some of their technology. When the dot-com boom ended, however, E-Prints was too small to thrive on its own. The company's intellectual property was sold to Kodak in 2001. Hunting for something new, Dane helped MIT build out its online education initiative (OpenCourseWare) for a few years. He also joined forces with some Rhode Island innovators who were taking apart encyclopedias and reassembling them for the web. Their talents and approach appealed to him, especially if he could have a hand in setting strategy.

Finally, in 2006, all the pieces came together. Dane teamed up with David Durand, a PhD computer scientist, and a couple of other colleagues to create a company that would help publishers make the jump from print to digital. They borrowed the name Tizra from Arabic; the word refers to the leaves of a shrub used to make bookbinding leather more pliable. Aided by some venture capital, they built a software platform suitable for niches such as textbooks and professional-society publications. They weren't targeting a giant market, but their ability to adapt to the quirks of each customer kept competition away.

Today, Tizra has a few dozen clients, many on long-term contracts. Dane talks about them as if they were his friends—and as far as I can tell, the fellowship is mutual. Later, when I chat with some of Tizra's customers, they express gentle wonder at Dane's and Durand's intense desire to fix every bug in the software even if there's nothing in the contract language obliging them to do so. That is the kind of company that Tizra's founders want to run.

In his early fifties, Dane finally is free to convene America's digital tinkerers on his terms. He's not much of a profit maximizer; at one point, he confides that Tizra's clients haven't ever protested that the software company is charging too much. "Perhaps that means we should raise our prices," he tells me. Then again, customers are happy, and they recommend Tizra to their friends. Word of mouth keeps the business growing. In the two-income Dane household (Abe's wife, Jan, runs a cooking-supply store), risk and reward somehow balance out each year. The Danes can afford a few pieces of original art on the walls and good schools and music lessons for their children. Silly luxuries like candleholders can wait.

For someone like Abe Dane, autonomy is the extra ingredient that transforms a turbulent but satisfying career into one that becomes a winner in all dimensions. Such well-paced shifts are wonderful when they happen. For other people, autonomy is more like a desperately needed gasp of air after being stuck under water too long. In career terms, it's a lifesaver.

In 1993, Gregg Newby found himself stationed at a U.S. Air Force base in Saudi Arabia, certified at age twenty-five as an Arabic-English translator. This wasn't the usual destination for a recent graduate of Mississippi's Millsaps College (BA, history and religion, 1991). But Newby wasn't a typical college student. "I grew up living in foster homes," Newby told me one afternoon as we chat in an office park just outside Jackson, Mississippi. "The government moved me five times, starting at age seven. I kept to myself and read a lot, mostly Victorian thrillers. I started with *Oliver Twist*. It resonated."

Shaken by this hard-luck upbringing, Newby never felt in step with the easygoing rhythms of college life. He savored his classes but moved off-campus after freshman year because he didn't want to shower in public. "The dorms felt like another boys' home to me," he confided. "I couldn't stand it." To pay his bills, he agreed to help other students with their term papers, either as an offi-cially recognized tutor or…not. Unsure what to do after gradua-tion in 1991, Newby seized on one certainty: he wanted to move as far away from Mississippi as possible.

For the next fifteen years, Newby careened through a series of stressful, highly constrained jobs. Regardless of whether he was translating phrases for the military or staffing a library's help desk, he constantly was tasked with problems of other people's making. He never got to be the boss or even an independent oper-ator. Time and again, he became the unappreciated peacemaker, trying to create a good outcome in the face of anger or apathy on all sides.

Newby's tour of duty as a military linguist lasted six years. (The translation dilemmas that he faced cannot be shared in a book intended for general audiences.) Eventually, he headed back to the United States and earned a master's degree in history. He tried teaching at several universities but didn't enjoy it. "I can't learn for a student," he told me resignedly. "They have to do it themselves." A few years later, he became an in-house historian and archivist for the public libraries of Memphis, Tennessee. At least, that is what he thought his job entailed. Then he began meeting the library's patrons. One woman insisted Newby show her how to play an online basketball game on the library's computers. When he politely explained that he was a historian who didn't know anything about her game, she erupted. "You're responsible for it," she shot back. "It's on the Internet."

Even when Newby retreated to his historian's desk, on the top floor of the library, the eccentrics wouldn't leave him be. One befuddled patron claimed to be a direct descendant of Ulysses S. Grant and wanted Newby to help prove this. Another insisted that she owned a mirror left in Memphis by Nicholas II, the last czar of Russia, during his visit to the city. (No such visit ever took place.) "They always wanted me to authenticate what they had," Newby told me. "They couldn't imagine that they might be wrong."

Battered by fate but never crushed, Newby eventually found a new line of work graced with the flexibility and dignity that his earlier jobs denied him. Now he takes on business-writing projects for clients whose values meet his expectations. In his most lucrative year, he earned six figures writing about diseases and cures on behalf of a major health insurer. At his current employer, a social-media company called EdgeTheory, he oversees a creative team cranking out Facebook posts on everything from restaurants to vacation rentals. Bosses appreciate his nimble way with words. He welcomes the freedom to choose tasks that appeal to him and avoid nightmares in the making.

By this point in our conversation, it was almost dusk. Just about everyone else at Newby's company had gone home. We were sitting alone in a conference room, and as I gathered up my notepads, I asked one last question: Did his college education help? Newby took a while to answer. "We were taught to be passionate about big topics," he said. That turned out to be a foundational strength, sustaining him through many lean years. He never lost his curiosity or his desire to learn more about new topics.

Mastery

Jessica Benjamin is about to give a master class in selling. We've been chatting on the phone for about half an hour. Much of our conversation covered her college days, back in the early 1990s. She started out studying philosophy at Penn State before transferring to Reed College and switching her major to English. We've shared respectful murmurings about the writings of Herman Melville and Virginia Woolf. She has taken me through her rocky moments too, including a series of junior-year exams that went very badly. "Reed was like being on an ice floe, trying to figure out what was going on," she confides.

I know Benjamin now works as a sales manager in Massachusetts on behalf of Monster.com, which sells recruitment advertising software and services. There's big money involved; the packages that she and her team sell to corporate recruiters can total sixty thousand dollars or more. My fundamental question is obvious to both of us, even before I put it into words: *What's an English major like you doing in a job like this?*

"I inadvertently got well prepared for this," Benjamin tells me. "I can talk to people about almost anything. If they want to talk about art, we can talk art. If they want to talk about how to fix cars, I can give that a try, even if I don't know a great deal about it.

It's just basic shooting the breeze. It's very easy to be in sales if you can do that."

There's more. "Much of my job involves making sense of the unfamiliar," she says. "A background in liberal arts helps when it comes to scoping out a new product. If we're launching something new at Monster, I'm the one who asks: 'Who would want to use this? How would they use it?' That whole perspective builds on skills I developed at Reed."

Finally, when Benjamin gets involved in a client presentation, she takes a moment to figure out the best way of connecting with this new person's decision-making process. "Monster's basic products can be explained in three different ways," she tells me. "If people want to hear a technical version, I tell them about the ways we use cookies to track users, showing them job ads that are similar to what they've been looking at. If people are more comfortable with an analogy, I tell them that what we do is similar to the way that when you look at shoes online, the next site you visit will be showing you shoe ads. And if they just want data, I tell them our system will give you a twenty percent uplift in the number of people that click on your job ads." She's equally comfortable with all three explanations; she's an expert in knowing which one will work best.

With her liberal arts background, Benjamin didn't leave college expecting to migrate from *A Room of One's Own* to "a sales quota of one's own." After graduation, she initially wanted to be a journalist. When she discovered how poorly that field paid, especially at the community newspapers that appealed to her, she reconsidered. Later, she spent three years in law school, thinking that new expertise in deal structuring and contract negotiations might qualify her to become a publishing executive. Those aspirations withered quickly too. She was trying to make a mark in a shrinking industry with too many publishing executives already. Whenever she landed an interesting job, a subsequent merger or restructuring would scramble her chances.

Over and over, though, Benjamin discovered that she could sell...and that she liked doing so. In college, she sold pizzas to pick up spare cash. At the *Willamette Week,* she sold newspaper ads. At Reed Elsevier, she sold recruitment ads for *New Scientist* magazine. Coming to Monster "has felt like a second resurgence in my career," she tells me. Even when clients get angry about some perceived problem, she resolves matters quickly without getting dispirited.

"Nobody in the business world ever gets as mad as a person who got pizza with the wrong toppings," she observes. "If you can sort out a pizza order gone wrong—at age twenty—you can deal with the mix-ups that happen when people buy a hundred thousand dollars of job ads."

Does it matter that decades ago, Jessica Benjamin was an English major and the author of a senior thesis on Virginia Woolf? Is there any significance to Abe Dane's college-age infatuation with the poetry of Wordsworth and Coleridge? Or would the two of them have journeyed toward the same sorts of multistage careers even if they had majored in business instead? We never know how all the different alternate-reality scenarios of our lives might have played out. Still, in this situation—and in many similar ones—we can make pretty good guesses.

In Dane's case, people with vocational degrees don't make so many wild, fortuitous leaps in the early years of their career. They certainly don't win admission to select fellowship programs at MIT with well-thought-out programs of study in mind and then jettison those in favor of radically different alternatives that caught their eyes. Serendipity plays a large role in the full arc of many

liberal arts graduates' careers. Train in a more tightly defined discipline, and you are less likely to let the hunger for new experiences drive your career.

In Benjamin's case, a business degree could have led her into a
similar, sales-focused career with ease. Yet her version of mastery
probably wouldn't have been the same. Every time I've spoken
with her, I've come away with the sense that her internal scorekeeping ranges well beyond business metrics that traditionally
define sales success. She adheres to the Conrad test. Her ledger
includes a lot of room for making work emotionally comfortable
and satisfying too.

In Benjamin's words: "I try to put a lot of fun into my work. I'll
send out handwritten notes to people, and I'll tell them they are
fun to work with, whether it's true or not." The payoff? "Often it
will make them more fun to work with."

A few years ago, I served on a middle-school board with David
Satterwhite, a Berkeley history major (BA, 1989) who has been
running software-sales teams in Silicon Valley for nearly twenty
years. Like most people in this book, he bounced around in a variety of jobs early in life. He tried to make it as a musician; he briefly
toiled as an accountant; he spent some time in frontline sales
himself.

It wasn't until 1997 that he tried overseeing teams of salespeople. As he later told me: "I knew two things at the end of the first
week. I was completely underwater—and I loved it."

Ever since, Satterwhite has become an unusual sort of specialist. He's the sales-management expert that start-ups hire when
they reach about fifteen million dollars a year in sales. Typically,
he stays three or four years, helping to grow revenue rapidly. Then
he moves on when the start-up becomes takeover bait and a giant
corporate owner with its own sales-management team steps in.

Stock-options payouts have been big enough to permit some *long* vacations, but that's not his style. Work is where he finds himself, both in renewed opportunities to build winning teams and in the constant quest to do it better each time.

What's his edge? Satterwhite takes me back to his college days, studying Germany's destiny after World War II. "I learned in college that there's never just one reason why things happen. Most people can't accept that. Everyone wants there to be just one reason. But in Germany's case, you had to keep an eye on Truman, Stalin, the Cold War, the French, and so on. In sales, you need to see the whole picture too. Your product, the competition, the industry cycle, and the role of each person in the negotiations. It's complex. I like that."

Purpose

After David Risher graduated from Princeton, he spent more than a decade acting like a "sleeper spy" trying to infiltrate an unfamiliar culture. Marching through a series of demanding corporate jobs, he met quarterly objectives and kept his bosses happy. Looking at his résumé from those days, you'll find it hard to see any trace of the unsettled, restless literature major who drew inspiration from Joseph Conrad's darkest work. Instead, Risher resembled the sort of person who kept Alfred Sloan's *My Years with General Motors* by his bedside for late-evening reassurance.

To pay off his student loans, Risher started with a two-year stint in the high-paying world of management consulting. His bosses encouraged him to try Harvard Business School next, and he did. That led him to Microsoft, where he spent six years, chiefly as a manager in charge of the software company's first database product. His final place of employment during this corporate phase was Amazon.com in the late 1990s, just as the Internet retailer was coming of age. Risher thrived in each job. At Amazon, he rose to become one of the company's five most important executives, overseeing the online sale of books and much more.

Then the searcher reawakened. In early 2002, Risher quit Amazon without offering much of a reason why. He recast himself as a business-school instructor at the University of Washington for a few years, and then grew restless again. He and his wife moved to Barcelona, thinking it would be interesting to raise their young daughters in a different culture. Settling into Spain, he lectured at times at the local business schools but stopped working at anything full-time.

After a few years, Risher took even bolder steps to unmoor himself from his past. The Rishers boxed up their possessions, headed to the Barcelona airport, and set off to see the world. They became philanthropy pilgrims, building a house in Vietnam one month, teaching English in China the next. They homeschooled (or road-schooled) their children, bringing Amazon Kindle readers on the trip and loading up the devices with worthy books. At age forty-three, the longtime corporate achiever was trying to find himself.

In Ecuador, Risher's journey finally paid off. He was doing some volunteer work in an orphanage when he became intrigued by a padlocked building with books inside. "That's our library," the orphanage director told him. When he asked why it was closed, she explained that most of the books inside were misguided donations from far away with no relevance to her students. It was safer to keep the door locked so animals wouldn't get in. When he asked to take a look anyway, she told him that wouldn't be possible, explaining: "I think I've lost the key."

Years later, Risher still describes that orphanage encounter as if it happened an hour ago. "Everything in my life came into focus in a different way," he says. "I'd spent a lot of time sending millions of books to people who could afford them. My kids were reading on Kindles all around the world. I thought: Why not come up with a way to give books to people who can't afford them, so their lives can be changed?"

A few months later, Risher was back in Spain forming a nonprofit that became known as Worldreader. He wheedled thirty free Kindles out of Amazon, to see if a Kindle donation program could work in a single school. When that pilot program clicked, Risher called on the U.S. Agency for International Development and lined up enough support to stock a half dozen schools in Ghana with Kindles. A few months later, Kenya.

By the end of 2016, more than five million people in Africa, India, and Latin America had started at least one Worldreader book via their smartphone apps. The company had placed more than 22,000 e-readers in schools across fourteen African countries. Worldreader's library consisted of more than 50,000 digital books, chosen to satisfy a wide range of possible student readers. Early selections tilted heavily toward American staples such as Mary Pope Osborne's Magic Tree House series. More recently, Worldreader's collection has been growing mostly through the addition of indigenous writers' work, such as William Kamkwamba's Malawi story of a farming village, *The Boy Who Harnessed the Wind*.

Decades ago, Risher himself was the family bookworm, savoring titles such as C. S. Lewis's *The Lion, the Witch, and the Wardrobe* and Edward Eager's *Half Magic*. "I used to read books on the walk to school, with my nose down, oblivious to everything else," he recalls. "People would call my parents, saying: 'David could get run over!'" Now, he takes a vicarious delight in visiting African classrooms and meeting with each school's top reader.

When the students want to chat him up, that's even better. One Ghanaian, Okanta Kate, said she wanted to become the most famous writer in the world. She had already written an anthology of poems, including one called "Agony of a Woman." Could Risher help get her poetry published? There was only one possible answer to that question. Kate's poetry is now available in Worldreader's digital library. The last time I checked, "Agony of a Woman" was the twentieth-most-downloaded work. (She has the gift. Take a look.)

In financial terms, of course, David Risher is an outlier. Thanks to his business success at Microsoft and Amazon, he enjoys an investment portfolio worth many millions of dollars. He can pay himself a nonprofit-size salary of $79,000—far less than he earned during his peak corporate years—and still live quite comfortably in San Francisco. He can pursue a line of work that's rich in social purpose without making the economic sacrifices that someone from a more meager starting point would face. He doesn't have to contend with a broken-down car, a heating bill that can't be paid, or all the other hardships a social crusader from a less fortunate start would face.

Yet there's another dimension of Risher's journey that speaks to everyone's career. To promote global literacy, he didn't need to set up Worldreader himself. He could have accomplished nearly as much by sending checks to worthy organizations and letting them do all the work. He didn't, though, and his reasons turn out to be intensely personal.

Growing up in the suburbs of Washington, DC, Risher constantly straddled two worlds. His mother is white; his father is black. As a result, something as simple as going to summer camp in the 1970s wasn't simple at all. Over coffee one afternoon, Risher tells me of a fellow camper who confronted him the evening before parents were going to visit. The other boy's comment: "It must be embarrassing for you, having one white parent and one black parent." The incident happened more than forty years ago, and Risher recounts it quite calmly. At the end, though, he says: "I still remember his name."

Being seen as an outsider can create an edgy, relentless internal drive that propels people to great heights. "I'm probably one of them," Risher says. During his corporate days, he spent fifteen years working around the clock to get good at logistics, good at finance, good at negotiating and a dozen other business skills. In each setting, he needed to apply those skills to meet expectations defined by other people long before he showed up. Even his most creative work, ultimately, was just the implementation of someone else's desires.

It's different at Worldreader. "This is me," Risher says. "This is what I do." Every time he puts his corporate skills to work, he is trying to bring his own dream a little closer to fulfillment. With Worldreader, Risher gets to link the two most disparate parts of the earth, every day.

"What I like is *in* the work—the chance to find yourself."

Part Four

Your Tool Kit

12

Telling Your Story

When Eventbrite was tiny, the online-ticketing company wouldn't hire anyone until co-founder Julia Hartz took stock of the leading candidate. Today, San Francisco–based Eventbrite employs more than five hundred people—and sells more than forty million tickets a year. If you've ever bought a ticket to a beer-tasting festival, a fringe-theater production, or a webinar, you've probably done business with Eventbrite. Amid all of the company's rapid growth, however, one custom has endured. Before anyone gets a job offer, he or she needs to meet with Hartz. It's a short but crucial conversation, centered on a simple request:

"Tell me your story."

When Hartz poses that challenge, she is willing to hear anything. No response is automatically right or wrong. What she's looking for, as she explained to me over lunch one day, is a sign of each person's motivation, stumbles, ambitions, and heroes. Responses can cover everything from your hometown to the time you hiked the Appalachian Trail. The more she knows about what makes you tick, the easier it is to ensure that if you're hired, you will be slotted into the right sort of job and be managed in an authentic, effective way. As Hartz often tells candidates, "Your résumé chronicles your background in black and white. Now I want to hear about it in color."

For anyone with an eclectic liberal arts background, the invitation to tell your story is an unparalleled chance to shine. This is the moment when hiring stops being a grim-faced hunt for candidates with the safest résumés—and instead becomes an optimistic search for newcomers with potential. If you're lucky, the question will be an obvious, prominent part of the interview, much like the way Julia Hartz poses it. More often, the opportunity to tell your story will arise obliquely, and you will need to be mindful of entry points that aren't always obvious. Either way, seizing command of the situation helps you avoid the frustrating rebuff "We don't think you have enough experience." It's your opportunity to build instead toward a happier finish, with recruiters or hiring managers declaring: "We think you could be really good at this."

In the next few pages, let's talk about ways you can make this transformation happen. Some clues already have been sprinkled through earlier chapters. Think of how Sonia Vora won a job at Morningstar by recounting her intellectual jousts in philosophy class. Look at the way Arthur Motch excelled on Wall Street by becoming known as the classics major who was trained to read every footnote. Or consider how Mai-Ling Garcia invoked her sociology training to define herself as a bureaucratic ninja who deserved a shot at co-leading digital-media initiatives with the City of Oakland.

There's a pattern to these strivers' success. It's highly transferable. Knowing how to talk boldly about your own journey can pay off if you're trying to get a job at a start-up, a giant company, a nonprofit, or a government agency. It doesn't matter whether your supposedly useless degree is in history, English, sociology, or any other discipline in the humanities or social sciences.

The central insight: At some point in the hiring process, seize an opportunity to explain what makes you tick. By sharing the key moments of your life, you transcend the drudgery of retracing the whats and whens of your résumé. You start to reveal the whys and hows in your life. You share the dreams that inspire you, the hardships you have overcome, or the parts of your personality that make you so distinctive. For the first time in the interviewing ritual, you and your interviewer will feel it's okay to let go of the standard script and just be human for a few minutes. You start to bring candor and trust into the conversation. If everything goes right, by the time you've finished sharing a bit of yourself, the person on the other side of the table will be thinking: *We need to hire you.*

Your chance to make this connection can arrive at any time, starting with in the earliest stages of your job exploration. Think of casual networking at a party, a wedding, or an airport lounge. (That's how English major and part-time poet LeAnne Gault caught the attention of a kitchen-appliance CEO who needed a social-media wizard.) Even your cover letter can present an intriguing chance for you to be *you*. Most commonly, your moment will come partway through standard job screenings, particularly behavioral interviews that focus on the ways you handled specific situations in the past. Rise to the occasion with an answer your interviewer will remember for a long time.

Whatever the setting, you need to get good at talking about yourself. Practice by developing strong responses to the five types of queries that follow below. Drill yourself in at least two or three simulated interviews, either with a career-services professional or with a friend. Get good at telling a long version (and a short one!)

of your favorite stories. Bear in mind these opportunities may arise obliquely. Interviewers aren't perfect. Often, they aren't fully prepared. When a question is hazy, you can reframe it into something that works to your advantage. After all, this is *your* interview too.

The Grit Question

How have you dealt with failure? How do you overcome setbacks? Tell me about the longest project you ever worked on.

In recent years, recruiters and hiring managers have loaded their cheat sheets with inquiries like these. They take their cue from Penn's Angela Duckworth, the psychology professor who has demonstrated the importance of tenacity in everyday life. Her book *Grit* shares fascinating research about this trait's benefits in settings ranging from kindergarten to West Point. This line of inquiry sounds terrifying at first, because it seems to draw attention to the weakest aspects of your candidacy. In fact, you should regard this as a showcase opportunity to highlight your appeal.

What your interviewer really wants is a story about a hard-won triumph. If you've prevailed in the face of financial troubles, prejudice, or family crisis, let your interviewer know (briefly) about the harshest moment—and then focus on how you battled back. Salute the people who helped you. Finish with an allusion to the ways this tenacity has helped you in college and will help you in the workplace. You create a triple-strength positive impression when you work through such a question, establishing not just your grit, but also your team-building skills and your relevance to the specific job you are seeking. It took about 2,300 words to tell Mai-Ling Garcia's story in chapter 3, and I'd hate to surrender a single syllable.

You don't need to be the brave pilot in *Sully*, the plucky street renegade in *Slumdog Millionaire*, or other heroes in nail-biting films to make this dynamic work. If you want a refresher on how the darkest details can reinforce your story, pay attention to the way Hollywood defines gritty triumphs in each weekend's batch of new releases. Even the ups and downs of completing your college major can win an interviewer's admiration. Ask Tess Amodeo-Vickery, a Wesleyan English major who got hired as a Wall Street analyst, without taking the math and finance courses that dotted rival candidates' transcripts. "My boss later told me that what impressed him the most was the story I told him about having to fight to keep my undergraduate thesis," she explained. Her professor thought her topic was too big; she disagreed. Staying up late at night, she cranked out a vastly more detailed outline of her proposal. The prof took a look the next morning—and conceded the point.

Can You Guide People to *Yes?*

Victoria Taylor wanted the job. I represented one of the last barriers before she could have it. We were sitting in a tiny, windowless conference room at Reddit.com's headquarters in San Francisco. She aspired to be Reddit's new community manager, a position with duties that included coordinating the site's wildly popular Ask Me Anything feature. My role, on that August afternoon in 2013, was to impersonate five versions of agitated site visitors and find out if she could handle the strain.

She parried everything. We argued about everything from atheism to the Boston Marathon bombing. I made up "facts" with impunity and accused Reddit of all sorts of bias. She calmly marshalled counterarguments when they existed and politely wound down the conversation when the craziness reached absurd levels. A week later she was hired. Over the next two years, she took Reddit's AMAs to greater heights, allowing site visitors to chat with everyone from astronaut Buzz Aldrin to hip-hop legend Nas and movie stuntwoman Laura Dash. Now she is director of digital community at WeWork, a shared-space start-up valued at nearly seventeen billion dollars.

What did Taylor learn as a Marquette student (BA, communications, 2007) that made her right for the rough-and-tumble tempo of Reddit, the self-styled front page of the Internet? Lots of elements of her background stand out, but perhaps the most important was a stint as president of the Milwaukee university's undergraduate art club. As a junior, she coordinated several art shows at one of Milwaukee's most elegant museums, which meant intricate protocol, high expectations, and no way of knowing how attendees might react. Long before Reddit came into her life, Taylor had shown she could guide people to *yes*.

In a behavioral interview, you're likely to be asked a lot of questions about how you motivate people, deal with conflict, build coalitions, or prevail in hostile settings. It's rare to be dragged into scenarios as explosive as the Reddit interview, but you can still be quizzed about your capabilities as a leader and as a communicator. Here's a simple truth to keep in mind. Every leadership question is really about communications. And every communications question is actually a leadership question in disguise. Tie your responses to these questions' deeper purpose, and you can win both ways.

Think of how Alex Maceda, the Dartmouth classics major, recounted the uplifting (and funny) highlight of her academic trip to Greece, in which she walked the grounds of the Temple of Delphi explaining its mysteries to her classmates. She brought ancient Greece to life so vividly that Australian tourists started tagging along in the mistaken belief she was a certified guide. With such strong presentation skills, it's no wonder she got a job at Bain, the elite consulting firm, straight out of college. Her panache won her an exemption from the economics/finance track that carries many other graduates into such firms.

Companies always need people who can read the room and inspire others. Showcase those strengths, and you solve a big problem for your next employer.

How Good Are Your Technical Skills?

Shortly after graduating from Indiana University with a bachelor's degree in psychology, Rachel Allen was hanging out with her parents in Wisconsin when the recruiters started messaging her. They had come across her LinkedIn profile. They liked what they saw. They encouraged her to interview for a job with Qualtrics, the fast-growing Utah market-research company.

Allen doesn't have a deep background in computer science, the field that comes to mind when most people think of technical skills that you can acquire in college. What she came to realize, however, is that today's liberal arts curriculum imbues you with a valuable collection of less-famous technical skills too. In her case, she could work comfortably and quickly with analytical tools such as MediaLab, SPSS, Excel, and Qualtrics survey software. She had built spreadsheets; she had analyzed data on everything from sports-fan attitudes to courtroom scenarios. For Qualtrics and its customers, those are winning skills.

Take credit for mastering the research methods involved in *any* field — and bear in mind that what seems simple and obvious to you may be rare and precious to a future employer. When Patrick Tyler Haas went job hunting in 2013, he thought mainstream employers would yawn at his bachelor's degree in classics and his master's in classical archaeology. Not so. He got offers from a consulting firm and a nonprofit focused on global literacy. It turned out his experience organizing field notes in a Greek archaeological dig was highly transferable to both those jobs.

Take note of the way, too, that strivers such as Mai-Ling Garcia improve their job-market prospects by completing relatively brief courses in digital technology from Code Academy, General Assembly, Startup Institute, GrowthX, or other organizations. Most offer a wide range of hybrid specialties such as digital marketing, design, or user experience. These courses straddle the divide between pure technical skills and humanistic strengths such as aesthetics and interpersonal relations. Adding such a workplace credential to your résumé is far quicker (and cheaper) than trying to complete a new college major.

Are You a Good Match for Us?

Peel the entire hiring ritual down to its essentials and interviewers are trying to assess you on three simple dimensions: *Can you do the job? Will you do the job? Will you fit in?* Of those three, the final one, compatibility, is the hardest one to pin down. It's also the screening standard most likely to serve as the tiebreaker when organizations are trying to decide among several strong finalists.

In days gone by, employers used awkward ploys to hunt for compatibility. The FBI used to ask prospective agents what books they read until an underground network of tipsters figured out the ideal answer: "Tom Clancy spy novels." Once word got around, every candidate professed to be a Tom Clancy fan, and the question lost its utility. In other cases, questions about church membership, political views, and other non-work-related topics came to be seen as ill-advised and outright discriminatory. Employers now tend to probe for compatibility with stunningly bland questions that invite you to volunteer whatever aspects of your life and values come to mind. Three of the most common such questions are as follows: *What do you know about us? Why do you want to work here? Where do you see yourself in five years?*

Seize the initiative! Put your critical-thinking research skills to work and come into the interview having studied not just the organization's website, but also recent news articles, research reports, and online resources such as Glassdoor, SlideShare, YouTube, and the U.S. Patent Office's searchable directory. Speak well of the organization but don't come across as fawning. Steer the conversation toward the organization's growth aspirations and how someone with your background and skills can make those goals come true faster. Parry the "five years" question (which is out of step with the unpredictable nature of modern jobs) by talking about ways you'd like to help the organization conquer new challenges by advancing beyond your entry-level job.

Most important, establish compatibility by asking thoughtful questions yourself. Ask to hear more about the organization's most innovative (or controversial) new initiative. Invite your interviewer to share his or her story: getting hired, first month on the job, current duties, best part of the job, advice to new hires. People generally like talking about themselves. Coming across as genuinely interested in the organization counts for a lot.

What's Fascinating About You?

If sociology major Oliver Meeker hadn't spent four years in Vietnam, would he still have been as intriguing a hire for IBM? And what about all the other achievers in this book whose zeal, wit, and ingenuity come through—loud and clear—when they share stories about everything from delivering pizza to filming documentaries in Bali?

We'll never know for sure, but in the noisy stampede of entry-level hiring, you don't want to be the bland candidate that no one even remembers two hours after the interview is over. Stand out from the crowd, and there's a lot that can go right. Even if you don't get the job, your interviewers are more likely to give you a call back and a fresh chance to brainstorm with them about what your next career move should be.

In a plain-speaking world, interviewers would actually ask: "What's fascinating about you?" Nobody dares be that direct, though. So your opportunity to inject a bit of personality into the conversation is likely to come in the course of standard, seemingly lifeless prompts like these: *Tell me about yourself. How do you deal with stressful situations? What's been your greatest accomplishment?* And the notoriously overused classic: *What are your greatest strengths and weaknesses?*

Take your time with each of those questions. You want to start your answer with something directly responsive, establishing yourself as a candidate taking the interview seriously. It's crucial to find a good fit with the organization and opportunity at hand. Once you've covered the basics, though, look for a way to share the robust side of you. Don't forget to wrap up your anecdote with a verbal bridge that connects your story to the job opening at hand.

In the course of researching this book, I hosted a lunchtime pizza chat with liberal arts majors at Reed College. For the first fifteen minutes, Noah Samel seemed like the quietest of the bunch. He was an English major with strong grades and some experience working in China. Self-effacing to a fault, he described himself as a "one-trick pony" who wasn't sure how to portray himself to employers. Then I asked about his lodging arrangements in China.

Boom! Out tumbled a story of living illegally in ten-dollar-a-night hotels. Even something as routine as getting his laundry done was full of adventure and terror. Bats swooped down at night, threatening to soil clothes left on a rooftop to dry. Pimps accosted him, certain that he must want a date for the night. When he said no, they screamed insults and tried to break into his room. After barricading his door all night, he showered in the morning and headed into work, doing his best to act as if nothing had happened.

By the time Samel was done, I wanted to hire him. From that moment onward, if anyone asked him about stressful situations, he possessed a story that would enthrall his interviewers. All he needed was permission to be himself. *Permission granted.*

13

Getting Paid Properly

Earning two hundred dollars a week teaching English in a small French town. Fetching coffee as an editorial assistant in Manhattan. Fetching coffee as a legislative assistant in Washington. Wearing borrowed clothes to a business meeting because you can't afford to upgrade your wardrobe. Sticking to a bare-bones budget by regarding a Subway sandwich as a perfectly adequate dinner.

Come out of college with a liberal arts degree, and there's a good chance your first job will involve a brush with lean times. You won't be earning nearly as much as you'd like. You may be stuck, at least at first, in a job that doesn't do justice to your education or your potential. It's faintly reassuring to hear outsiders insist this is just a brief rite of passage. Large-scale studies (such as the PayScale and Hamilton Project data cited in chapter 7) keep demonstrating that salaries for liberal arts graduates rise briskly in the first decade after college. Today's humbling circumstances won't seem so bad if a wave of opportunity is coming your way, vindicating the importance of your college training and your "try anything" mind-set.

Still, if better times lie ahead, shouldn't the secret for escaping new-graduate poverty be right in front of you *now*?

It's time to get tactical. Earlier chapters of this book have been packed with stories about strivers who started near the bottom and made everything work out. That low-paid English teacher in France was Emory Zink, years before she made her way to a nice analyst's job at Morningstar. The fellow in the borrowed sport coat: Harvard classics graduate Tim O'Reilly before he started his own media company. That sandwich-eating legislative aide: Maine senator Susan Collins, in her first job out of college. And so on. Now it's time to analyze what they did to get paid properly—and show how those techniques can be applied to almost any career.

Here's a distillation of winning techniques, presented in a seven-stage model.

Step 1: Get Started — Anywhere

Spend your first year out of college building your portfolio on whatever terms the market offers. Say yes a lot. If you want to be a designer, bid for online work at sites such as 99designs.com. If you want to be a foreign-policy analyst, make the rounds of think tanks and find out who needs an extra chapter of a report written in a hurry. (Someone always does.) If you want to be a diplomat specializing in an unusual language, look for short-term translation opportunities with nonprofits and academic organizations.

As much as possible, don't stress about pay. Share an apartment; take public transportation; put up with that older-model phone for one more year. Live at home if you and your parents can abide each other. Keep expenses under control so you can invest heavily in your own future. Embrace a five-hundred-dollar freelance assignment if you think it could boost your worth to employers by two thousand dollars or more. You may take on a few projects you never want to do again. But the era of cheap labor and dining at Subway won't last long. As you gain experience, the pieces of your emerging portfolio will combine into an impressive mosaic of professional skills.

After six to twelve months, you will have an achiever's résumé. You will stand out in a crowd. Better still, you will enjoy a wealth of contacts in the field you care about. Partners and hiring managers will know your work. They will keep you in mind if something closer to a full-time position opens up. They will introduce you to their friends and peers. It's amazing how often a short-term consulting contract can turn into a full-time job. Employers discover you're good at what you do! They also come to realize that their short-term problem isn't going away and that they need a long-term solution if their enterprise is going to thrive.

Be adventurous. History major Chris Chrysostom has done a lot over the years to establish his credibility as a computer software engineer, regardless of his educational background. He has held down full-time jobs at eight companies, including 3M and CVS/Caremark. Even so, the credential that catches everyone's eye—and wins him rapid consideration in a crowded field—is a freelance gig building a three-dimensional model of a crime scene. Over a two-month period, Chrysostom combined police photos, Google Earth images, and blood-spatter calculations to show how the vile deed must have taken place. Put something like that on your résumé, and employers will be itching to meet you. Take their calls, even if it's unclear whether they want to hire you or merely find out more about your fascinating life.

Step 2: Zero In on Your Best Prospects

This is the most crucial power move of all. Once you've found a pool of people who appreciate what you can do, stop saying yes to everyone. Start putting your discernment to work. Focus on the business partners that can do the most to brighten your life. Perhaps they pay you the most. Maybe they speak most highly of your work. If they stand at the top of your chosen field, good. If they simply steer the steadiest volume of work your way, that's fine too.

Regardless of how you draw this inner circle, draw it. Then start pitching more ambitious projects to your most desired partners. Develop an understanding of how they make money or meet their biggest obligations. Pay especially close attention to their pain points: elements of their businesses that aren't going well right now and need a talent infusion to get back on track. Present yourself as the ingenious fresh thinker who can solve big problems if given sufficient time, resources, and money.

Make sure you're pitching your services to people with big enough budgets to act on your ideas. As digital-content expert Andy Anderegg explained to me, if you're dealing mostly with a section editor at a media site, he or she may not have authority to do more than buy articles one at a time from freelancers at low prices. Connect with the managing editor instead. Now you're talking to someone with a much bigger budget who thinks in terms of story packages and entirely new channels. Rather than sell your expertise in tiny slivers, you start proposing six-month projects that approach full-time work. Suddenly, your pay conversations have an extra zero at the end.

Steer the conversation toward value-based pricing too. You've endured the frustrations of being paid the minimum you can tolerate on an hourly or piecework basis. Look for opportunities to migrate the money conversation to a healthier framework, centered on the value of what you create, regardless of the time involved. If you're ready to play an important role on a project that could bring in five hundred thousand dollars of revenue for an organization, it's allowable to argue that you should get 20 percent of that revenue for your contribution. Pick an ambitious (but not crazy) number, and then get ready to negotiate. If they bargain you down, that's not a bad outcome at all. Even at 15 percent, you'll be earning seventy-five thousand. Stylish clothes and trendy restaurants can become part of your new life.

Step 3: Make Yourself More Valuable

If Qualtrics, the Provo, Utah, market-research company, hires you straight out of college, you're likely to spend your first few months in an apprenticeship program of sorts, called QUni. Most of the time, you will be fielding customer-service calls, but there's a deeper agenda at work too. Marking time on client calls helps you learn the full intricacies of Qualtrics' business; it's also a fine way for you to devise a useful project that will make other departments want to hire you. Every month, Qualtrics' high-prestige specialty areas take a look at QUni's current pool of people. Impress the bosses, and you get "drafted" out—much like college athletes being picked for the pros.

Caroline Poole, a 2014 Furman graduate (BA in sociology), rocketed out of QUni in a hurry after she came up with a reverse-authentication tool to ensure that the same people didn't get asked to participate in an anonymous survey twice. She also launched a user contest that invited Qualtrics customers to share offbeat ways they used the company's market-research tools. Those displays of initiative won her a spot on Qualtrics' partner-services consulting team, where recent college graduates routinely earn seventy thousand dollars a year or more.

Even if companies don't offer a classic career-development track, put that QUni ethos to work on your own. Look at the way English major Andy Anderegg developed a training module for Groupon's newest hires within a month or two of her own arrival. Take note, too, of the way that she became a leader in the company's recruiting efforts. Within a year, those two initiatives had helped boost her pay 42 percent. The two areas that she picked—training and recruiting—are uniquely well suited to newcomers on the rise. You don't need ten years of experience to emerge as a leader in those fields. In fact, you're an instant expert, thanks to your own discoveries while getting hired and learning the job.

Step 4: Use Leverage Boldly to Win a Raise

For most of us, asking for a raise is awkward. We want to believe that our bosses recognize good work and don't need to be badgered to do the right thing. After all, that's (usually) the way professors mete out college grades. It's jarring to realize that most workplaces don't function that way. About 40 percent of workers tend to ask for raises every year, and they generally get them, according to PayScale data. As for everyone else…in too many cases, the quiet vigil for better pay yields nothing.

What can you do about it?

The challenge is especially intense if you are the liberal arts go-getter who started out with an unconscionably low salary and now is rising rapidly in terms of job responsibilities, output, and caliber of work. You're still underpaid. You should be getting hefty raises to bring your pay in line with industry norms. Unfortunately, most corporations address such inequities quite languidly, if at all. The ugly truth is that managers' own metrics tend to reward them for keeping costs down and productivity high. From afar, the injustice of your situation resembles good management.

The remedy, of course, is to ask for a raise anyway. Take a tip from Facebook chief operating officer Sheryl Sandberg, who, in her book *Lean In,* offers a five-step approach to getting better pay without seeming self-serving. She wrote for a primarily female audience, but her advice transcends gender. Cite other people's comments about your effectiveness. Remind your bosses of the gap between your current pay and industry pay norms. Let go of any bitterness about your treatment (at least for the moment), and look for ways to portray yourself, your manager, and your organization as a harmonious trio destined to promote one another's best interests.

I've got two more points to add. First, start the pay conversation a little earlier than you think you should. Research shows that male/female disparities in pay can be attributed in part to the fact that men ask for raises more often — and more bluntly. Even if managers reply, "We're sympathetic; we just can't do anything right away," that can be a useful first step. Begin your hunt for a raise when a few months of corporate inertia about the decision won't infuriate you.

Finally, muster as much confidence as you can. If the strains of being judged by a wary boss seem unbearable, imagine that the real you is staying at home today, reading a book in a cozy armchair. The person doing the negotiating is your doppelgänger, equipped with a dossier that explains why you deserve a raise. Let this sci-fi clone do the hard work. He or she is an animated advocate on a simple mission: to champion your ingenuity, your hard work, and your impact.

Step 5: Take Command of a Project

If you're working in a fast-growing field, it doesn't take much seniority to be regarded as management material. Show up on time, do a good job, get along with your colleagues, and you are most of the way there. Bring some commonsense ideas into the conversation about how to make the business run better, and you will be regarded as a can't-miss candidate for promotion.

Even if you don't see yourself as a domineering, corner-office personality, embrace the idea that you can have a bigger impact — and a more fulfilling job — if you're helping to set the tempo. Look at the way Andy Anderegg, LeAnne Gault, and Bridget Connolly all emerged as project chiefs, simply because they were doing a good job in areas where extra (and more junior) people needed to be hired. Experience and good judgment can make you an effective leader without forcing you to adopt a radically different personality.

Although some organizations still pay lip service to the idea that talented frontline workers can earn as much as some bosses, that egalitarian approach is becoming rarer all the time. A 2014 survey by Hay Group found that the pay gap between relatively senior U.S. bosses and lower-level employees now amounts to a four-fold difference in pay — and has widened more than 10 percent since 2008.

Don't forget about stock options, guaranteed bonuses, restricted stock — and all the other perks that can come from moving into management. The class divide between skilled workers and low-level management may have narrowed from the 1950s to the 1970s, but it has been widening ever since. Relatively low-ranking managers can quietly add as much as 20 percent to their overall earnings by participating in various stock-based compensation programs that are reserved for the bosses. By contrast, even the most valued frontline workers are hardly ever invited into this inner circle.

As a result, the economic rewards for leadership have never been so attractive; the financial penalties for lingering too long without a promotion have never been so severe.

Step 6: Keep Investing in People

Tim O'Reilly, the classics major who founded O'Reilly Media, has a wonderful piece of advice for anyone whose influence is on the rise: "Try to create more value than you capture." As promotions pile up, it's tempting to hoard power by clinging to what's already working or by maneuvering for the upper hand in each new situation. Leave those strategies to the wary. You can do better by sticking with the open-minded methods that have brought you this far.

Get to know younger talent and look for ways to bring rising stars onto your team. The higher you rise in an organization, the more your success will be judged by how well you develop other leaders too. Speak at conferences. Teach. Blog. Share your work. You will become more widely known and more widely admired. In the process, you gain a widening circle of allies — and a lot more serendipity in your life.

One of the reasons philosophy major Stewart Butterfield's start-ups rise higher each time he starts afresh is that the best people associated with his earlier projects are eager to work with him again. When a consummate networker like Ashley Introne wants to switch jobs, lots of people whom she has helped along the way are looking out for her too. That reputation for doing well by others makes it easier for you to switch jobs gracefully — and to prosper even in turbulent times.

Being well networked has another payoff too. As you become better known, you will start getting unsolicited offers from potential new employers excited about the possibility of adding your dynamism in their organization. Say yes to the very best of those offers; use the rest as gentle (or not-so-gentle) bargaining chips with your current employer. While you can't get ahead in the long run by threatening to quit every six months, you are allowed a few junctures in your career where you actively bargain for better. Tell your boss (or your board) that you'd love to stay, but you're worried about being stuck in a situation where you're earning 20 percent below what a leading competitor is willing to pay you right now. The usual reply: "What would it take to keep you?" Once that question is on the table, you're probably only a few hours away from a big raise and roomful of smiling people.

Step 7: Keep Investing in New Ideas

K. Anders Ericsson, a psychology professor at Florida State, has attracted a lot of attention in recent years with his findings that the best classical musicians spend enormous amounts of time practicing the hard stuff, often before age eighteen. (You may recognize his research through the popularized variant of the 10,000-hour rule as portrayed by author Malcolm Gladwell.) If you want to excel in a field where standards of excellence were well defined more than a hundred and fifty years ago, Ericsson and Gladwell are right. There are no shortcuts.

Fortunately, most disciplines don't work that way! New ideas keep coming along all the time. Early innovators reap gigantic rewards long before they have put in ten thousand hours at anything. They had the wonderful good fortune to be first, when opportunities were huge and no one else was fighting for them.

Think of the way Soleio showed up at Facebook in 2005 with a music degree from Duke and some self-taught ideas about good design. Right place, right time. After Soleio created the "Like" icon, his fame and financial success in graphic design were assured.

Keep looking for such opportunities. Remember that most people crave predictability and are willing to endure very low growth in opportunities or income just to be able to keep doing what's familiar, month after month. The effective habits that have propelled you into higher-paying situations also mean that you're well positioned to spot the next big trend—and to harness it to your advantage.

The most successful journalists, bankers, historians, and entrepreneurs that I know periodically ask themselves: "If I were just starting out today, what would I be working on?" Often such opportunities arise at the junctures between two disciplines, where longtime experts lack the flexibility to see new ways of doing things. Newcomers welcome! Seize those chances. A decade later, as the rewards become clear, people will be asking: "How did you know?"

Acknowledgments

Every book is a team effort. This one especially benefited from wise advice and helping hands at every stage. Long before I dared imagine this book, Henry Riggs, Don Fehrenbacher, Lois Amsterdam, and William Mills Todd III stretched my horizons in college. John Kelliher and Norm Pearlstine kept me on track during a college-to-career transition that could have gone south many times.

This book's central arguments gradually took shape in the pages of *Forbes* magazine, where editors Randall Lane, Caroline Howard, and Bruce Upbin offered patient support along with some inspired bits of word craft. During that formative period, from 2012 to 2015, Marc Bodnick at Quora, Larry Rout at the *Wall Street Journal,* Nanette Byrnes at *Technology Review,* and Daniel Roth at LinkedIn also provided excellent platforms for a writer trying to make sense of his own material.

In the autumn of 2015, Christine Cavalier, Josh Stephens, Nanci Schiman, Vicki Reid, Malcolm Reid, and Brian Eule helped me clear out the clutter in early drafts of my book proposal. They ensured that each iteration (and there were a lot!) became a little crisper. My agents at Inkwell Management, Kim Witherspoon and William Callahan, were exceptionally thoughtful about helping this book find the right publishing home. At Little, Brown and Company, executive editor John Parsley provided the perfect blend of encouragement and exhortation. He believed in this book's message with a conviction that inspired me to work harder and more resourcefully than on any other project I've tackled in the past twenty years. It's a privilege to be one of his authors.

Being a solo researcher for many months can be the hardest part of making a book come together. This time around, I was fortunate to connect with allies new and old at every stop along the way. Alice Harra, Kevin Myers, Beth Throne, Tammy Halstead, Sonia Elliot, Ma'Ayan Plaut, Chris Teare, Jane Salerno, Sharon Jones, Paul Christesen, Loni Bordoloi, Desiree Vasquez, and Frank Christianson were gracious hosts during campus visits and conference sessions. Each introduced me to more helpful people than I can count. Mark Tomljanovich, Pancho Savery, Brian Stinchfield, and Carol Auster invited me into their classrooms; I appreciate their bravery in doing so. Carling Spelhaug, Aimée Eubanks Davis, Mara Zepeda, Laurie Friedman, Joe Stadlinger, and Will Bunker broke down barriers in the employer and alumni communities with equal gusto.

Peggy Raybon transcribed interviews with good cheer and precision. Jay Penn set me up in a fine office. On the road, longtime friends Loch Rose and Andy Davis in Illinois, Dwain Doty in Mississippi, and Brett Fromson in New York made sure I did not go hungry. Our noisy, messy meals together were the best. Jeff Bailey, Sophie Egan, Alan Drummer, Charlene Drummer, John Rosenberg, Heather Parry, and Sara Schiman all shared valuable feedback on chapter drafts.

Little, Brown's publishing team brought this book to the finish line with great skill and professionalism. Gregg Kulick designed a brilliant cover. Gabriella Mongelli helped make each chapter better, with consistently excellent questions and suggestions. Artificial intelligence will never take over the world as long as Tracy Roe is copyediting; her knowledge of everything from Irish history to crime-scene research helped make this a more accurate book. Lauren Velasquez brought ingenuity and excitement to our marketing meetings; Zea Moscone did the same on the publicity front. Pamela Marshall and Elisa Rivlin were unfailingly sure hands as they guided the manuscript through production and legal review.

This book isn't a memoir, but its structure and message have been influenced greatly by the events of my own family's life. My parents were both educators, and I'm grateful for the ways their curiosity spilled into my upbringing. My wife, Betsy Corcoran, has rebuilt her career in thrilling ways the past few years; she is the first person I think of when someone says, "You can do anything." As for our sons, Matthew and Peter, they have become the first readers of many chapter drafts. They're fearless, they're funny—and they're usually right. If I had not had such close family support, this book wouldn't have been possible.

Snacks for the Road

I'm a nibbler. Pretzels aren't safe when I'm around. Almonds, carrots, and grapes are in peril too. Perhaps you have similar frailties. If so, it's likely you infuse any big learning project with this snack-minded focus. Granted, a buffet of the mind ought to be constructed with full-length books in the center. Even so, short-term treats also deserve a place in our research. Watch a few TED Talks? Sure. Add some high-profile thinkers to your Twitter feed? Why not? Bookmark some interesting web pages? Of course.

On the theory that grazing is a virtue, I will offer many bite-size suggestions for further exploration in the next few pages. If you have enjoyed *You Can Do Anything* and want a second helping, I'm serving. You can find short updates and articles at www .georgeandersbooks.com, but these pages will draw attention to other people's work. Everything from a blog post to an online community can be of value. That's especially true for the big themes of this book: how to rebuild your spirits, how to get a job, how to make the most of your college experience, and how to improvise your way to a successful career.

The lists that follow are front-loaded with small, instant pay-offs. You will encounter plenty of recommendations in the first half of this section that take five minutes or less to consume. If you prefer something more substantial, keep going. A suggested reading list showcasing a dozen books with enduring value appears at the end. I've curated the list carefully, thinking hard about which standouts deserve a few hours of concentrated attention. Find the right book, and its insights could help you for years to come.

Handy Facts for Any Argument

Picking the liberal arts path is controversial. Telling people what you're doing can invite puzzled looks, blunt criticism — even a few taunts. You needn't run from these doubters. If an acquaintance, parent, or know-it-all seatmate on an airplane starts questioning the utility of your college major, comprehensive, multiyear data will keep the skeptic at bay. Shore up your response with the following resources.

If you chose the liberal arts track at a big university, you're in good company. Bolster your defense/rebuttal with data from this Brigham Young University presentation, which shows how English majors, history majors, et cetera establish strong careers in a wide range of fields: http://humanitiespathways.byu.edu/.

If you opted for a small liberal arts college, Cereus Data has compiled a remarkable run of data, going back to 1935, showing how Williams College graduates with various different majors find their careers. The circular displays and multicolored palettes create beautiful swirling patterns that look a bit like maypoles in mid-dance. A link is here: web.williams.edu/mathematics/devadoss/careerpath.html.

If you want evidence that a liberal arts degree can lead to strong midcareer incomes even if the first few years after graduation are bumpy, three national sources stand out. Data from the Association of American Colleges and Universities is here: www.aacu

.org/nchems-report. Information from the Brookings Institution's Hamilton Project is here: www.hamiltonproject.org/charts/career _earnings_by_college_major/. Also useful is the biennial college salary report compiled by PayScale, a Seattle labor-data company; it can be found here: www.payscale.com/college-salary-report/ degrees-and-majors-lifetime-earnings.

The Best of Twitter

Get the right people and organizations into your Twitter feed, and you create a customized flow of timely updates about topics that matter to you. I've set up a ready-made list of accounts to follow at @GeorgeAnders/lists/YCDA resources, but if you'd rather build your own cohort, a handy starting point is @SmartColleges, which provides upbeat messages about the value of a liberal arts degree. For career advice on everything from negotiating a raise to interview-day wardrobes, consider @CareerBuilder, @TheMuse, and Hannah Morgan (@careersherpa). If you prefer a dash of wit (or snark!) blended into career tips, you can't go wrong with Liz Ryan (@HumanWorkplace).

If you want big-picture updates about the college-to-career pathway without the time drain of reviewing each new batch of charts and economic bulletins, Twitter can help. These six experts sift through everything and then share what's newsworthy via lively, 140-character updates. Click on the tweets that interest you; glide past the rest. The accounts to follow are education writer Jeff Selingo (@JSelingo), Georgetown University's Center on Education and the Workforce (@GeorgetownCEW), the National Association of Colleges and Employers (@NACEOrg), and the job-related sites @PayScale, @Vault.com, and @BLS_gov.

TED Talks to Brighten Your Life

For a soothing blend of information and entertainment, TED Talks are hard to beat. The speakers are brilliant, the pacing is quick, the production values are excellent, and so on. These archived videos present the key findings and arguments of best-selling authors, usually in about eighteen minutes. It's no wonder these authors' talks routinely attract thirty times the audience of their books.

As it happens, several authors already cited in this book are ready to say hello, free of charge, via their TED Talks. You can find Daniel Pink talking about motivation (www.ted.com/talks/dan_pink_on_motivation) and Angela Duckworth talking about the importance of grit (www.ted.com/talks/angela_lee_duckworth_grit_the_power_of_passion_and_perseverance).

Plenty of well-targeted encouragement can be found in Susan Cain's talk about the power of introverts (www.ted.com/talks/susan_cain_the_power_of_introverts), Brené Brown's presentation on the ways vulnerability can work for you (www.ted.com/talks/brene_brown_on_vulnerability), and Elizabeth Gilbert's remarks on your elusive creative genius (www.ted.com/talks/elizabeth_gilbert_on_genius).

If you're intrigued by the notion of telling stories with numbers, don't miss the late Hans Rosling's TED Talk on "The Best Stats You've Ever Seen" (www.ted.com/talks/hans_rosling_shows_the_best_stats_you_ve_ever_seen). If you want to be a more effective storyteller or public speaker, take inspiration from talks by Chimamanda Adichie (www.ted.com/talks/chimamanda_adichie_the_danger_of_a_single_story) and Julian Treasure (www.ted.com/talks/julian_treasure_how_to_speak_so_that_people_want_to_listen). Finally, if you'd like a refreshing—and hilarious—perspective on helicopter parents and the importance of getting out of the way, Julie Lythcott-Haims is not to be missed (www.ted.com/talks/julie_lythcott_haims_how_to_raise_successful_kids_without_over_parenting).

Career Advice That Shouldn't Be Free (But Is)

Most career advice costs money, but some of the best does not. With an Internet browser, you can benefit from the information that leading universities and liberal arts colleges share with their own students. These online resources are refreshingly practical and free of bombast. If you're a student or recent alum with full access to your own campus's career-services department, you may have all the resources you need. If you're outside that inner group, however, or if you just want to see best-practices offerings from other schools, these standouts have caught my eye. All are accessible to the public at no cost (you don't need to be a registered student), or at least they were at the time this book went to press.

Start with the early stages of learning about a possible career. If you're wondering how to conduct a preliminary informational interview with someone already in the field, this tip sheet from Amherst College covers the basics very nicely: www.amherst.edu/system/files/media/Informational%2520Interviewing%2520Redesign%25202015-16.pdf.

If you're writing a résumé for the first time, Wake Forest University has an excellent set of templates and pointers that match many common situations and show you how to highlight various campus activities, such as study-abroad programs, sports, performing arts experiences, and summer jobs. Go to http://career.opcd.wfu.edu/write-a-resume-or-cover-letter/resumes/.

If you're in the running for a specific opening with an actual job interview coming up, try these pointers from Occidental College: http://cache.oxy.edu/sites/default/files/assets/Interviewing%20 Guide.pdf. Focus on the eight common interview questions listed there and collect your thoughts ahead of time so that you can be at your best.

If you have been out of college for a few years and want some pointers on getting a traditional résumé in shape, Marc Cenedella is ready to help. He runs TheLadders.com, a job-finding website for high-paying positions. In this blog post, Cenedella explains what mainstream firms are looking for and how to keep them satisfied: https://medium.com/the-mission/the-best-resume-template -based-on-my-15-years-experience-sharing-resume-advice -9f2a0bb0547.

Some Favorite Books

Brooks, Katharine. *You Majored in What?: Mapping Your Path from Chaos to Career.* New York: Viking, 2009.

Bruni, Frank. *Where You Go Is Not Who You'll Be: An Antidote to the College Admissions Mania.* New York: Grand Central Publishing, 2015.

Burnett, Bill, and Dave Evans. *Designing Your Life: How to Build a Well-Lived, Joyful Life.* New York: Knopf, 2016.

Cain, Susan. *Quiet: The Power of Introverts in a World That Can't Stop Talking.* New York: Crown Publishers, 2012.

Deresiewicz, William. *Excellent Sheep: The Miseducation of the American Elite and the Way to a Meaningful Life.* New York: Free Press, 2014.

Duckworth, Angela. *Grit: The Power of Passion and Perseverance.* New York: Scribner, 2016.

Dweck, Carol S. *Mindset: The New Psychology of Success.* New York: Random House, 2006.

Grant, Adam. *Originals: How Non-Conformists Move the World.* New York: Penguin, 2016.

Huth, John Edward. *The Lost Art of Finding Our Way.* Cambridge, MA: Harvard University Press, 2015.

Moretti, Enrico. *The New Geography of Jobs.* Boston: Houghton Mifflin Harcourt, 2012.

Pink, Daniel. *Drive: The Surprising Truth About What Motivates Us.* New York: Riverhead Books, 2009.

Sandberg, Sheryl. *Lean In: Women, Work, and the Will to Lead.* New York: Knopf, 2013.

Selingo, Jeffrey. *There Is Life After College.* New York: HarperCollins, 2016.

And a Few Songs

I can't claim that this list will work for everyone, but it's a start. If you've got some other favorites, e-mail me via the links posted on www.georgeandersbooks.com, and I'll try to add your suggestions to a later printing of this book.

Clark, Guy. *Boats to Build.* Elektra Entertainment, 1992. The metaphors in the title track ("Boats to Build") do a fine job of conveying any new project's sense of hope and purpose. "Jack of All Trades" is a job-hopper's delight. "Picasso's Mandolin" is indecipherable and enchanting.

Dvořák, Antonín. Symphony no. 9 in E Minor, *From the New World.* In 1969, astronaut Neil Armstrong took a recording of this work to the moon; he returned with good memories to a hero's acclaim. The composition works for shorter trips too.

Ratatat. *Magnifique*. Because Music, 2015. Electronic music that will energize you in a hurry; Bridget Connolly (chapter 4's protagonist) recommends this band. The best-known tracks from this album are "Cream on Chrome" and "Abrasive," but it's all good.

Notes

Chapter 1

3 no idea how to find a job: Most details of Josh Sucher's journey from Bard to Etsy were reconstructed during an interview on April 5, 2016, as well as via e-mail and phone exchanges in September 2015, January 2015, and December 2016. Additional information comes from various websites Sucher has built to chronicle different stages of his life, including Blockfactory.com and http://interactiondesign.sva .edu/projects/by/josh-sucher.

3 Bard's graduation speakers: The text of Leon Botstein's address is archived at www.bard.edu/commencement/2007/ botstein.shtml. Michael Bloomberg's remarks can be found at www.bard.edu/commencement/2007/bloomberg_speech .shtml.

5 the Cave of Altamira: Raphael Minder, "Back to the Cave of Altamira in Spain, Still Controversial," *New York Times*, July 30, 2014.

6 Its alumni: https://en.wikipedia.org/wiki/List_of_Bard_Col lege_people.

8 a fondness for people with eclectic backgrounds: Chad Dickerson, "Why Liberal Arts Education Matters: The Story of a Drucker (Mis-)Quote," Chad Dickerson's blog, September 29, 2013, https://blog.chaddickerson.com/2013/02/03/liberal-arts-matter/; Lillian Cunningham, "How to Craft a Successful Career: An Interview with Etsy CEO Chad Dickerson," *Washington Post*, November 20, 2014.

9 **published a landmark study:** David H. Autor, Lawrence F. Katz, and Melissa S. Kearney, "The Polarization of the U.S. Labor Market," National Bureau of Economic Research (January 2006), www.nber.org/papers/w11986.

10 **at risk of being automated:** Michael Chui, James Manyika, and Mehdi Miremadi, "Where Machines Could Replace Humans—and Where They Can't (Yet)," *McKinsey Quarterly* (July 2016), www.mckinsey.com/business-functions/digital-mckinsey/our-insights/where-machines-could-replace-humans-and-where-they-cant-yet.

10 **"Software is eating the world":** Marc Andreessen, "Why Software Is Eating the World," *Wall Street Journal*, August 20, 2011.

10 **8.8 million Americans were thrown out of work:** Christopher J. Goodman and Stephen M. Mance, "Employment Loss and the 2007–09 Recession: An Overview," *Monthly Labor Review* (April 2011), www.bls.gov/mlr/2011/04/art1full.pdf.

11 **Barack Obama repeatedly urged teenagers:** https://phys.org/news/2015-03-obama-240m-pledges-stem.html.

11 **Of the 10.1 million net new jobs:** The Bureau of Labor Statistics publishes annual reports on U.S. employment levels for more than seven hundred occupations, ranging from chief executives to parking lot attendants. The bureau's tallies from 1989 through 2016 can be found here: www.bls.gov/oes/tables.htm. Industry-specific calculations for this

chapter are based on the growth (or shrinkage) in notable occupations from 2012 to 2016.

14–15 **Average salaries range from $43,000 to $90,000:** "National Occupational Employment and Wage Estimates," U.S. Bureau of Labor Statistics, www.bls.gov/oes/current/oes_nat.htm.

16 **"In times of drastic change":** Eric Hoffer, *Reflections on the Human Condition* (Titusville, NJ: Hopewell Publications, 2006).

19 **"the habit of attention":** William Johnson Cory, *Eton Reform* (London: Longman, Green, Longman, and Roberts, 1861).

20 **The full linkages:** Angela Duckworth, *Grit: The Power of Passion and Perseverance* (New York: Scribner, 2016).

21 **"openness to new experiences":** See Arthur E. Poropat, "A Meta-Analysis of the Five-Factor Model of Personality and Academic Performance," *Psychological Bulletin* 135, no. 2 (2009): 322–38. In this ambitious paper, Australian researcher Arthur Poropat carries out a meta-analysis of nearly two hundred studies looking at possible correlations between five leading personality traits and success in school or later life. He found that conscientiousness correlated most closely with success, but openness to experience ranked second. Other factors such as amiability, neuroses, and introversion or extroversion didn't have significant correlations.

23 **"get a job at Starbucks instead":** Megan McArdle, "Why a BA Is Now a Ticket to a Job in a Coffee Shop," *Daily Beast*, March 27, 2013, www.thedailybeast.com/articles/2013/03/27/why-a-ba-is-now-a-ticket-to-a-job-in-a-coffee-shop.html. In an e-mail exchange in February 2017, McArdle remarked: "I was an English major, and I am not working at Starbucks, so obviously I'm aware that there are career paths

beyond the major. However, I came out of college more than 20 years ago (gulp), and things have gotten a lot harder for liberal arts grads since then."

23 **"We need more welders"**: Shoshana Weissmann, "Rubio: 'We Need More Welders and Less Philosophers,'" *Weekly Standard*, November 10, 2015, www.weeklystandard.com/ rubio-we-need-more-welders-and-less-philosophers/ article/1062072.

23 **"working at Chick-fil-A"**: www.youtube.com/watch?v=qtjov E9HjVE.

24 **willingness to relocate:** "Americans Moving at Historically Low Rates, Census Bureau Reports," U.S. Census Bureau, November 16, 2016, www.census.gov/newsroom/press-releases/ 2016/cb16-189.html.

25 **novels of Romain Gary:** Judge for yourself. Many people admire Gary's *The Roots of Heaven,* an interlocking series of tragedies set in French-controlled Africa shortly after World War II; many others can't abide its tone and technique.

Chapter 2

26 **renowned introductory course Antiquity Today:** The Dartmouth course-catalog listing for Antiquity Today is here: http:// dartmouth.smartcatalogiq.com/en/current/orc/Departments -Programs-Undergraduate/Classics-Classical-Studies-Greek -Latin/CLST-Classical-Studies/CLST-1. A fuller sense of the class can be found in this YouTube video: www.youtube.com/ watch?v=A4t6rlWQoHs&feature=youtu.be. Paul Christesen provided further information on enrollment trends in a series of e-mail exchanges with the author in July 2016.

27 **the most admired professors:** www.ratemyprofessors.com/blog/toplist/the-2015-2016-annual-top-lists-are-here/.

28 **biography of Andrew Carnegie:** Steven Perlstein, "Meet the Parents Who Won't Let Their Children Study Literature," *Washington Post*, September 2, 2016.

28 **sheer cost of college:** Because of merit scholarships, need-based scholarships, and tuition discounting, many students aren't charged the full prices that colleges post. The best gauge of actual charges for tuition, room, and board comes from the College Board, which provides data for four-year public institutions: https://trends.collegeboard.org/college-pricing/figures-tables/average-net-price-over-time-full-time-students-public-four-year-institution, and for four-year private schools: https://trends.collegeboard.org/college-pricing/figures-tables/average-net-price-over-time-full-time-students-private-nonprofit-four-year-institutions.

28 **Jill Lepore, chair of Harvard's history and literature program:** Tamar Lewin, "As Interest Fades in the Humanities, Colleges Worry," *New York Times*, October 30, 2013.

33 **"protean" careers:** The argument for protean careers—and it's a good one!—can be traced back to this 1996 paper: Douglas T. Hall, "Protean Careers of the 21st Century," *Academy of Management Executive* 10, no. 4 (1996): 8–16.

34 **Paul Christesen plays that role at freshman orientation:** www.youtube.com/watch?v=jV4vfGKZW7s&feature=youtu.be.

35 **Ally Begly:** Ally Begly, phone interview and e-mail exchanges with the author, May 2016.

36 **Undergraduate Sarah Murray:** Paul Christesen, phone interview and e-mail exchanges with the author, July 2016; Sarah

Murray, e-mail exchanges with the author, December 2016 and January 2017.

37 **"Manet's *Olympia*":** Hui Min Chang, interview with the author, June 6, 2016; phone interview with the author, February 2017.

39 **Evan Golden:** Evan Golden, phone interview with the author, May 2016; e-mail exchange with the author, February 2017.

39 **Arthur Motch:** Arthur Motch, phone interview with the author, May 2016; e-mail exchanges with the author, January 2017.

41 **Isabelle Abrams:** Isabelle Abrams, interview with the author, August 18, 2016; phone interview with the author, January 2017.

42 **Amy Pressman:** Amy Pressman, interview with the author, September 3, 2016.

43 **Helene Meyers:** Helene Meyers, "Feeding English Majors in the 21st Century," *Chronicle of Higher Education* (January 25, 2016), www.chronicle.com/article/Feeding-English-Majors -in-the/235042.

45 **Joe Indvik:** Joe Indvik, phone interview with the author, January 2016; e-mail exchange with the author, January 2017.

45 **"as if she had seen a devil":** Kari Dallas, phone interview with the author, June 2016; e-mail exchange with the author, January 2017.

46 **Susan Farris:** Susan Farris, interview with the author, May 19, 2016.

47 **"I humanize things":** Bryce Nobles, interview with the author, August 18, 2016.

48 *strong speaking skills:* www.aacu.org/leap/public-opinion-re search/2015-employer-priorities.

49 Alexandra Maceda: Alexandra Maceda, interview with the author, January 20, 2016. Additional details of her Delphi talk come from a Dartmouth-in-Greece blog: https://greecefsp2009.wordpress.com/.

Chapter 3

51 Her grades were ragged: Mai-Ling Garcia, interviews with the author, May 4, 2016, and August 12, 2016.

51 King of the Cage: Timothy Guy, "Soboba: King of the Cage Comes Home to San Jacinto," *Riverside Press Enterprise,* March 11, 2015.

51 Popular classes include: Information about Mount San Jacinto's classes is at www.msjc.edu/ScheduleofClasses/Pages/CurrentSchedule.aspx.

52 "She didn't sit": Maria Lopez-Moreno, phone interview with the author, July 2016.

53 Her annual salary, benefits, and bonus: Government employees' salaries are publicly disclosed in California; information comes from http://transparentcalifornia.com/salaries/search.

55 In 2015, the Bureau of Labor Statistics: www.bls.gov/news .release/pdf/nlsoy.pdf.

56 De Anza College: De Anza student Ron Gonzales (who later earned a BA in community studies from the University of California, Santa Cruz) served as mayor of San Jose, California, from 1999 to 2006. De Anza student D. J. Patil (who later earned a BS in math from the University of California, San Diego) became chief data scientist of the United States in 2015.

58 LinkedIn data analyst: www.linkedin.com/pulse/you-dont -need-know-how-code-make-silicon-valley-alice-ma.

59 **Richard Detweiler set out to study:** George Anders, "To Earn $100,000 or More, Roam Outside Your College Major," *Forbes,* June 21, 2016.

60–61 **"My long and winding journey":** Jennifer Kohn, interview with the author, April 4, 2016.

62 **Chris LaRoche:** Chris LaRoche, phone interviews with the author, September 2015 and January 2017.

65 **Brian Anderson:** Phone interview with the author.

66 **a "brain hub":** Enrico Moretti, *The New Geography of Jobs* (Boston: Houghton Mifflin Harcourt, 2012).

66 **typical graduates earn:** Data on median college-graduate earnings sorted by individual institution can be found on the U.S. Department of Education's website in its College Scorecard section: https://collegescorecard.ed.gov/.

67 **LeAnne Gault:** LeAnne Gault, interviews with the author, May 18 and May 19, 2016.

70 **She won a Shorty Award:** Gault was honored in the Social Commerce category. Details are here: http://shortyawards .com/4th/leanne-gault.

74 **Oakland's Digital Front Door:** Mai-Ling Garcia described her role in our interviews. Additional information comes from Howard Dyckoff, "Oakland's Code for America Summit Emphasizes Diversity and Inclusiveness," *East Bay Times,* November 17, 2016, as well as this 2014 SlideShare presentation by Code for America: www.slideshare.net/codeforamerica/2014-code-for-america -summit-designing-with-people-digital-front-door.

Chapter 4

79 **coast of Hawaii's Big Island:** On the Big Island of Hawaii from 1986 to 2009, the Kilauea lava flow created 475 acres of

fresh land, and it continues to add more. Some fascinating photos are here: "Kilauea Lava Enters the Ocean, Expanding Coastline," CoastalCare.org, http://coastalcare.org/2010/11/kilauea-lava-enters-the-ocean/. Other parts of the Hawaiian coast are eroding, making the jobs/coastline metaphor applicable in both directions.

81 **the Notorious B.I.G.:** Bridget Connolly, interview with the author, March 29, 2016.

82 **42 percent of all hires:** Steven J. Davis et al., "The Establishment-Level Behavior of Vacancies and Hiring," National Bureau of Economic Research, www.nber.org/papers/w16265.

84 **166,000 new jobs in market research and marketing:** This figure reflects a giant surge in category 13-1160, "Market research and marketing specialists," as reported by the Bureau of Labor Statistics. In 2010, the BLS counted 261,780 people in the United States working in this category. That number soared to 506,420 in 2015. Full data can be found here: www.bls.gov/oes/tables.htm.

84 **surveys happen weekly:** Rachel Emma Silverman, "Are You Happy at Work? Bosses Push Weekly Polls," *Wall Street Journal*, December 2, 2014.

85 **"If it's predictable":** Cliff Latham, interview with the author, August 18, 2016.

85 **Caroline Poole:** Caroline Poole, interview with the author, August 18, 2016.

86 **more than four hundred thousand openings a year:** "The Art of Employment: How Liberal Arts Graduates Can Improve Their Labor Market Prospects," Burning Glass Technologies, 2013, http://burning-glass.com/wp-content/uploads/BGTReportLiberalArts.pdf.

87 **Max Menke:** Max Menke, phone interview with the author, February 2017.

88 **73,000 new jobs:** This figure reflects a brisk pickup in category 13-1071, "Human resources specialists," as reported by the Bureau of Labor Statistics. In 2010, the BLS counted 417,880 people in the United States working in this category. That number rose to 491,090 in 2015. Full data can be found here: www.bls.gov/oes/tables.htm.

88 **Mike Junge:** Mike Junge, interview with the author, August 29, 2016, and phone interview with the author, February 2017.

91 **Brie Lowry:** Brie Lowry, phone interview with the author, August 2016.

91 **"a deep conversation":** Jennifer McCrea and Jeffrey C. Walker, *The Generosity Network: New Transformational Tools for Successful Fund-Raising* (New York: Random House, 2013).

92 **Soleio Cuervo:** Geoffrey Fowler, "The Man Who Got Us to 'Like' Everything," *Wall Street Journal*, August 13, 2011; Ralph Gardner Jr., "At 34, a Facebook Elder Statesman," *Wall Street Journal*, April 24, 2016.

94 **Amazon hires lots of project managers:** Job-ad search on Indeed.com conducted in September 2016.

94 **Just ask Bridget Connolly:** This account is based on Bridget Connolly's interviews with the author on March 29, April 13, and August 30, 2016, as well as on the author's phone interviews with multiple wikiHow colleagues and his personal interview with wikiHow chief executive Jack Herrick on March 17, 2016. Postings on wikihow.com corroborated many details; so did documents that Connolly and her colleagues shared with me.

97 **"I know we've been talking":** Elizabeth Douglas, phone interview with the author, April 2016.

98 **"Try using an IF command":** Chris Hadley, phone interview with the author, April 2016.

Chapter 5

106 **Frontiers Conference:** Tim O'Reilly's prepared remarks and a video of his talk are here: https://medium.com/the-wtf -economy/wtf-whats-the-future-e52ab9515573#.qkaz 85dwy. Details on the overall conference are here: www .frontiersconference.org/.

108 *Wired* **magazine profile:** Steven Levy, "The Trend Spotter," *Wired*, October 2005.

109–110 **split into two camps:** C. P. Snow, "The Two Cultures" (repr., New York: Cambridge University Press, 1998).

111 **hybrid job openings:** http://burning-glass.com/research/ hybrid-jobs/.

111 **Phunware:** E-mail exchange with the author, April 2017.

111 **Skycatch:** Mimi Connery, presentation at a Williams College event in San Francisco, February 20, 2016.

112 **"You're really differentiated":** Bracken Darrell, "Debating the English Major: 'Have a Back-Up Plan,'" *Wall Street Journal*, June 10, 2013.

112 *blockchain:* IBM's strategy will doubtless keep evolving, but this article from the company's own website describes the state of play in 2016: www.ibm.com/blockchain/what-is -blockchain.html.

112 **Oliver Meeker:** Oliver Meeker, phone interview with the author, September 2016, and e-mail exchanges, February 2017.

117 **"Statistics is not math":** William M. Briggs, "Statistics Is Not Math," January 27, 2013, http://wmbriggs.com/post/3169/.

117 **close look at OpenTable:** OpenTable explains the basic elements of its business on its website: http://press.opentable.com/. Additional details come from the author's phone interviews with OpenTable executives in December 2014 and February 2015.

118 **hop in a car:** Firsthand observation of Shawna Ramona's visits by the author, February 9 and February 10, 2015.

121 **Danielle Sheer:** Elizabeth Segran, "Why Top Tech CEOs Want Employees with Liberal Arts Degrees," *Fast Company,* August 29, 2014, www.fastcompany.com/3034947/the-future-of-work/why-top-tech-ceos-want-employees-with-liberal-arts-degrees.

122 **NeKelia Henderson:** NeKelia Henderson, phone interview with the author, August 2016.

125 **Tim O'Reilly's story:** Tim O'Reilly, interview with the author, April 12, 2016; Linda Walsh, phone interviews with the author, April 2016; Tim O'Reilly, *Frank Herbert* (New York: Ungar, 1981); Levy, "The Trend Spotter."

Chapter 6

129 **Bess Yount is about to tell:** Firsthand observation by the author during a visit to Facebook headquarters, April 6, 2015.

130 **Facebook's fast-growing advertising ecosystem:** Facebook's quarterly financial statements are archived here: https://investor.fb.com/financials/?section=secfilings.

132 **Douglas Adams famously observed:** Douglas Adams, "How to Stop Worrying and Learn to Love the Internet," Sunday *Times,* August 29, 1999, www.douglasadams.com/dna/19990901-00-a.html.

133 **fifty minutes a day on Facebook:** https://techcrunch.com/2016/04/27/facediction/.

134 **median age of an American:** www.statista.com/statistics/241494/median-age-of-the-us-population/.

134 **"It can't be B-to-C":** Stephanie Meyer, e-mail exchange with the author, January 2017.

135 **"exactly the people I'm looking for":** Michael S. Malone, "How to Avoid a Bonfire of the Humanities," *Wall Street Journal*, October 24, 2012.

136 **seventy-four gigabytes of data a day:** "How Much Media?," Institute for Communication Technology Management, University of Southern California, https://news.usc.edu/56894/americans-consume-media-in-a-major-way-study-finds/.

137 **Andy Anderegg:** Andy Anderegg, phone interviews with the author, June and November 2016.

140 **affluent Americans tend to be more narcissistic:** P. K. Piff et al., "Higher Social Class Predicts Increased Unethical Behavior," *Proceedings of the National Academy of Sciences* 109, no. 11 (2012): 4086–91.

140 **"through many lenses":** Eric Fridman, "Empathy and the Liberal Arts," *Executive Coaching* (blog), July 15, 2016, https://fridmancoaching.com/2016/07/15/empathy-and-the-liberal-arts/.

141 **givers, takers, or a bit of both:** Adam M. Grant, *Give and Take: A Revolutionary Approach to Success* (New York: Viking, 2013).

142 **Mary Helen Smith:** Firsthand observation by the author, August 17, 2015; Mary Helen Smith, phone interview with the author, August 2016.

144 **Robert Cialdini:** Robert B. Cialdini, *Influence: The Psychology of Persuasion* (New York: Collins Business, 2007).

144 **Solomon Asch's pioneering research:** Solomon E. Asch, "Studies of Independence and Conformity: A Minority of One Against a Unanimous Majority," *Psychological Monographs: General and Applied* 70, no. 9 (1956): 1–70.

146 **Litterati, a socially minded enterprise:** Jeff Kirschner, phone interviews with the author, September 2015 and January 2017.

Chapter 7

149 **Stewart Butterfield:** The counterculture adventures of the Butterfield family are richly described in the following articles: Mat Honan, "The Most Fascinating Profile You'll Ever Read About a Guy and His Boring Startup," *Wired*, August 2014; Alec Scott, "How Stewart Butterfield Built a Billion-Dollar Company in 8 Months," *Canadian Business*, January 5, 2015. The Lord's Prayer anecdote is from the author's interview with Stewart Butterfield, July 17, 2015.

150 **he started talking about *eudaemonia*:** Butterfield interview.

153 **Typical Starting Earnings:** PayScale's 2016–2017 report on college graduates' earnings by majors can be found here: www.payscale.com/college-salary-report/degrees-and-majors-lifetime-earnings. The full report covers more than three hundred majors with lots of drop-down menus and adjustable sliders that make it easy to carry out customized comparisons.

155 **High Achievers' Lifetime Earnings:** Full information on the Hamilton Project's methodology and results can be found here: www.hamiltonproject.org/charts/career_earnings_by_college_major/. The findings are presented in a highly

interactive way, making it easy to search for specific majors and income trends at different stages of life.

156 **Herb Allison:** Laurence Arnold, "Herbert Allison, Ex-Merrill President Who Ran TARP, Dies at 69," Bloomberg .com, July 15, 2013, www.bloomberg.com/news/articles/2013 -07-15/herbert-allison-jr-former-merrill-lynch-president -dies-at-69.

157 **Roger Ferguson:** Ferguson's life story is well summarized here: Adam Bryant, "Roger Ferguson of TIAA-CREF: Always Act as if You're an Owner," *New York Times*, November 29, 2014. The 2008 news release announcing his appointment is archived here: "TIAA-CREF Names Roger W. Ferguson, Jr., President and Chief Executive Officer, Succeeding Herbert M. Allison, Jr.," TIAA-CREF website, www1.tiaa-cref.org/ public/about/press/pressrelease236.html.

158 **The most reliable route:** Christian Stadler, "How to Become a CEO: These Are the Steps You Should Take," Forbes.com, June 14, 2015, www.forbes.com/sites/christianstadler/2015/ 03/12/how-to-become-a-ceo-these-are-the-steps-you -should-take; Christian Stadler, *Enduring Success: What We Can Learn from the History of Outstanding Corporations* (Stanford, CA: Stanford Business Books, 2011).

158 **Spencer Stuart analyzed:** The firm's 2005 findings on CEO education can be found here: www.cluteinstitute.com/ojs/ index.php/JBER/article/download/694/680. Other data and context come from Spencer Stuart executive Bennett R. Machtiger, phone interviews and e-mail exchanges with the author, September 2016.

160 **Maine senator Susan Collins:** Colin Woodard, "Collins, Fiancé 'Bring Out Best in Each Other,'" *Portland Press Herald*, July 28, 2012.

163 **"the abstract came first":** George Soros, *The Alchemy of Finance* (Hoboken, NJ: John Wiley and Sons, 2003), 1.

163 **"you have to think beyond that":** Moira Forbes, "7 Career Lessons from Billionaire Abigail Johnson," Forbes.com, October 13, 2014, www.forbes.com/sites/moiraforbes/2013/11/01/seven-career-lessons-from-billionaire-abigail-johnson.

164 **Carl Icahn:** Carl C. Icahn, "The Problem of Formulating an Adequate Explication of the Empiricist Criterion of Meaning" (undergraduate thesis, Princeton, 1957).

165 **Reid Hoffman:** "'Fail Fast' Advises LinkedIn Founder and Tech Investor Reid Hoffman," BBC News, January 11, 2011, www.bbc.com/news/business-12151752.

167 **"driven by ideas":** As quoted in John D. Spooner, *No One Ever Told Us That: Money and Life Lessons for Young Adults* (Hoboken, NJ: Wiley, 2015), 65. Sprung's own career embodies his message: he studied classics at Harvard in the 1980s and then went on to create a highly successful translation company.

167 **Nicole Sahin:** Nicole Sahin, phone interview and e-mail exchanges with the author, December 2016, and Alix Stuart, "How This Founder Grew Her Company to $17 Million in 4 Years," Inc.com, August 17, 2016.

167 **"know how to sell":** Patrick Chung, interview with the author, September 24, 2015.

168 **Paint Nite's edge:** Paul Keegan, "How Paint Nite Started a Party-Planning Revolution," *Inc.*, January 15, 2015, www.inc.com/magazine/201502/paul-keegan/art-stars.html.

168 **John Mackey:** John Mackey and Rajendra Sisodia, *Conscious Capitalism: Liberating the Heroic Spirit of Business* (Boston: Harvard Business Review Press, 2013).

169 **"always experimenting"**: Alyson Shontell, "The CEO of $11 Billion Pinterest Reveals His Thoughts on Going Public, Crazy Private Markets, and Advice for Founders Who Don't Want to Fail," *Business Insider,* April 21, 2016, www.business insider.com/ben-silbermann-interview-pinterest-ceo-on -ipo-startups-2016-4.

169 **Stewart Butterfield's career:** Daniel Terdiman, "Watching the Birth of Flickr Co-Founder's Gaming Start-Up," CNET .com, February 9, 2010, www.cnet.com/news/watching-the -birth-of-flickr-co-founders-gaming-start-up/; Honan, "The Most Fascinating Profile."

170 **"tin is in my blood"**: Stewart Butterfield's Yahoo resignation letter can be found across the Internet; one notable home is here: Jemima Kiss, "The Alpaca Resignation Letter—Can You Do Better?" *Guardian,* June 20, 2008, www.theguardian .com/media/pda/2008/jun/20/thealpacaresignationletter.

171 **named Slack in 2013:** Carmel DeAmicis, "Third Life: Flickr Co-Founder Pulls Unlikely Success from Gaming Failure. Again," Pando.com, April 5, 2014, https://pando .com/2014/04/05/third-life-flickr-co-founder-pulls-unlikely -success-out-of-gaming-failure-again/; Jeff Bercovici, "Slack Is Our Company of the Year. Here's Why Everybody's Talking About It," *Inc.,* December 2015.

172 **Slack as dominant in communication:** Omar El Akkad, "From Flickr to Slack: B.C.'s Silicon Valley Golden Boy Finds Success in Failure," *Globe and Mail,* December 5, 2014.

172 **"It's just terrible"**: Rachel Metz, "Three Questions with Slack's CEO," *MIT Technology Review,* February 18, 2015, www.technologyreview.com/s/532606/three-questions -with-slacks-ceo/.

172 **"the ability to interpret people":** George Anders, "Your HR Team Needs to See Slack's Defiant Take on 'Values,'" *Forbes*, July 29, 2015, www.forbes.com/sites/georgeanders/2015/07/29/your-hr-team-needs-to-see-slacks-defiant-take-on -values.

Chapter 8

177 **Sonia Vora:** Sonia Vora, interview with the author, June 6, 2016, and phone interview with the author, February 2017.

178 **Morningstar, a Chicago investment firm:** John Cook, "The Quiet Billionaire: Morningstar CEO Joe Mansueto," *Chicago*, June 2006; Neil Munshi, "The Monday Interview: Joe Mansueto, Morningstar CEO," *Financial Times*, October 20, 2013.

179 **Jim Murphy:** Jim Murphy, interview with the author, June 6, 2016.

179 **Emory Zink:** Emory Zink, interview with the author, June 6, 2016.

181 **an hour with John Rekenthaler:** John Rekenthaler, interview with the author, June 6, 2016.

187 **Deloitte prefers STEAM:** Larry Quinlan, phone interview with the author, March 2015.

189 **says Brian DeChesare:** Brian DeChesare, "From Liberal Arts to Finance: Shakespeare with Swag or Mission Impossible?," *Mergers and Inquisitions* (blog), www.mergersandinquisitions.com/liberal-arts-to-finance/.

190 *Nordstrom needs to save money:* "Nordstrom Cut Costs in Cleaning Services Division," Management Consulting Case

Interviews, www.consultingcase101.com/nordstrom-cut-costs
-in-cleaning-services-division/.

191 **ReD Associates:** Christian Madsbjerg, phone interview
with the author, July 2016; Drake Bennett, "Heidegger's
Marketing Secrets: What German Philosophers Know
About Selling TVs," Bloomberg.com, February 21, 2014,
www.bloomberg.com/news/articles/2014-02-20/inno
vation-firm-red-shows-clients-how-to-use-philosophy-to-sell
-stuff.

192 **Stanford's Jennifer Aaker:** Professor Aaker's comments were
made in a 2013 Stanford lecture, viewable in its entirety on
YouTube: www.youtube.com/watch?v=CdO9a41WUss.

195 **economist Milton Friedman:** Friedman's quote, and some
fiery debate about its applicability, can be found in this
Harvard Business Review article: https://hbr.org/2012/04/
you-might-disagree-with-milton.

195 **Etsy, the online crafts marketplace:** Tom Foster, "The Story
of Etsy's Distinctly 21st-Century Management Challenge,"
Inc., December 2013.

197 **Willa Cather or F. Scott Fitzgerald:** This example is culled
from the State Department's practice exam for the Foreign
Service test as posted online in December 2016: https://
careers.state.gov/fsopracticetest/.

197 **Suggested Reading List:** https://careers.state.gov/uploads/
ff/03/ff03e644688fe25f74ff3b0641c59e9d/Updated
_FSOT_Reading_List_Aug2013.pdf.

199 **McMaster-Carr:** Sarah Williams, "From English Major to
Software Developer: Up Close with McMaster-Carr," *Wildcat Career News*, November 10, 2016, http://wildcat-career
-news.davidson.edu/alumni-and-networking/from

-english-major-to-software-developer-up-close-with
-mcmaster-carr/.

200 **"We focus more on the soft skills":** Melissa Suzuno, "How
Enterprise Recruits and Develops Diverse New Grad Talent," Employer.AfterCollege.com, October 15, 2014, http://
employer.aftercollege.com/enterprise-recruits-develops
-diverse-new-grad-talent/.

Chapter 9

201 **"You're too impulsive":** Most of the opening section's details
come from the author's phone interviews with Kaori Freda
in November and December 2016 as well as from her travel
blog, https://rainagainblog.wordpress.com/category/japan/.
Additional information about the islands comes from the
Japan National Tourism Organization website: www.jnto
.go.jp/eng/regional/tokyo/ogasawarashotou.html.

202 **"The longer wanderers drift":** Jeffrey Selingo, *There Is Life
After College* (New York: HarperCollins, 2016).

206 **tips began streaming in:** An archived record of Kaori Freda's exchanges exists at www.reed.switchboardhq.com.

207 **college graduates do the most job-hopping:** www.bls.gov/
news.release/nlsyth.t02.htm.

209 **"I started out as a bookworm":** Polly Washburn, phone interviews with the author, November 2016 and January 2017.

210 **Oberlin, for example, has drawn more than eighteen hundred:** Ma'ayan Plaut, manager of social strategy and projects
in Oberlin's Office of Communications, phone interview
with the author, November 2016.

212 **Mara Zepeda:** Mara Zepeda, interview with the author,
June 9, 2016, plus phone interviews in November 2016.

Zepeda's list of two hundred allies is here: www.marazepeda
.com/about/.

213 **Kevin Greer dreamed:** Kevin Greer, phone interview with
the author, November 2016.

215 **Kelli Smith:** Direct quote is from Eric Coker, "New Fleish-
man Center Director Stresses Collaboration," *Inside Binghamton University,* September 11, 2014, www.binghamton.edu/
inside/index.php/inside/story/9213/new-fleishman-center
-director-stresses-collaboration/. Additional information is
from the author's phone interviews and e-mail exchanges
with Kelli Smith in November 2016.

218 **"If the Metropolitan Opera":** Michelle Bata, phone interview with the author, April 2016.

219 **Evelyn Perez-Landron:** Evelyn Perez-Landron, phone interview with the author, December 2016, and e-mail exchange
with the author, January 2017; Evelyn Perez-Landron, "A
Woman of the World," *Gates* (blog), May 4, 2016, https://
blog.mtholyoke.edu/thegates/a-woman-of-the-world;
Mount Holyoke College, "LEAP Pathway: Evelyn Perez-
Landron," YouTube, April 29, 2016, www.youtube.com/
watch?v=LWPdaYstJfo.

222 **April Dennis:** April Dennis, phone interview with the
author, November 2016.

223 **Amherst's online alumni portal:** George Anders, "Can't
Donate a Building? Alumni with Job Tips Win New Respect,"
Forbes, June 9, 2016, www.forbes.com/sites/georgeanders/
2016/06/09/cant-donate-a-building-just-help-eager-grads
-find-jobs.

223 **National Association of Colleges and Employers:** Louisa
Eisman, "First Generation Students and Job Success," *NACE
Journal* (November 2016): 16.

Chapter 10

225 **Gallup-Purdue survey:** www.gallup.com/poll/199307/one -six-grads-say-career-services-helpful.aspx.

230 **Wake Forest president Nathan Hatch:** Nathan Hatch, "State of the University, 2011," WFU.edu, November 7, 2011, http://president.wfu.edu/speeches/2011-state-of-the -university/.

230 **looked like a winner:** Susan Dominus, "How to Get a Job with a Philosophy Degree," *New York Times,* September 15, 2013.

230 **initiatives that have sprung up at Wake Forest:** Andy Chan, phone interview with the author, January 2017.

232 **surveys of graduates' first destinations:** http://opcd.wfu .edu/first-destination-data/.

233 **Brigham Young University:** John Rosenberg and Danny Damron, interviews with the author, March 3, 2017.

234 **Eilis Wasserman:** Eilis Wasserman, phone interview and follow-up e-mails with the author, August 2015.

239 **"I want to produce graduates":** Adam Falk, interview with the author, February 19, 2016.

240 **she asks students to use Pinterest:** Alicia Ellis, interview with the author, April 7, 2016.

241 **Dyllan Brown-Bramble:** Dyllan Brown-Bramble, phone interview and multiple e-mail exchanges with the author, January 2017.

242 **"Keep it real":** Josmar Tejeda, phone interview with the author, January 2017.

243 **Each major is its own story:** Joe Pinsker, "Rich Kids Study English," *Atlantic,* July 6, 2015. Pinsker's article is based on federal data analyzed by Kim Weeden, a sociology professor at Cornell University.

243 **"Then they discover anthropology"**: Daniel Porterfield, interview with the author, October 13, 2016.

244 **"The power of the cohort"**: Shirley Collado, phone interview with the author, January 2017. In February 2017, Collado took up a new post as president of Ithaca College.

245 **She set up Braven:** Aimée Eubanks Davis, interview with the author, February 15, 2017; phone interviews and e-mail exchanges with the author, December 2016 to February 2017.

Chapter 11

247 **his yearbook epigram:** Danielle Newnham, "David Risher: The Quiet Revolutionary," Medium.com, August 27, 2016, https://medium.com/swlh/david-risher-the-quiet -revolutionary-1e6d1512eadb.

249 **when Cicero positioned:** Bruce A. Kimball, *The Liberal Arts Tradition: A Documentary History* (Lanham, MD: University Press of America, 2010).

250 **the Latin term *humanitas*:** Michael Lind, "Why the Liberal Arts Still Matter," *Wilson Quarterly* (Autumn 2006), http://archive.wilsonquarterly.com/essays/why-liberal-arts -still-matter.

250 **"a lifetime of genuine success"**: George Forsythe, "The Global Citizen: Finding Practicality in a Liberal Arts Education," *Huffington Post,* www.huffingtonpost.com/george -forsythe/liberal-arts-education-careers_b_1755679.html.

250 **"a more fulfilling life"**: Marvin Krislov, "The Enduring Relevance of a Liberal-Arts Education," *Hechinger Report,* February 12, 2015, http://hechingerreport.org/the-enduring -relevance-of-a-liberal-arts-education/.

251 **joint polling initiative by the Gallup Organization and Purdue University:** "Engagement in College, Engagement in the Workplace: Findings from the Gallup-Purdue Index," Association of American Colleges and Universities, June 13, 2014, www.aacu.org/aacu-news/newsletter/engagement-college-engagement-workplace-findings-gallup-purdue-index.

251 **autonomy, mastery, and purpose:** Daniel H. Pink, *Drive: The Surprising Truth About What Motivates Us* (New York: Riverhead Books, 2009).

253 **Tizra, a software company:** Abe Dane, interview with the author, October 15, 2016; David Durand, phone interview with the author, December 2016; Wade Roush, "Tizra Puts Publishers Back in Control of Their E-Books," *Xconomy*, February 24, 2009, www.xconomy.com/boston/2009/02/24/tizra-puts-publishers-back-in-control-of-their-e-books; Rhonda J. Miller, "Tizra Software Bringing Einstein Papers Online," *Providence Business News*, December 2, 2013.

257 **Gregg Newby:** Gregg Newby, interview with the author, May 19, 2016, plus phone follow-up in January 2017.

259 **"like being on an ice floe":** Jessica Benjamin, phone interview with the author, February 2016.

262 **"I knew two things":** David Satterwhite, interview with the author, March 9, 2016.

263 **To pay off his student loans:** David Risher, interview with the author, January 5, 2017.

Chapter 12

271 **Julia Hartz:** George Anders, "Before We Hire You, Step into Our Founder's Office for a Chat," Forbes.com, May 22, 2014,

www.forbes.com/sites/georgeanders/2014/05/16/
before-we-hire-you-step-into-our-founders-office-for-a-chat.

274 **the importance of tenacity:** Angela Duckworth, *Grit: The Power of Passion and Perseverance* (New York: Scribner, 2016).

275 **Tess Amodeo-Vickery:** Tess Amodeo-Vickery, "Dear Ezra: Wall Street Was No Match for a Liberal Arts Degree," *Good*, February 22, 2012, www.good.is/articles/dear-ezra -wall-street-was-no-match-for-a-liberal-arts-degree.

277 **Rachel Allen:** Rachel Allen, interview with the author, August 18, 2016.

277 **Patrick Tyler Haas:** Patrick Tyler Haas, interview with the author, October 18, 2016.

280 **a verbal bridge:** Occidental College provides some excellent advice on how to draw these connections via a "problems- actions-results" format: www.oxy.edu/sites/default/files/assets/ job-interviews.pdf. Amherst offers a four-step version of the same concept, recast as "situation-task-action-result": www .amherst.edu/system/files/media/Interviewing%2520Redesign %25202015.pdf.

280 **Noah Samel:** The meeting took place September 13, 2016, on the Reed campus at the Center for Life Beyond Reed.

Chapter 13

284 **blood-spatter calculations:** Chris Chrysostom, phone inter- view with the author, December 2016.

286 **QUni:** Mike Maughan and Dave Gilbert, interviews with the author, August 18, 2016.

286 **reverse-authentication tool:** Caroline Poole, interview with the author, August 18, 2016.

287 **boost her pay 42 percent:** Andy Anderegg, phone interview with the author, August 2016.

287 **PayScale data:** Jen Hubley Luckwaldt, "You Won't Get What You Don't Ask For," PayScale.com, www.payscale .com/salary-negotiation-guide/whats-holding-you-back -people-who-ask-for-raises-earn-more.

288 **offers a five-step approach:** Sheryl Sandberg, *Lean In: Women, Work, and the Will to Lead* (New York: Alfred A. Knopf, 2013).

288 **male/female disparities:** John Bussey, "Gender Wage Gap Reflects the 'Ask' Gap," *Wall Street Journal*, October 10, 2014.

289 **2014 survey by Hay Group:** www.haygroup.com/en/press/ pay-gap-between-senior-managers-and-lower-level -workers-surges-worldwide/.

291 **K. Anders Ericsson:** His landmark publication is the 901-page *Cambridge Handbook of Expertise and Expert Performance* (Cambridge: Cambridge University Press, 2006), edited by K. Anders Ericsson et al.

291 **the 10,000-hour rule:** Malcolm Gladwell, "The 10,000 Hour Rule," Gladwell.com, http://gladwell.com/outliers/ the-10000-hour-rule/.

Index

About the Author

GEORGE ANDERS is a senior editor at large at LinkedIn, exploring issues related to careers, education, and innovation, and a certified LinkedIn Influencer, with 170,000 followers. He is the author of five books, including *Merchants of Debt, Health Against Wealth*, the *New York Times* bestseller *Perfect Enough*, and *The Rare Find*. Earlier in his career, George served as a staff writer for the *Wall Street Journal, Fast Company* magazine, and *Bloomberg View*. In 1997, he shared a Pulitzer Prize for national reporting. He and his wife live in Northern California. Their two sons are starting their own college adventures.